Reading from the Margins
Textual Studies, Chaucer, and Medieval Literature

edited by Seth Lerer

Huntington Library
San Marino, California

Cover illustration
Frontispiece to J. Stanbridge, *Vulgaria* (1519)
printed by Wynkyn de Worde

Simultaneously published as *Huntington Library Quarterly*, vol. 58, no. 1

Library of Congress Cataloging in Publication Data
Reading from the margins : textual studies, Chaucer, and Medieval
    literature / edited by Seth Lerer.
            p. cm.
        "Simultaneously published as Huntington Library Quarterly, volume
    58, no. 1"—Copr. p.
        Includes bibliographical references (p.).
        ISBN 0-87328-163-2 (alk. paper)
        1. Chaucer, Geoffrey, d. 1400—Criticism, Textual.
    2. Illumination of books and manuscripts, Medieval. 3. Literature,
    Medieval—Criticism, Textual. 4. Chaucer, Geoffrey, d. 1400—
    Manuscripts. 5. Manuscripts, Medieval—Editing. I. Lerer, Seth,
    1955–   .
    PR1939.R43 1996
    821'. 1—dc20   96-31096
                                                                              CIP

Printed in the United States of America

Contents

Acknowledgments

This book began as a special issue of the *Huntington Library Quarterly* timed to coincide with the biennial meeting of the New Chaucer Society held in Los Angeles in 1996. That issue and this book could not have been prepared without the guidance, support, and welcome editorial contributions of the *Quarterly*'s editor, Susan Green. I am also grateful to Joseph A. Dane for collaborating with me on the introduction to this volume and for advice throughout its production. The contributors, too, deserve thanks for their enthusiasm and for the vigor and promptness of their work on these essays.

Support for this project was provided by research funds made available from Stanford University and by the staff of the English Department of Washington University in St. Louis, where I had the privilege of serving as the Hurst Visiting Professor during the winter of 1996.

Seth Lerer

Introduction

What Is a Text?

SETH LERER AND JOSEPH A. DANE

We are all now for "bibliographical" methods, keenly on the watch for every least indication of disturbance in the accurate transmission of a text, sorting out by many subtle and ingenious methods the first, second, or third stage of the composition, the original draft, the first completed form, the revision of this, that, and the other purpose, and so on. But there is much more in these modern methods of research than used to be understood by "bibliography," and I am not sure that the recent extensions of the term have been altogether justifiable. The virtues of bibliography as we used to call it were its definiteness, that it gave little scope for differences of opinion, that two persons of reasonable intelligence following the same line of bibliographical argument would inevitably arrive at the same conclusion, and that it therefore offered a very pleasant relief from critical investigations of the more "literary" kind.[1]

R. B. McKerrow's remarks of sixty years ago may well stand as an epigraph for this volume of essays. We are now, too, all for "bibliographical" methods: advances in computer science and the attendant technologies of collation, ideological critiques of the presuppositions of textual criticism itself, and the sheer volume of newly discovered manuscripts and early printed volumes have all made bibliography a central topic of academic debate. Few might still claim that the province of bibliography lies with the unarticulated intuitions of "persons of reasonable intelligence," but many would likely agree that what we mean by "textual scholarship" necessitates a knowledge of the historicity of texts and readers and that such scholarship can only benefit from the communication among critics of many and various fields.[2] Nonetheless, although

1. R. B. McKerrow, *An Introduction to Bibliography* (New York, 1927), 2.
2. See D. C. Greetham, *Textual Scholarship: An Introduction* (New York, 1992), 2.

"textuality" has become something of a term to conjure with—and disciplines as diverse as film studies, cultural anthropology, and the history of science imagine themselves working with the meaning and the mode of "texts"—the processes of transcribing, collating, describing, and editing books and manuscripts of earlier historical periods remain, for the most part, relatively familiar. Editions from the age of McKerrow may seem, at first glance, pretty much the same as those from the atelier of Jerome McGann. And, to a large degree, debates framed by the Bédierists and Lachmannians of nearly a century ago still find themselves played out in the prefaces and articles of professional editors.[3]

The question still evades us: What is a text? Or, to ask it more precisely, what are the relationships between the methods of textual study and the privileging of a class of objects called texts? How does an artifact become a text? Does it become one only when subjected to the inquiries of textual analysis? For that matter, can a text lose its status and revert to the merely artifactual?

Such questions guide our inquiries into the elements of textuality itself. Are pictures—illustrations, marginalia, historiated initials—texts, and how can the editor incorporate such information in the making of the modern edition? For example, no modern scholarly edition of *The Canterbury Tales* (excluding, for the moment, facsimiles) prints the pilgrim portraits with the General Prologue. Yet Frederic Furnivall's late-nineteenth-century edition of Hoccleve's *Regiment of Princes* prints a facsimile of Hoccleve's portrait of Chaucer precisely where it appears in one of the earliest manuscripts of the poem (British Library, MS. Harley 4866).[4] We may ask the question more radically: Can texts themselves function as pictures? Can, in other words, displays of writing function not as strings of words to be conveyed and edited but rather as icons of something else? The very notion of "facsimile" implies a transformation of text back into picture. And, as current photographic technologies improve, the spate of new facsimiles may come to stand as virtual (in both senses of the word) replacements of old texts. The facsimile of the famous Ellesmere manuscript, recently copublished by the Huntington Library and Yushodo Co., Ltd., is no simple reproduction, how-

3.   Witness, for example, the exchanges in the essays collected in Stephen G. Nichols, ed., *The New Philology*, a special issue of *Speculum* 60 (1990); and see Tim William Machan, *Textual Criticism and Middle English Literature* (Charlottesville, Va., 1994).

4.   F. J. Furnivall, ed., *The Regiment of Princes A.D. 1411–12, from the Harleian MS 4866*, Early English Text Society, extra series, 72 (London, 1897). Of the forty-three manuscripts of this work, only a few contain, or ever did contain, a Chaucer portrait where the text seems to demand one. See M. C. Seymour, "The Manuscripts of Hoccleve's *Regiment of Princes*," *Edinburgh Bibliographical Society Transactions* 4, pt. 7 (1974): 253–97.

ever; and a number of textual scholars have argued directly that the entire enterprise of facsimile production is editorial from beginning to end.[5] In a postscript
to this volume of essays, Anthony G. Cains describes the rebinding and conservation of the Ellesmere manuscript that was undertaken as a component of the
recent facsimile publication. He reveals the ways in which binding affects the production of a facsimile—what one can see of the page, both generally and in detail.
More broadly, his analysis suggests the difficult boundary between the textual and
the artifactual; not only natural degradation but also the various bindings and
repairs have interfered with the pigments and inks, the decoration of the manuscript in particular, which, as other essays in the volume show, is increasingly the
subject of textual inquiry.

In what ways does the availability of facsimile editions alter the character of
textual questions? For the Ellesmere Chaucer, the answer lies in the future. But
for, say, *Beowulf,* the evidence has been around for centuries. One need only recall
the reading *wundini gold*—a phrase long thought to evidence the linguistic
archaism of the poem—to reflect on how editors working from a transcription (in
this case the Thorkelin transcripts of the *Beowulf* manuscript) could discern a
piece of text not to be found in the actual manuscript and then incorporate that
text in published facsimile and critical editions.[6]

What, then, are the elements of textuality? At the local level, where do we
draw the line between a "variant" and an "error"? In the vicissitudes of scribal
copying, how can we distinguish between a lapse and an intrusion—and, in the
case of what appear to be intelligent and meaningful intrusions, how do we distinguish between the variant and wholesale rewriting?[7] The transmission of

5,   See, for example, T. H. Howard-Hill, review of Michael Warren, *The Complete King Lear (1608–1623)*
      (Berkeley and Los Angeles, 1989), *Review of English Studies,* n.s., 43 (1992): 420–22.

6.   The phrase *wundini gold* in *Beowulf* had been understood to be a survival of an early Old English instru
      mental form, and thus was valued as evidence for an early date (seventh or eighth century) of composition of
      the poem. Kevin Kiernan demonstrated that this reading appears as an editorial conjecture in the transcript
      of the poem made by G. J. Thorkelin in the late eighteenth century. It was then reproduced in Julius
      Zupitza's transliteration of the text in his published facsimile (*Beowulf, Reproduced in Facsimile* [London,
      1882]) and was maintained by twentieth-century editors (notably C. L. Wrenn), who had not consulted the
      original manuscript. Kiernan's examination of that manuscript shows that the reading should, in fact, be
      wundmi gold —scribal nonsense, but one that may be more conservatively edited as *wundum gold,* not an
      archaic phrase at all and one consistent with the date c. 1000 for the manuscript. See Kiernan, *Beowulf and
      the Beowulf Manuscript* (New Brunswick, N.J., 1980), 30–37.

7.   This question has been explored for a variety of vernacular literatures in such recent studies as Sylvia Hout,
      From Song to Book: The Poetics of Writing in Old French Lyric and Lyrical Narrative Poetry (Ithaca, N.Y.,
      1987); Seth Lerer, *Chaucer and His Readers: Imagining the Author in Late Medieval England* (Princeton, N.J.,
      1993); and John Dagenais, *The Ethics of Reading in a Manuscript Culture: Glossing the "Libro de beun amor"*
      (Princeton, N.J., 1994).

medieval literary documents has been an obvious site for such reflections. To some, variation is the mark of unreliability, the distinctive manifestations of what Chaucer would lament as the miswriting and mismetering "for defaute of tonge" that he imagines as the scribal afterlife of *Troilus and Criseyde*. To others, variation offers testimony to the creatively fluid nature of the medieval and the early modern text. Barry Windeatt incorporates such miswritings into his edition of *Troilus and Criseyde*. He presents Chaucer's poem "in the context of the corpus of variants drawn from the extant manuscripts, not only because those variants can be of editorial value, but also because they are held to be of a positive literary value, to embody in themselves a form of commentary, recording the responses of near-contemporary readers of the poetry."[8] But variation did not end with the advent of print. In a curious troping on Chaucer's envoy, Stephen Hawes concluded the *Pastime of Pleasure* (first published by Wynkyn de Worde in 1509) with his fears not of scribal but of typographical error:

> Go lytell boke I pray god the saue
> From mysse metrynge / by wronge Impressyon.[9]

And it went on. Phenomena recorded as variants by modern editors may all too often be the mere mistakes of the compositor. Sir Thomas Wyatt's "Satire to John Poynz" condemns the courtiers, "Of them that list all vice for to retain," a line mangled in Tottel's *Miscellany* to "Of them that list all nice for to retain" (a reading, by the way, corrected back to "vice" in the first three reprintings of the volume, yet again transformed to "vile" in later ones).[10] And more significantly, many Shakespearean variants have recently been revealed to be not witnesses to competing versions of the plays but similar mistakes at the print shop. Some dif-

8.   B. A. Windeatt, ed., *Chaucer: Troilus and Criseyde* (London, 1984), 25.

9.   W. E. Mead, ed., *The Pastime of Pleasure by Stephen Hawes,* Early English Text Society, original series, 173 (London, 1928), lines 5803–4. For a discussion of this passage in the context of a larger argument on Hawes's thematic attentions to print culture and literary fame, see Lerer, *Chaucer and His Readers,* 176–93.

10.   Tottel's reading is recorded as a variant in the edition by Kenneth Muir and Patricia Thompson, *Collected Poems of Sir Thomas Wyatt* (Liverpool, 1969), 88; and in the study by Richard Harrier, *The Canon of Sir Thomas Wyatt's Poetry* (Cambridge, 1975), 171; though not in the edition by Ronald A. Rebholz, *Sir Thomas Wyatt, The Complete Poems* (Harmondsworth, England, 1978). It is likely that his reading is not a true variant but rather a compositor's mistake: perhaps not the printing of an *n* but of a turned *u* (where the compositor misread *vice* and *uice*). Such turned letters are commonplace in the printings of the *Miscellany;* see the list of variant readings and misprints in Hyder E. Rollins, *Tottel's Miscellany (1557–1587),* 2 vols. (1928–29; reprint, Cambridge, 1965), 1:263–326. The specifics of the line in the "Satire to Poynz" are recorded on 283 (keyed to 1:85, line 41).

ferences between the Quarto and Folio editions of *King Lear*, for example, may well be missettings of a marked up copy-text.[11]

The instability of medieval and early modern literary texts is thus a problem not only for the editor but also for the author and the reader. Chaucer's attentions to miswriting in the *Troilus*, together with his well-known lament to Adam Scriveyn, suggest a thematic attention to the vagaries of textual transmission.[12] The author's words are always subject to the garblings of others. As Chaucer put it to his Adam: "And all is through thy negligence and rape." But often, the mistakes of writing hands are not due to the ministrations of the scribe but to the anxieties of authorship itself.

> And now my penne, allas, with which I write,
> Quaketh for drede of that I most endite.[13]

This couplet from the proem to Book IV of *Troilus and Criseyde* stands not just as a mark of Chaucer's narratorial self-consciousness. In the century after his death, it also came to articulate the position of any author writing in the post-Chaucerian tradition. Lydgate mimes these lines half a dozen times, as do a string of poetasters stretching into the sixteenth century.[14] Even Sir Thomas Wyatt complains, "My hand doth shake, my pen scant doth his part," in a ballade that queries the very possibility of authorial control of the literary text.

> I do remain scant wotting what I write,
> Pardon me, then, rudely though I indite.[15]

If the instabilities of texts give voice to the anxieties of authors and their readers, they have become the nodes of celebration for more modern, theoretically minded critics. Late-twentieth-century attentions to the reader's affective responses to

---

11. See Joseph A. Dane, "'Which is the Iustice, which is the theefe': Variants of Transposition in the Text(s) of *King Lear*," *Notes and Queries* 42 (1995): 322–27. For some of the broader implications of mechanical variation in Shakespearean texts, see Peter W. M. Blayney, *The Texts of* King Lear *and Their Origins*, vol. 1, *Nicholas Okes and the First Quarto* (Cambridge, 1982); and, more generally, the discussion in Greetham, *Textual Scholarship*, 285–90.

12. "Chaucer's Wordes Unto Adam, His Owne Scriveyn," in Larry D. Benson et al., eds., *The Riverside Chaucer*, 3d ed. (Boston, 1987), 650. For a discussion of the place of this poem in Chaucer's thematics of correction, together with a broader argument about the "openness" of medieval manuscript culture, see Gerald L. Bruns, "The Originality of Texts in Manuscript Culture," *Comparatve Literature* 32 (1980): 113–29.

13. Windeatt, *Troilus and Criseyde*, IV.13–14.

14. For Lydgate's uses, see Hans Kurath et al., eds., *Middle English Dictionary* (Ann Arbor, Mich., 1954–), s.v., *quake*.

15. Rebholz, *Complete Poems*, CLXXVII.19, 23–24.

a work, together with poststructuralist predilections for the *jeu* of signs and signifying, may lead editors as well as critical interpreters to celebrate the variation that inheres in textual transmission. The ideal of the editor as an intentionalist and of the critical edition as recovering the meaning of a work as posed by its originary author may well be past. As David Greetham puts it, "it seems that all we have are competing texts and competing readers."[16] What we are "all for," to return to McKerrow, is just about everything—be it cultural studies, history, materialism, politics, the problematics of representation. It might be hard now to distinguish between editing as a professional practice and "critical investigations of the more 'literary' kind."

The interfaces of the history of authorship, the practices of scribes and printers, and the institutions and the ideologies of the academy lead us to ask not only "What is a text?" but also "What is a textual critic?" The discipline of bibliography may have originally seemed a handmaiden to the literary: editions were produced to make texts available to readers, critics, and appreciators. Recently, however, textual work has taken on an increasing independence. To some degree, Jerome McGann's plea for a new "critical editing" offers a manifesto of the bibliographer's autonomy.

> Both linguistic and bibliographical texts are symbolic and signifying mechanisms. Each generates meaning, and while the bibliographical text typically functions in a subordinate relation to the linguistic text, "meaning" in literary works results from the interactive agency of these two semiotic mechanisms operating together.[17]

From this position, it may seem a short step to Greetham's "Textual Forensics," in which textual scholarship is not merely on a par with literary criticism but also in some way profoundly apart from it, yet a powerful influence over it.

> Textual scholarship is an antidiscipline because it does not occupy a permanent or consistent epistemological position and because it has no definable *Fach*, or subject matter. And textual scholarship is a postmodernist antidiscipline because it consists of coopted and deformed quotations from other fields.[18]

---

16. Greetham, *Textual Scholarship*, 342. Remarks in this paragraph are indebted to Greetham's general discussion of the relations between new developments in textual criticism and literary theory (pp. 341–46).
17. Jerome J. McGann, "What Is Critical Editing," *TEXT* 5 (1991): 27.
18. D. C. Greetham, "Textual Forensics," *PMLA* 111 (1996): 32.

For Randall McLeod, who has called our attention to, in Greetham's words, "a technical and epistemological disjunction between the local evidence derivable from analytical bibliography and the generalized evidence resulting from reading,"[19] the very act of writing and publishing textual scholarship becomes a tour de force of typographical invention. One need only scan the concatenation of visual codes in McLeod's work—facsimiles of First Folio type, photographs of signatures, skewings of lineation and justification, orthographic representations of verbal garblings, right down to the presentation of the critic's name as, variously, "Random Clod" and "Random Clovd"—to see the building blocks of textual scholarship reassembled into something of an abstract expressionism of the word.[20] McLeod's text becomes an object of textual study itself. One can imagine the nightmare of proofreading such a document; more to the point, one might note that the critic's own work enacts his dicta of textual scholarship: that we must avoid *reading* texts in order to *see* them.[21]

This volume of essays seeks to engage these directions in textual scholarship from a variety of critical positions, and it does so stimulated by the occasion of the New Chaucer Society's biannual meeting, held in Los Angeles in 1996. That such an occasion should provoke a volume that may seem to query the very idea of authorial autonomy may be something of a paradox. Ralph Hanna III and A. S. G. Edwards, in the first essay in the volume, treat the annotations and ephemera surrounding the text of *The Canterbury Tales* in the Ellesmere manuscript—including Rotheley's poem on the De Vere family, written on the opening flyleaves of the manuscript—not merely as curiosities of history but also as testimony to the historicity of Chaucer. They explore the provenance of Ellesmere to discern how Chaucer's work was read and understood by late-medieval audiences and also to recognize that such an understanding was a profoundly social and political act. Their new edition of Rotheley's poem, presented as an appendix to the essay, illustrates the ways in which the methods of traditional textual scholarship may be pressed into the service of decentering the canonical text.

For Julia Boffey also, the recovery of a new text is central to recalibrating Chaucerian authority—here, not as the author of a single canonical work but as the name attached to a canon of shorter poems. The poet as proverbialist is important to much fifteenth- and sixteenth-century reception of Chaucer, and

19. Ibid., 37.
20. Random Clod, "Information Upon Information," *TEXT* 5 (1991): 241–81.
21. See the picture of McLeod reading upside down and the discussion in Greetham, "Textual Forensics," 39.

Boffey explores the ways in which a little stanza of proverbial verse by Walton came to be misattributed to Chaucer. Bringing to bear the contexts of late-medieval patronage on manuscript production, Boffey's essay helps us understand the ways in which Chaucer's poems were brought together to define late-medieval literary writing itself. In the context of Boffey's ongoing project of revising the *Index of Middle English Verse,* the essay also provokes insight into the critical presuppositions underlying the construction of such reference works. The original *Index* organized autonomous poems by first lines; it created hierarchical relationships between "texts" and "fragments." Many Middle English lyrics are cut out or cobbled together from longer narrative poems. Bits and pieces of Chaucer's *Troilus and Criseyde,* Lydgate's *Temple of Glass,* Stephen Hawes's *Pastime of Pleasure,* and other works were often excised, reassembled, and recast into short lyrics of desire or verse letters of complaint. Where do we draw the line between quotation and a new text? When does an extract become a new poem? How do the organizational principles of a project such as the *Index of Middle English Verse* shape the answers to these questions, and in the process, how does such a scholarly resource redefine the canon—and the very materials to which it provides the index?

Such questions also motivate Ardis Butterfield's contribution to this volume. Her close examination of the manuscripts of *Troilus and Criseyde* not only reveals the modes of late-medieval reading in terms of the *ordinatio* of layout, rubrication, heading, gloss, and commentary; it also helps us to appreciate the ways in which the *Troilus* embedded a variety of genres in its narrative. Lyrics, songs, and epistles are, to some degree, the building blocks of Chaucer's amorous and philosophical story, and Butterfield shows in great detail how the scribes of the poem indicated these various generic distinctions in their manuscripts. Such distinctions, too, may draw on the habits of French manuscript organization, and this essay points toward further research in the historical recovery of medieval notions of the text. *Troilus and Criseyde* may not be best considered as a single text but rather, as the scribes perhaps indicate, an arrangement and a synthesis of different forms of discourse, each signaled visually by distinctive codes of textual representation.

Textual representation is at the heart of David Boyd's account of Chaucer's Cook's Tale in Bodleian Library, MS. 686. Like the preceding contributions, Boyd's essay locates textuality in the material and social conditions of making and reception. He reads this version of the fragmentary, difficult, and both poetically and politically challenging Cook's Tale in terms of the social positions of its likely audience. Situating a single tale in a single manuscript, he nonetheless enlarges the issue to query the very nature of an authorized, or authorial, text. Any historicist approach to literature, and by implication any historicist conception of textual criticism, must recognize, he argues, that "an authorial text . . . exists socially and historically as the author's (s') Work . . . to a particular group of readers and owners of particular versions." This revisionist claim leads to a particularly postmodern conception of both the medieval text and the profession of medieval studies. "We cannot separate," Boyd concludes, "the processes of medieval book production, construction, and transmission from our study of medieval texts or from issues of ideology, politics, and power, all of which are naturalized in the specific manuscript matrices within which and through which they operate."

For David Greetham, the possibilities of postmodern medieval or textual studies lie not so much in exposing the politics of literature or the literary profession as in exploring the controlling metaphors that have shaped modern editorial practice. The images of filiation, lineal descent, and genealogy; the notion of the text as a member of a family or a branch of a tree; the social paradigms of linearity and patriarchy that govern training in literary scholarship generally—all find themselves laid bare for the cultural figurations that they are. Through analogies to Indo-European philology, comparative biology, and physical paleoanthropology, Greetham shows how all forms of historical inquiry define the objects of their study in familial, linear, or generative terms. What Greetham offers, in the end, is not a rejection of these models as such but a personal recalibration. He posits "a model of embedding rather than descent," a notion of the text as finding its place not on the tree of textual life but in the rhizome of textual diversity. And he suggests, in closing, that "the hypertextual model of free-floating links," for all its seeming postmodernity, "is a better simulacrum of medieval textuality than the fixed critical text of the codex ever was; or at least of some types of medieval textuality, the *scriptible* rather than the *lisible.*"

Read individually, each of these essays exemplifies a tone, a technique, and a tradition of textual criticism in medieval literary study. Read in sequence, however, they trace an arc that leads us from the historical document to our own historical positions as scholars and readers. Along that arc we may be able to locate, if not a definitive answer to this introduction's titular question, then at least some points of reference for posing definitions. For what each of these contributors suggests—sometimes explicitly, sometimes implicitly—is that a text is whatever is reproducible as an object of concern. The Rotheley poem to the De Veres, a proverbial stanza of Chaucerian attribution, annotated manuscripts of *Troilus and Criseyde,* manipulated forms of the Cook's Tale, even the documents of professional editorial practice: all are "texts" worthy of study. Or, perhaps to put it differently, what we witness here are the ways in which bibliographical study transforms physical artifacts into objects of study, and furthermore, the ways in which the practices of editing, in turn, transform these objects of study into "texts." As scholars, we are all aware of these processes (this is what intellectual history *is*). Yet what this collection may enhance is our appreciation of the many and competing forces that disturb, mediate, or occlude such an awareness. As textual scholars, we all stand at the nexus of object and artifact: of physical thing and constitutive subject of institutional study. It may seem, in the end, merely reductive to define a text as whatever textual scholars study. But by exploring the vicissitudes of textual study itself—its methods, histories, controlling metaphors, and ideologies—we might well, in the end, see more clearly what McKerrow called the "virtues of bibliography."

Stanford University
University of Southern California

Rotheley, the De Vere Circle, and the Ellesmere Chaucer

RALPH HANNA III
A. S. G. EDWARDS

From William Caxton's first printings through those of Wynkyn de Worde, Richard Pynson, and William Thynne, the works of Geoffrey Chaucer were presented as a formed poetic canon.[1] All writings deemed relevant—that is, legitimate authorial effusions together with others fortuitously or circumstantially connected to them—appear between covers in arranged format (as small volumes in Caxton's and de Worde's versions, as a three-volume set in Pynson's edition, and finally as one large folio book in Thynne's). The model of the "complete works" established by Pynson and Thynne, perhaps owing something to the example of complete texts of Latin and Greek authors, has set the standard, not just for our understanding of the work of Chaucer, but also for our conception of the English literary canon as a whole. Chaucer's *Works*, in their modern, single-volume *Riverside* edition, now sit easily next to those of Shakespeare, Milton, and Keats.[2]

But before Caxton, Pynson, and Thynne, during the productive period of Middle English literature, things were quite different. Even such masterworks of the Poet as *The Canterbury Tales* and *Troilus and Criseyde* circulated in fitful and surprising ways, often as separate works in loose quires and booklets. And the fate

This essay is a full collaboration, inasmuch as both of us stand behind the views expressed in the whole. However, different portions reflect our individual research—Edwards on Drury and Bury books, Hanna on the De Veres and Rotheley, both of us on the Paston books. Hanna is particularly grateful to Rita Copeland, who presented for him an earlier version of his work to the New Chaucer Society meeting held in Dublin in 1994. And we both appreciate the editorial ministrations of Joseph A. Dane and Seth Lerer.

1. See Edwards, "Chaucer from Manuscript to Print: The Social Text and the Critical Text," *Mosaic* 28, no. 4 (1995): 1–12.
2. In other contexts, Hanna has written on the distinction between the medieval and modern circulation/consumption of Chaucer's poetry; see *Pursuing History: Middle English Manuscripts and Their Texts* (Stanford, Calif., 1996), 115–30, 140–55; and cf. Charles A. Owen Jr., *The Manuscripts of* The Canterbury Tales (Cambridge, 1991), passim, on Chaucer's self-modeling as a canonical poet. With regard to the next several paragraphs, see also *Pursuing History*, 174–94.

of Chaucer's "minor poems"—both in the peculiarities of their transmission and in the demonstrably substantial losses of copies as well as whole works—suggests the even greater randomness one might expect with less substantial, hence less clearly canonical or literarily central, products of the author. Fifteenth-century book producers and readers often had to recreate the poems from fragments, inevitably in unique and idiosyncratic ways. While such personalization is a substantial irritant from the perspective of modern textual criticism, it is equally a strength in enabling certain kinds of provocative historicization of "Chaucer"— not the poet *in se*, but the poet as received, read, and responded to in medieval literary culture. Hence the value of provenance studies, which seek the particular material circumstances of a specific audience.

Situating medieval books compels attention to the historical record, and this, in turn, may identify readerly interests and enthusiasms far removed from and even critical of the moment of poetic composition. In the prenational literary scene of fifteenth-century England, such localization is a desideratum, for local literary communities often express particularistic interests and motivated uses of cultural artifacts that are eventually suppressed in the development of a national literary canon. Provenance studies reveal the ways, often particularly difficult for modern readers to grasp, in which Chaucer was appropriated by fifteenth-century manuscript audiences. Chaucer comes to us marked as "Literature" in ways that he himself programmed and that we have thoroughly internalized as the English literary tradition,[3] a gesture that was not all-compelling to medieval audiences accustomed to other versions of literary culture. We would suggest that the study of provenance potentially shatters the raison d'être for the gathering this volume commemorates: our modern sense of Chaucer's unique and transhistorical importance.

In this context, we turn to the most splendid model for the canonically received Chaucer, Huntington Library, MS. EL 26 C 9, the Ellesmere manuscript. We moderns view the book, with its copious *demivinets* and pilgrim portraits, as a magnificent bearer of Chaucer's text. But the overly authorized canonical object we value is appropriate to the world of print, not that of fifteenth-century book consumption. Consequently, we attend to those portions of this book that comprise the Ellesmere *Canterbury Tales* and ignore the rest as extranea.[4] But highly

---

3. See *Pursuing History*, 267–79.
4. The opposite view is expressed in the effort to denigrate uncollected (and thus noncanonized) forms of fifteenth-century transmission, e.g. the "flyleaf circulation" of Chaucer's lyric *Truth* (the form of the text in Ellesmere). Cf. Aage Brusendorff, *The Chaucer Tradition* (Oxford, 1925), 202–3, 205–6; and Hanna, *Pursuing History*, 172–73.

relevant for ascertaining the later use of the manuscript is one piece of "extranea" that began as a separate eight-leaf quire, fully pricked and ruled in a form consonant with the elaborate format of the manuscript, within which the producers of Ellesmere had the book bound.[5] This unused quire was split into two four-leaf chunks to protect the intricately decorated first and last leaves of the book. These chunks attracted, in the course of the fifteenth and sixteenth centuries, a variety of materials, all of value for imagining the readership of Ellesmere and for imagining several readings of book and *Tales*, unintended by either the uninvolved author or the production team but equally part of the volume.

Broadly, the information on the Ellesmere flies points to early readership and ownership of the volume, suggesting that the book had been, for a long time, in an area on the borders of Essex and Suffolk.[6] Ignoring a great deal of further, in the main later, material, we can say that the binding leaves include three items that may be described as distinctly literary. On folio vii[v] a late-fifteenth-century reader wrote a table of contents for *The Canterbury Tales*, matching tellers with brief descriptions of content, usually names of leading characters but sometimes notations of theme. For example, the Wife of Bath's contribution is described as "Of what thyng þat women louen best." A second major addition is securely Chaucerian, the lyric *Truth* copied in on folio viii during the first half of the fifteenth century. And on folios ii[v]–iv, near the head of the volume, appears a poem of nearly two hundred lines, copied by a hand probably trained in the third quarter of the century. This contribution is said to be "Per Rotheley," which could be the name of either scribe or author. The poem includes a panegyric to the De Vere earls of Oxford, whose principal seat was at Castle Hedingham in Essex. In the appendix to this article we offer a new edition of this poem (see n. 39).

But in addition to such literary items, the flyleaves bear some entries that point to a precise Ellesmere readership. Ian Doyle has suggested that the book was available to the Paston family of Norfolk at some point in the fifteenth century. He notes that the family motto "de mieulx en mieulx" appears twice (on folios iv and vii[v]; he should also have noted the very indistinct appearance on folio ii), in

---

5. See M. B. Parkes, "The Planning and Construction of the Ellesmere Manuscript," in Martin Stevens and Daniel Woodward, eds., *The Ellesmere Chaucer: Essays in Interpretation* (San Marino, Calif., 1995), 41–47 at 42 and 45, for the suggestion that the quire was prepared to handle a possible conclusion to the Cook's Tale, should it have appeared. In *The Ellesmere Manuscript of Chaucer's* Canterbury Tales: *A Working Facsimile* (Cambridge, 1989), although text leaves are presented washed of bounds, rules, and pricks, the format shows clearly in the reproductions of the flies.

6. See the characteristically exuberant discussion of provenance in John M. Manly and Edith Rickert, *The Text of* The Canterbury Tales, 8 vols. (Chicago, 1940), 1:152–59.

what he characterizes as a "hand of the fifteenth century and probably of the first half." Doyle concludes that "if these are not the original owners, . . . it would be surprising if they were remote."[7] And although other scholars have queried the distinctiveness of the motto as an identification of the Pastons, the family had close ties—as did the Drurys of Hawstead in Suffolk, the line to which we turn next—with the candidates for ownership we are most concerned with here, the De Vere earls of Oxford memorialized in "Rotheley's" poem.[8]

Before discussing the Drurys, we review well-known information about Paston book ownership.[9] One family booklist, datable 1474–79, survives: it includes, inter alia, at least three Chaucer manuscripts (no. 2, a *Troilus;* no. 3, a courtly anthology with *Legend of Good Women, Parliament of Fowls,* Lydgate, and "La Belle Dame"; and no. 5, an anthology with similar contents, including *Parliament*). Other volumes (nos. 7, 8, 11) provide materials exemplifying another Paston association, this one with Sir John Fastolf of Caister in Norfolk and his circle. There are also tantalizing references to what might be alliterative poems, the *Morte* and *Gawain,* but more likely their stanzaic parallels (nos. 1, 3). And the list ends (no. 11) with heraldic materials, including "my boke off knyghthod" (the surviving manuscript now British Library, MS. Lansdowne 285), which Paston possibly had produced from another, also surviving, book, Morgan Library, MS. M 775, then the property of Sir John Astley K.G. of Warwickshire (who died in 1486), perhaps an acquaintance through Fastolf.[10]

7. A. I. Doyle, "English Books in and out of Court from Edward III to Henry VII," in V. J. Scattergood and J. W. Sherborne, eds., *English Court Culture in the Later Middle Ages* (London, 1983), 163–82 at 172 and n. 21.
8. Consuelo Dutschke remarks that "it seems unlikely that the manuscript could have belonged to the [Pastons in the early fifteenth century]" (*Guide to Medieval and Renaissance Manuscripts in the Huntington Library,* 2 vols. [San Marino, Calif., 1989], 1:50). J. Norton-Smith, in his edition *John Lydgate: Poems* (Oxford, 1966), notes the occurrence of the phrase in *Temple of Glass,* line 310 (as also in 530). He describes it as "a common French literary phrase (cf. Deschamps, *Lay Amoureux* 206). It came to be used much later as a motto, in England, by the Pastons" (p. 183). It would seem that both the early date of the inscription and its evident literary currency could militate against the likelihood of Paston ownership. Cf. Hanna, introduction to *Working Facsimile,* 1; and see nn. 28, 38, and 49, below, on the connections of the Pastons with the De Veres.
9. See the discussion by G. A. Lester, "The Books of a Fifteenth-Century Gentleman: Sir John Paston," *Neuphilologische Mitteilungen* 88 (1987): 200–217.
10. For the booklist, see Norman Davis, ed., *Paston Letters and Papers of the Fifteenth Century, Part I* (Oxford, 1971), 516–18. On the "boke off knyghthod," see A. I. Doyle, "The Work of a Late Fifteenth-Century Scribe, William Ebesham," *Bulletin of the John Rylands Library* 39 (1957): 298–325; and G. A. Lester, *Sir John Paston's "Grete Boke": A Descriptive Catalogue, with an Introduction, of British Library MS Lansdowne 285* (Cambridge, 1984), a work to be used with some caution, especially with regard to its discussion of the mode by which the book was produced.

If connection with the Pastons has seemed tenuous to some, the flies include one certain early indication of ownership. A note on folio 1ᵛ associates the book with Sir Robert Drury (1455–1536), probably at some time in the period 1528–36, given the references to his children. Sir Robert was a London barrister whose townhouse faced on the lane that still bears his name. He entered Lincoln's Inn in 1473–74, was a bencher of the Inn by 1490, Commons Speaker in 1495, and a privy councillor under Henry VII. He was knighted in 1497. Drury acquired his rural seat Hawstead, just south of Bury St. Edmunds and perhaps ten miles north of the De Vere seat at Castle Hedingham, in 1504.[11] The descent of the manuscript from him to its current residence in the Huntington Library is entirely mappable.

Following Manly and Rickert, scholars have usually assumed that Drury came by this Chaucer manuscript through his local rural connections. Drury, one of the twelve executors of the will of a great nobleman, was among other things the scion of a noble family. John De Vere, the thirteenth earl of Oxford, left Drury an annuity of ten marks, one of his four largest extrafamilial bequests. It has usually been assumed that the tantalizing reference in the inventory of the earl's property to "A Chest full of frenshe and englisshe bokes" in the college at Sudbury in Suffolk glances at books like Ellesmere. Certainly, the association of both Pastons and Drurys with the manuscript offers a kind of triangulation that points toward possible early De Vere ownership and, although the will makes no explicit mention of such a legacy, to the possibility that Drury acquired Ellesmere in the bequest.[12]

Nor would interest in the book have been at all foreign to Robert Drury, for the family included a number of book owners in the fifteenth and sixteenth centuries. For example, Sir Robert's father Roger Drury willed his son William (who died in 1536) "ij. English books called Bochas of Lydgates making"—that is, a two-volume copy (or two copies?) of *The Fall of Princes*.[13] A manuscript of the Vulgate (Christ's College, Cambridge, MS. 4) contains on its flyleaves a register

11. See R. C. Bald, *Donne and the Drurys* (Cambridge, 1959), 9–11. Robert's father, Roger, had previously settled in an adjacent manor in Hawstead.

12. See William H. St. John Hope, "The Last Testament and Inventory of John de Veer, Thirteenth Earl of Oxford," *Archaeologia* 66 (1915): 275–348, esp. 318 (on the executors and the Drury annuity) and 342 (on the Sudbury book chest).

13. See Manly and Rickert, *Text of* The Canterbury Tales, 1:156. Robert was left "books of Latin lying in [Roger's] chapel or belonging thereto;" see Bald, *Donne and the Drurys*, 10–11, for the suggestion that the bequest included the next book we mention.

of the Drury family. "Robertus Drury miles" (Sir Robert's son?) gave Gonville and Caius College a manuscript of Latin homilies (now MS. 243) in 1568.[14] The same man also owned Bodleian Library, MS. Hatton 4, a Book of Hours decorated by two of the Ellesmere artists.[15] British Library, MS. Harley 4826 contains Lydgate's *Life of St. Edmund and Fremund*, Burgh's *Secreta secretorum*, and Hoccleve's *Regiment of Princes*. It was apparently also in the possession of the Drury family in the sixteenth century, if not earlier; it contains an epitaph on Sir William Drury (who died in 1579).[16] A printed missal with added manuscript sequences and collects, now Norwich Cathedral, MS. 5 (fragments from the Middle English Robert of Gretham translation were only joined with this material in the nineteenth century), contains a request for prayers "pro anima Iohannis Drory pro statu Willelmi." And a *Registrum brevium* now in Worthing Public Library has the inscription "Robtus Drury est pocessor huius libri."[17] The name "Anne drure" appears in a copy of *The Prick of Conscience* (Cambridge University Library, MS. Add. 6693).[18]

We thus cannot pinpoint Ellesmere ownership in the fifteenth century with complete assurance. But substantial evidence suggests that the manuscript was available to persons in Suffolk by the early fifteenth century, and a substantial portion of the evidence points toward the neighborhood of Bury St. Edmunds, a locale important to Pastons, Drurys, and De Veres.

One largely unremarked aspect of the Ellesmere manuscript's history is that in the second quarter of the fifteenth century it appears to have been in close proximity to a presentation copy of Lydgate's *Siege of Thebes* (now British Library, MS. Arundel 119), apparently made for William de la Pole, duke of Suffolk,

14. See M. R. James, *A Descriptive Catalogue of the Western Manuscripts in the Library of Christ's College, Cambridge* (Cambridge, 1905), 4–5; and *A Descriptive Catalogue of the Manuscripts in the Library of Gonville and Caius College, Cambridge*, 2 vols. (Cambridge, 1907–8), 1:294–95, respectively.

15. See Kathleen L. Scott, "An Hours and Psalter by Two Ellesmere Illuminators," in Stevens and Woodward, *Ellesmere Chaucer*, 87–119 at 109, 112.

16. See M. C. Seymour's description, "The Manuscripts of Hoccleve's *Regiment of Princes*," *Transactions of the Edinburgh Bibliographical Society* 4, no. 7 (1974): 255–97 at 268–69 (with no notation of scribal dialect). Nicolas Barker, in *Two East Anglian Picture Books: A Facsimile of the Helmingham Herbal and Bestiary and Bodleian MS. Ashmole 1504* (London, 1988), miscites this book as Harley 4830 (p. 58); Barker offers further examples of De Vere and Drury associations in the early sixteenth century.

17. See N. R. Ker (completed by A. J. Piper), *Medieval Manuscripts in British Libraries,* 4 vols. (Oxford, 1969–92), 3:418–20, 532–34; and 4:689–90, respectively.

18. Robert E. Lewis and Angus McIntosh, in *A Descriptive Guide to the Manuscripts of* The Prick of Conscience (Oxford, 1982), tentatively identify the scribal language as "Berkshire, Oxfordshire, or Northamptonshire?" (pp. 45-46).

probably within a decade of its initial composition in the early 1420s.[19] A possible occasion for his commissioning such a manuscript was his marriage to Chaucer's granddaughter Alice in 1430. Both she and her father, Thomas, the poet's son, had patronage links to Lydgate.[20]

Lydgate's *Thebes* is explicitly a continuation of *The Canterbury Tales*, and one of the distinctive features of the Arundel manuscript is its *ordinatio*—the use of rubricated Latin marginal glosses, in addition to its *demivinets* and frequent large decorated initials. Such an *ordinatio* might be construed as an allusion to Lydgate's predecessor text, and it insistently recalls the page format of the only early *Canterbury Tales* manuscript to be so elaborately presented, Ellesmere. But the relationship between Ellesmere and Arundel 119 is also more particular and textual, for a gloss unique to Ellesmere also appears in the prologue to Arundel 119, at a point where Lydgate is imitating Chaucer's prologue. At General Prologue, line 8 ("Hath in the Ram his hal[ve] cours ironne"), Ellesmere has the unique gloss, "*id est sol in ariete.*" The first gloss in Arundel 119, to the opening line of Lygate's poem, "Whan briȝte phebus passed was the ram," is "Phoebus in ariete."[21] The recurrence of the same otherwise unrecorded gloss in the same context in these two manuscripts suggests a direct connection between them.

As Jeremy Griffiths has shown, the scribe of Arundel 119 copied at least three other manuscripts. All these books transmit Middle English verse: the *South English Legendary* (now in a book owned by Toshiyuki Takamiya, Tokyo, MS. 54); Gower's *Confessio Amantis* (Pembroke College, Cambridge, MS. 307); and John Walton's *Boethius* (in the Schøyen collection in London and Oslo, MS. 615).[22]

---

19. Samuel Moore noted the Suffolk arms in the manuscript in his seminal study "Patrons of Letters in Norfolk and Suffolk, *c.* 1450," *PMLA* 27 (1912): 188–207; *PMLA* 28 (1913): 79–105 at 27:203. For a brief description, see Axel Erdmann and Eilert Ekwall, eds., *Lydgate's Siege of Thebes*, 2 vols., Early English Text Society, extra series, 108 and 125 (1911–30), 2:37–42. There seem to be reasonable grounds for assuming that Lydgate's poem was written in 1421; see Johnstone Parr, "Astronomical Dating for Some of Lydgate's Poems," *PMLA* 67 (1952): 251–58 at 256.

20. Lydgate addressed a poem to Thomas; see Norton-Smith, *John Lydgate: Poems,* for the most recent edition (pp. 4–7). He also composed "ad rogatum domine comitisse de Suthefolchia," "The Virtues of the Mass" (see Moore, "Patrons," at 27:203). A list of manuscripts Alice owned survives in Bodleian Library, Ewelme Muniments A.VII.47 (3); see Historical Manuscripts Commission, 8th Report, Appendix I, i:629a. The most interesting of the volumes there listed (nearly all are either service books or texts in French, including Christine de Pisan's "le citee de Dames") is "a boke of English, in paper, of the pilgrymage, translated by domine John Lydgate out of fresnh." Alice's second husband, Thomas Montacute, earl of Salisbury, commissioned this verse translation of de Deguileville's *Pilgrimage of the Life of Man*, although modern scholars have sometimes queried the ascription to Lydgate.

21. We are grateful to Stephen J. Partridge for the information on the Ellesmere gloss. Partridge's study of glosses in *Canterbury Tales* manuscripts is forthcoming from Boydell and Brewer.

22. See Jeremy Griffiths, "Thomas Hyngham, Monk of Bury and the Macro Plays Manuscript," *English Manuscript Studies* 5 (1995): 214–19. The first book was purchased at Sotheby's, London, 24 June 1980,

The third of these manuscripts is of particular interest since it was certainly in Bury in the latter half of the fifteenth century. Then it was owned by the monk Thomas Hyngham, perhaps best known for his work on the Macro Plays.[23] But other Bury connections surface continually: Lydgate, himself a monk of Bury, was available to the Suffolks. The confraternity of the abbey included members of the three families in which we are most interested: John Paston I was admitted in 1429; Elizabeth Drury and Henricus Drury in 1440; and Elizabeth, wife of the twelfth De Vere earl of Oxford, was also a member.[24] Moreover, Elizabeth Drury was married to John Baret, Lydgate's copensioner, and Baret's will, written in 1463 and proved in 1467, made bequests to the Drury family, and included, among other books, "my boke with the sege of Thebes in englysh"—which might even be Arundel 119.[25]

There are yet further Bury St. Edmunds connections. Kathleen L. Scott has provided an authoritative account of the work of a group of scribes and decorators concerned mainly with the production of copies of *Edmund and Fremund* in the 1460s.[26] Among the volumes to be associated with this workshop is the Drurys' copy of the poem, Harley 4826. The derivation of the iconographic program in Harley 4826 and related books from the surviving presentation copy (British Library, MS. Harley 2278), produced for Henry VI (ca. 1434–39, prob-

---

lot 57; the second is described by M. R. James, *A Descriptive Catalogue of the Manuscripts of Pembroke College, Cambridge* (Cambridge, 1905), 273–75; the third is noted as the property of Mr. H. C. Pratt in A. G. Watson's *Supplement* to the second edition of Ker's *Medieval Libraries of Great Britain* (London, 1987), 6, 127.

23. It should be stressed that the book had other owners before coming into Hyngham's possession. As Griffiths shows, it was bequeathed by Elizabeth de Richmond to Sir Robert Godebowe before Hyngham owned it. It has not been possible to establish the whereabouts of these previous owners, although Godebowe is an Essex name. See also Richard Beadle, "Monk Thomas Hyngham's Hand in the Macro Manuscript," in Beadle and A. J. Piper, eds., *New Science out of Old Books: Studies in Manuscripts and Early Printed Books in Honour of A. I. Doyle* (Aldershot, England, 1995), 315–41.

24. On John Paston, see Rodney M. Thomson, ed., *The Archives of the Abbey of Bury St Edmunds*, Suffolk Records Society 21 (1980): 56 (item 82); on the Drurys (and Anne De Vere), see Craven Ord, "Account of the Entertainment of King Henry the Sixth at the Abbey of Bury St. Edmund's," *Archaeologia* 15 (1806): 65–71 at 70 n. 1; on Elizabeth De Vere, Victoria County History, Suffolk, 2:71.

25. Samuel Tymms, ed., *Wills and Inventories from the Registers of the Commisary of Bury St. Edmunds and the Archdeacon of Sudbury*, Camden Society 49 (1850): 15–44 at 35. Baret left this book to "sere John Cleye my cosyn, and preest with my maister Prisote"; an adjacent bequest of 3s. 3d. is directed to Osbern Bokenham (see below).

26. See "Lydgate's Lives of Saints Edmund and Fremund: A Newly Located Manuscript in Arundel Castle," *Viator* 13 (1982): 335–66; see 356–57 on Harley 4826.

ably late in the period) makes a Bury localization particularly likely. Nicholas J. Rogers has presented evidence to show that such manuscript production was being undertaken at Bury in the 1430s, when the Arundel manuscript of *The Siege of Thebes* was produced.[27]

∿ ∿

The most emphatic evidence for fifteenth-century Ellesmere provenance comes from the largest entry on the flyleaves, the poem honoring the De Veres. Certainly, the family need not have actually owned the book for this entry to be made there. Hence our attention to the Pastons, the Drurys, their books, and their associations: these provide an extended family context, a circle within which interest in the fate of this outstanding local family would have been entirely appropriate, if not absolutely expected.[28] We now consider what this poem can tell us about the context within which Ellesmere was used and about the nature of its use.

A logical place to begin is the signature attached to the poem by "Rotheley," whether poet or scribe. Identifying this figure has proved an intractable task, and in our researches we have been unable to improve on Ethel Seaton's suggestions.[29] The name seems to occur but six times in the public records of the mid- and later fifteenth century. Two sets of Rotheleys—members of a yeoman family from Dartford in Kent and a London goldsmith and his wife—seem most unlikely candidates for author of this poem. Perhaps more relevant are two figures from East Anglia, a Thomas Rotheley from Witham, in Essex, who acted as an attorney in 1489, and a Walter Rotheley who appears in a 1468 deed with Margaret Beaufort and may be identical with a collector of customs by that name in Boston, Lincolnshire, in the early 1480s.[30] Closest to home in terms of associa-

---

27. Nicholas J. Rogers, "Fitzwilliam Museum MS 3–1979: A Bury St. Edmunds Book of Hours and the Origins of the Bury Style," in Daniel Williams, ed., *England in the Fifteenth Century: Proceedings of the 1986 Harlaxton Symposium* (Woodbridge, England, 1987), 229–43.

28. See the index of Davis's *Paston Letters*, 2:646, for a variety of references to Paston involvement in De Vere affairs, especially in the family's times of ill fortune.

29. Ethel Seaton, *Sir Richard Roos, c. 1410–1482: Lancastrian Poet* (London, 1961), 421–25, esp. 422.

30. William Rotheley of Dartford appears in records ca. 1430–67; in a pardon for his participation in Cade's rebellion (1450), he is associated with Roger (in his only other appearance, of 1464, called Roger the elder, apparently dead in 1471; see Calendar of Fine Rolls, 1471–85:2). Roger the younger occurs in three records 1464–71 and is probably also the Roger Rotheley who seems to be associated with London in a patent roll record of 1472 (Calendar of Patent Rolls, 1467–77: 364). William Rotheley, goldsmith of London, occurs in records 1450–88; his wife Alice was still alive and a widow in 1491. For Thomas Rotheley, see Calendar of Ancient Deeds, A 7724 (and cf. A 7737, of 1475). For Walter Rotheley, see Calendar of Close Rolls, 1461–68: 465, CCR 1471–85: 746, 750, 813. In addition, a John de Rotheley was sheriff of Chester in 1462.

tions but relatively removed temporally—the only reference to him predates the poem by at least fifteen years—is one John Rotheley, apparently from a "Westchester" (? West Caister, Norfolk).

According to this garbled record,[31] Rotheley was among a half dozen men extended protection in February or March 1448. They were on their way to France "in the retinue of Edmund, marquis of Suffolk." As Seaton noted, the record is inaccurate: the only Edmund who held a marquisate at this time was John of Gaunt's grandson, Edmund Beaufort, nominally marquis of Dorset (although the title might be construed to have lapsed on his accession to the earldom of Somerset in 1444). He was in France at the time as lieutenant and governor general. The record may then conceal a small eyeskip, and may properly have read: "Edmund marquis (or duke?) [of Dorset (Somerset?) and William, duke] of Suffolk." We have earlier identified William de la Pole as the patron of Arundel 119, the Lydgate presentation volume that shares a gloss with Ellesmere: William on 9 March 1447/8 was appointed governor and protector of the Calais Staple and had probably been in France since the previous summer as a member of a peace embassy. His failure to protect English lands abroad was to lead to his attainder and fall within three years.[32] But such a Suffolk noble may have had connections with those circles, both social and literary, in which Oxford, Drury, and the Pastons participated.

Moreover, Rotheley's poetry smacks of Bury and the Suffolk circle. For although he writes alliterative metre—four-stress verses with regular heteromorphic second halflines—Rotheley's style is far removed from alliterative diction.[33] Rather, his lexicon is thoroughly imbued with the language of Bury's poet (and Alice Chaucer's poet and the duke of Suffolk's), Lydgate. Here perhaps most telling, as Seaton saw, is the use of the word *tarrage* (meaning "scent," at line 83): unlike many words in the poem with merely Lydgatian connotations, this word is exclusively Lydgatian—known in literary usage only from the writings of Bury's bard.[34] Although we can align the scribal language of Rotheley's poem with no

31. "Calendar of the French Rolls, Henry VI," in *Deputy Keeper of the Public Records*, 48th Report (1887): 217–450 at 376.
32. For brief biographies, see, for Edmund Beaufort, G. E. C., *The Complete Peerage*, 12, i:49–53; and for William de la Pole, ibid., 443–48.
33. On the subject of alliterative metre, see Hanna, "Defining Middle English Alliterative Poetry," in M. Teresa Tavormina and R. F. Yeager, eds., *The Endless Knot: Essays in Honor of Marie Borroff* (Woodbridge, England, 1995), 43–64.
34. *Middle English Dictionary* (ed. Hans Kurath et al. [Ann Arbor, Mich., 1954–]), s.v., "tarage," *n.*, gives twenty-two citations (overlooking this usage); of these, twenty are from Lydgate's poetry. In addition there is one from a legal text (London Letter Book K) and one from a recipe collection.

single profile in *A Linguistic Atlas of Late Mediaeval English* (Aberdeen, 1986), parallel spellings are found near Bury, in southwestern Suffolk and, to a lesser extent, in adjacent areas of northwest Essex.

Of course, beyond mutual association with the duke of Suffolk, Lydgate–De Vere connections might be construed as potentially intimate. The poet served for some years (1423–34), albeit largely in absentia, as prior of Hatfield Broadoak, in Essex, a cell of Bury, the patronage of which always belonged to the De Veres.[35] In a poem that might be construed a brief prospectus for the massive *Fall of Princes*, Lydgate included Robert, ninth earl of Oxford, banished by the Appellants after Radcot Bridge (1386), in his discussion of fallen kings and their favorites, "Of the Sudden Fall of Princes in Our Days."[36] Moreover, the only surviving vernacular book we can clearly associate with the thirteenth earl—whatever was in the chest at Sudbury—is a Lydgate manuscript: *The Life of Our Lady* (in British Library, MS. Harley 3862) bears the earl's arms.

Because the De Veres were involved in local literary efforts, they may well have patronized a poet like Rotheley. Elizabeth, wife of the ill-fated twelfth earl (of whom more shortly), was dedicatee of Osbern Bokenham's "Life of St. Elizabeth."[37] The surviving accounts for the thirteenth earl's household indicate a wealth of literary activities during Christmastide 1490–91. While none of these involves poetic commissions, the household plainly arranged its own "dysgysyng"

35. See Walter F. Schirmer, *John Lydgate: A Study in the Culture of the XVth Century,* trans. Ann E. Keep (Berkeley, Calif., 1961), 90–92; Derek Pearsall, *John Lydgate* (London, 1970), 160; and G. A. Lowndes, "History of the Priory at Hatfield Regis alias Hatfield Broad Oak," *Transactions of the Essex Archaeological Society,* n.s., 2 (1884): 117–52 at 146–47.

36. Edited by Eleanor Prescott Hammond, "Two Tapestry Poems by Lydgate: The *Life of St. George* and the *Falls of Seven Princes,*" *Englische Studien* 43 (1910–11): 10–26 at 23–25. The poem is extraordinarily evenhanded in political terms: it includes Richard II; his fallen favorite, the ninth earl; *and* Richard's uncle and eventual victim, Thomas of Woodstock, one of the Appellants who destroyed Robert De Vere. Thomas also was a prominent Essex figure: his principal seat was at Pleshy.

37. For further discussion, see Moore, "Patrons," 28:86–88; and Edwards, "The Transmission and Audience of Osbern Bokenham's *Legendys of Hooly Wummen,*" in A. J. Minnis, ed., *Late-Medieval Religious Texts and their Transmission: Essays in Honour of A. I. Doyle* (Cambridge, 1994), 157–67 at 166. Barker, *Two East Anglian,* discusses the thirteenth earl's arms in Ashmole 1504, in a form that must postdate 1509, but believes the book was produced for the Tollemaches of Helmingham in Suffolk (pp. 40–41). And the religious miscellany, British Library, MS. Harley 1706, was in the earl's household at this time, as the property of his second wife; see further Doyle, "Books Connected with the Vere Family and Barking Abbey," *Transactions of the Essex Archaeological Society,* n.s., 25 (1958): 222–43, esp. 235–39, with some information on the thirteenth earl's patronage of William Caxton.

and built its own "paugent" (stage); in addition, Castle Hedingham was visited by minstrels as well as troupes of players from both Chelmsford and Lavenham (? or Langham).[38]

Rotheley's poem purports to be written by one in despair because imprisoned (a detail that only emerges at the end, line 191).[39] The speaker is "of conforte full blynde" (line 16), since "All worldely ioy [is] passed and ouergone" (line 4). In this state of mind, one "agayne nature" (line 10), he finds himself incapable of any rational action (lines 7, 21, 23, 30, 39). The opening parodies the *topoi* of contemporary dream-visions: the poet is denied even the opportunity for a good amatory *insomnium* (lines 25–32) and cannot then escape into sleep. A divine voice twice rouses him and urges him to write, and he recognizes the voice as the restorative it is. His prayer (lines 49–72) suggests the possibility of reviving the divine image within himself: God is the source of "resonable vertues," which include "wyt, mynde, resone, and volunté" (lines 58–59). And when the poet writes, he turns not to love but to public actions; he appropriately presents a tale of a divinely inspired service and election—of the nobility and fidelity to kings that characterizes the De Vere line.

The poem is quite elaborately heraldic, and it interfaces neatly with the Chaucerian lyric *Truth* copied on one of the later flyleaves. Ever since their days as descendants of Vikings in the Contentin, the De Veres seem to have been given to elaborate punning. In the poem, this wordplay not only figures in the heraldic display but also, like medieval etymology generally, stands for a relationship with *trouthe*, "what is real"; it indicates precisely the nature of the De Veres as part of the nature of things (see n. 44 below). Most especially, the name Vere lends itself to connections with Latin *verus* "true"—the family motto was *Vero nichil verius*, "nothing is truer than truth/Vere."

But the truth the De Veres embody is scarcely limited by the terms of the Chaucerian lyric. In Rotheley's account, Vere is represented by the supporter to the family arms, the blue boar (true blue, of course), a device inspired by the sim-

---

38.   See John Payne Collier, ed., *Household Books of John Duke of Norfolk, and Thomas Earl of Surrey; temp. 1481–90* (London, 1844), 504–20, esp. 517 (519 for the "Lanham" players). Note also the payment of 3s. "to M. Sir John Pastons man for the bryngyng of v. storkys" on 17 September 1490 (p. 509). For Collier's misidentification of the household recorded in the accounts, see Melvin J. Tucker, "Household Accounts 1490–1491 of John de Vere, Earl of Oxford," *English Historical Review* 75 (1960): 468–74.

39.   The poem is only available in the sloppy reprint from Todd's *Illustrations* at Edwin Ford Piper, "The Royal Boar and the Ellesmere Chaucer," *Philological Quarterly* 5 (1926): 330–40 at 331–35 (an article that also includes some useful historical information). Consequently, we offer a new edition as an appendix and use this as our citation text.

ilarity of the surname and Latin *verres* "a boar." Moreover, this boar disports itself in spring, the season "Veer," contextually a reference both to God—as controller of the seasons and sponsor of rebirth—and to the opening of *The Canterbury Tales*. At the poem's head, Rotheley laments past losses and cannot conceive any productive future. But the fearless blue boar gives the lie to those anxieties: the De Veres are loyal both to that transcendent Truth whose incursion into the cell supposedly inspired Rotheley's verse and to God's designate in this world, "The lyon hys [the boar's] lorde" (line 113). Moreover, given the spring setting, another swerve from amatory vision (but not from Chaucer's natural world as invoked in the General Prologue, lines 1–11) is at issue: Rotheley hails "lusty Veer" (at line 100; see further 101–7), the family's extraordinary reproductive skill. In addition to their other virtues, the De Veres are, as Rotheley claims, England's "moste trwyste lynage" (line 135), in part because every generation since the conquest produced a male heir.

The poem further links the De Veres' reverent fidelity to God, king, and country ("the bore of grace," line 115) with the family's receipt of their arms (described in accurate detail in lines 146–49). This is a two-part narrative. First, "Aubray the Gryme" (line 141)—as we shall see, a well-recognized member of the line—is said to have won the blue boar "In hethenesse" (line 141), apparently by slaying the Saracen (?) champion who previously bore the device. Second, "A knyght of thys auncestery" (line 155), not necessarily Aubrey, offered support to a hard-pressed "kynge of Englande," again "in the land of hethynes" (line 154). In this originary act of service to a royal lion, the De Vere knight's prayer brought a divine light, the heraldic "v. poynte mollet" (line 171), into his shield, where it disconcerted the enemy and purchased victory and royal safety.

Some external evidence indicates that this tale of the De Vere "mollet" and blue boar represents at least family saga, even if its status as verifiable history is distinctly suspect. In his *Itinerary*, which dates from the 1530s and 1540s, John Leland provided a series of genealogical notes on the De Veres, including this account of the third Albericus/Aubrey De Vere:

> This Albry the 3., his father yet lyving, was at the conquest of the cites of Nicque, of Antioche, and of Hierusalem in the cumpanie of Robert Courtois Duke of Normandie.
>
> At the siege of the cite of Antioche in a batelle againe Solimant Prince of the Turkes aᵒ. D. 1097. a baner of S. George was taken from the Christians: the which after was won againe by this Abry the 3. Wherapon

Albry gave after the armes of S. George in his sheld.

In the yere of our Lord 1098. Corborant, Admiral to the Soudan of Perce, was faught with at Antioche and discumfited by the Christianes. The night cumming on yn the chace of this bataile, and waxing dark, the Christianes beyng 4. miles from Antioche, God willing the saufte of the Christianes shewid a white starre or molette of fyve pointes on the Christen host, which to every mannes sighte did lighte and arrest apon the standard of Albry the 3., there shyning excessively.

This Albry for his greatnes of stature and sterne looke was namid Albry the Grymme.[40]

This narrative differs from the poem, of course, in several striking ways. First, it definitely ascribes two different acts associated with the De Vere arms to Aubrey the Grim alone. Second, in placing these acts during the First Crusade, Leland describes a historical situation where no English king was present—although the association of English participants in the crusade with Robert, duke of Normandy, is accurate.[41] Third, although Leland's Aubrey wins new arms as a result of his exploits, the boar supporter is not among them, although the great English national emblem, the cross of St. George, is.

Moreover, whatever actual historical events may be enshrined in Leland's and Rotheley's accounts, some utter implausibilities surround both versions. On the side of "genuine history," in a night battle on 29 December 1087, a Turkish sortie out of Antioch was repulsed, but only after the loss of many French knights and a French standard. And Kerbogha, the atabeg of Mosul (Leland's "Corborant" recognizably reproduces the "Curbaram" of some Latin historians), led an expedition to relieve the siege; his army was destroyed on 28 June 1088, and the crusaders ranged far afield in pursuit of his fleeing troops.[42] Clearly, some

40. Lucy Toulmin Smith, ed., *The Itinerary of John Leland,* 5 vols. (1907–10; reprint, Carbondale, Ill., 1964), 4:146. Leland's information is widely repeated, with varying degrees of thoroughness and accuracy: see Arthur Collins, *Historical Collections of the Noble Families of Cavendishe, Holles, Vere, Harley, and Ogle . . .* (London, 1752), 219; Richard Almack, "Some Notes on the Family of De Vere," *Proceedings of the Essex Archaeological Society* 1 (1855): 83–88 at 83; Severne A. Ashhurst Majendie, *Some Account of the Family of De Vere, the Earls of Oxford, and of Hedingham Castle in Essex,* 2d ed. (Castle Hedingham, [1904]), 9. One De Vere genealogy we have not surveyed, Bodleian, MS. Top. Essex c.16 (notes from the mid-nineteenth century), may include original information.

41. The conclusion to the De Vere host's prayer, "do as thou wylt" (line 169), may well represent a confirmatory bit of First Crusade lore. The motto of this expedition was the approving shout first made in response to Pope Urban's sermon urging the Crusade at Clermont, 27 November 1095, "Deus le volt."

42. See Steven Runciman, *A History of the Crusades,* vol. 1, *The First Crusade and the Foundation of the Kingdom of Jerusalem* (Cambridge, 1951), 220–21 and 247–49, respectively.

combination of these pregnant details lies behind both Rotheley's and Leland's renditions of the De Vere legend.

But other information is more troubling. So far as we can tell, no surviving chronicle of English provenance describing the First Crusade offers any information like that provided by either Leland or Rotheley. And neither Aubrey the third nor his father can have been of suitable age to participate in this war. Although the first Aubrey (before 1040–1112), who came with the Conqueror, could have done so, no allusion to him as a crusader exists. Alternatively, the legend may refer to Aubrey the fourth, who could have been a crusader—certainly he was with Richard Lionheart in France in 1190. But again no English chronicle of this crusade provides any confirming detail.[43]

The legend appears to have attached itself to Aubrey the third precisely because of his standing within the family line. He was the most boarlike of all the De Veres—Grim Aubrey/Aubrey the Grim translates Latin "Albericus aper," for an *aper* "boar" in medieval etymology is also *affer*, from *ferus* "cruel, fierce."[44] His tombstone in the De Vere pantheon in the family foundation, the priory of Earl's Colne, Essex—according to sixteenth-century reports—noted his cognomen "grim" and stated that he was called such "propter summam Audaciam, et effrenatam Pravitatem."[45] He was also, as Leland did not recognize, the De Vere eventually rewarded with an earldom (by Matilda around 1142), and thus, in some sense, the head of his line. Early antiquaries connected him with the Crusades because of a Saracen's head on his tomb, although later students have

---

43. Cf. F. H. Fairweather, "Colne Priory, Essex, and the Burials of the Earls of Oxford," *Archaeologia* 87 (1937): 275–95: "Confusion has constantly arisen with reference to the early De Veres, as no less than four in succession, who were heads of the house, bore this same name [Alberic]" (p. 277). G. E. C., *The Complete Peerage*, 10:193–244 covers the medieval heads of the family, from the Conquest to the thirteenth earl; in addition to the first Alberic/Aubrey, there were Aubrey junior (before 1090–1141), Aubrey 3 (ca. 1110–94), and Aubrey 4 (ca. 1163–1214). Leland, in his *Itinerary*, splits the career of Aubrey 3 between him and Aubrey 4 (pp. 146–47), thus making it possible for Aubrey 3 to have had dates like ca. 1070–1150 and to be a member of the First Crusade. Almack ascribes the story to Aubrey 2, as does Majendie—who ascribes part of it to Aubrey 3 as well.

44. Cf. M. C. Seymour et al., eds., *"On the Properties of Things": John Trevisa's Translation of Bartholomaeus Anglicus De Proprietatibus Rerum: A Critical Text*, 2 vols. (Oxford, 1975), 2:1117/27–30. Instructively, given this supporting data, Rotheley identifies the De Vere materials of the poem as offering "proprietat[es] Veer."

45. For the epitaph, see Collins, *Historical Collections*, 220; G. E. C., *The Complete Peerage*, 10:207 note d; and Majendie, *Account of the Family of De Vere*, 13. Majendie includes very useful heraldic information; he argues that the "mullet" actually was a mark of cadency, probably first borne by Robert, the third earl (1170–1221), a younger son who succeeded to the earldom only owing to Aubrey 4's childlessness (p. 9). See also Piper, "Royal Boar," 336.

noted that this ornament was movable and its location at Earl's Colne may be a response to an already formed family legend rather than independent historical verification of it.[46]

We have mentioned Rotheley's alleged imprisonment. This is an important detail, because the poem's grandiloquent claims for De Vere fidelity (and fidelity to royalty) is a case of spin-control, of plastering over the obvious. The poem's misrepresentation of De Vere crusading is, in some sense, matched by a misrepresentation of modern De Vere history. Although the De Veres were springlike and prolific, their *verus* "trouthe" was significantly compromised by those commonplace public events of the fifteenth century that rendered the very notion of fidelity a particularly contested one. Through its reference to imprisonment and the death of hope, this poem should be associated with one of two attainders the family suffered for Lancastrian sympathies. In 1462, John, the twelfth earl, and his heir Aubrey were summarily executed by Edward IV, and the family estates conficated for two years.[47] Perhaps more significantly, in the wake of Barnet (1471), John, the thirteenth earl, second son of the twelfth and Robert Drury's friend, carried on several years of guerrilla warfare against Edward, eventually was imprisoned (safely outside England, near Calais) for a decade, and only regained full legal control of his patrimony in the early years of Henry VII.[48] Instructively, the great beneficiary of these vicissitudes of fortune was another heraldic boar, later Richard III, who twice confiscated a good many De Vere manors: at least one point of the poem might be a warning to Edward IV about who the king's real friends are: to favor the true blue boar over the white "Hogge." And the poem's prophetic promise, however discretely muted, is that a family that won its boar arms from the heathen who bore them might again overcome an evil boar.[49]

---

46. Collins mentions the Saracen's head on Aubrey 3's tomb (*Historical Collections,* 220); cf. Fairweather, "Colne Priory," 290 and n. 3.

47. John was buried at the London Austin Friars, one of only two pre-Renaissance heads of the family not interred at Earl's Colne; see Fairweather, "Colne Priory," 289.

48. See Majendie, *Account of the Family of De Vere,* 23–34 ("the greatest De Vere that ever bore the title of Earl of Oxford" [p. 23]); Piper, "Royal Boar," 336–37; and esp. C. L. Scofield, "The Early Life of John de Vere, Thirteenth Earl of Oxford," *English Historical Review* 29 (1914): 228–45.

49. On Richard's depredations—particularly his coercion of the twelfth earl's dowager, Elizabeth, and on the thirteenth earl's effort to clear title to these estates (with material aid from the Pastons)—see M. A. Hicks, "The Last Days of Elizabeth Countess of Oxford," *English Historical Review* 103 (1988): 76–95.

    Piper, in "Royal Boar," aptly cites the ballad "The Rose of England" (p. 337), There the white boar Richard destroys the garden of England and, with it, the Lancastrian rose bush. Henry Tudor uses Oxford to redress this destruction: "He brought the blew bore in with him / To encounter with the bore soe white" (stanza 8). In the ballad, Oxford shows an undue readiness to destroy all those who adhere to Richard

The De Vere poem represents a species of what Anne Middleton has called "kynde naming," in its standard chivalric form—the blazon explains the family's conception of its social work.[50] In his tale of earl Aubrey the Grim and his receipt of the family arms through prayer and divinely given prowess, Rotheley indicates what the life of the De Veres is—their Truth, in all the ways that the poem defines it, ranging from devotion and fearless service to springtime joy and sexual potency. We would suggest that the poem and the De Vere reception of Ellesmere resituate Chaucer within family saga. Rotheley inflects Chaucer's *Truth* in a new—and elaborately polyvocal—way. Rather than the sober Boethian disengagement Chaucer enjoined on Vache, his cowlike recipient, in the original, the De Vere boar points to the complications of public life and the ways in which "soothfastnesse" must be continuously reenacted for appropriate social effect. In so doing, the poem implies dense material acts of political lordship at least comparable to the dense and diverse Chaucerian offering in the book. This poem, Chaucer's *Tales*, declines Rotheley's tack of securely identifying De Vere identity through recounting an originary family myth; it deliberately disguises its author's social identity ("What man artow?"). And in contrast to the implicitly rich social marking of De Vere responsibilities and interests, *Tales* disperses its author's identity through the voices of his created world, marked only according to occupation. Rotheley claims for his De Vere patrons a force, integrity, and identity broadranging as that of the poet's *Tales*, not his *Truth,* and yokes those attributes with the implicit promise of their social action, the possibility that in a better, unimprisoned future they will actuate anew all the powers that are theirs.

But whatever value we may wish to accord to this interpretation of *Truth* and *Tales*, Rotheley's implicit reading of these poems uncomfortably reveals certain historical repressions at the center of Chaucer's career. For if not the product of imprisonment, *The Canterbury Tales* are the fruits of relative retirement, Chaucer's withdrawal from the central bureaucracy after 1386, a withdrawal associated with the triumph of the Appellant Lords in 1386–89. The De Veres in the 1460s and 1470s showed their fidelity, but to the wrong candidate for the throne; Chaucer in the 1380s adhered to the king's part but to the losing courtly party (one whose fall

---

(stanza 18), but provides truly heroic service in the vanguard at Bosworth Field (stanza 27). For the text, see Francis James Child, ed., *The English and Scottish Popular Ballads*, reprint, 5 vols. in 3 (New York, 1953), 3:332–33.

50. See "William Langland's 'Kynde Name': Authorial Signature and Social Identity in Late-Fourteenth-Century England," in Lee Patterson, ed., *Literary Practice and Social Change in Britain, 1380–1530* (Berkeley and Los Angeles, 1990), 15–82, esp. 27–30.

led to the exile of a De Vere earl). In Rotheley's account, De Vere despair in a situation of lost power was replaced by the hope of renewed worldly action. In contrast, the Ellesmere *Canterbury Tales* represents the glorious fountainhead of English literature, a triumph of culture that redresses the anxieties of lost power. But this triumph is predicated purely and only upon political failure—Chaucer's inability, in the event, to regain the outstanding courtly place he had held before. While John De Vere returned in triumph with Henry Tudor, Chaucer may simply have gone off to North Petherton. He exchanged some measure of political power for a much less clearly valuable cultural standing. The Ellesmere *Canterbury Tales* heroicizes that contribution; the De Vere circle's additions to the book's flyleaves may be read as a sober assessment of the losses inherent in such poetic heroism.

University of California, Riverside
University of Victoria

Rotheley's Poem on the De Veres

We provide a transcription of the poem, folios ii^v–iv of the Ellesmere manuscript, EL 26 C 9. We follow manuscript spellings (abbreviations appear in parentheses) but intrude modern punctuation and capitalization. Because the scribe writes *ff* almost universally, we have replaced it with *F* or *f* as appropriate. Interlined readings appear between slant lines. We have ignored a variety of otiose strokes typical of many fifteenth-century hands—for example, barred *ll* and *h* and ticks on final *-d, -g, -n*. We do expand the full loop on some medial and final *r*'s as *r(e)*, and we reproduce the few ornamental capitals, all in text ink, in bold face.

Halfe in a dede sclepe not fully revyued,	f. ii^v
Rudely mysylfe as I lay alone	
With trovbled dremes sore was I mevyd;	
All worldely ioy passed and ou(er)gone.	
Me semyd full sore I made my mone	5
Of tyme passed and leste and tyme to come.	
Mynde, thowght, resonable wyt hadde I none;	
Thus I lay sclomberyng a owre to my dome.	
As thus I lay avexed full sore	
In suche thynges as of right bythe agayne nature,	10
I herde a voyce seyyng, "sclepe thow no more.	
Aryse vp and wake; do thy besy cure.	
Thy mynde, thy hert, thy body thow alure	
To suche that wyll fall next tho thy mynde.	
Take thy penne in thy hand, stedfaste and sure.	15
Awake, awake, of conforte full blynde."	

Thys voyce well I herde and therto gaue audyens.
I felte the entent, but I stode amased;
I wyste not what it ment, for I saw no presens.
Thus in pencyfenes sore was I crased   20
And as a wytles man gretely adased.
I gaue no credenc(e); anon I fell in sclepe.
Frome all kyndely wyt clene was I rased,
So to hys wordes I toke no grete kepe.

    I supposyd yt to haue bene some noxiall fantasy   25
As fallyth in dremes in partyes of the nyght,
Which co(m)meth of ioy or of greuo(us) malady
Or of robuste metes which causeth grete myght.
Ouer(e)moche replet obscuryth the syght
Of naturell reasoune and causyth idyll thowgh,   30
Makyth the body heuy where hyt was lyght.
So schortly to co(n)clude of thys voyce I ne rowght.

    And not sclepte but a lytyll whyle
But thys voyce well I herde; to me he sayde:
"Awake and aryse; thow doste thysylfe begyle   35
Aryse from the place where thow art leyde."
Wyth that I awoke and from my slepe brayed
Maruelyng moch and sayde, "Benedicite,"
As a man vnresonable gretely dysmayed.
"Ey gode lorde, whate thyng may thys be?"   40

    Hugely trobled yet feythfully I beleuyd
That the voyce came frome the celestyall place.
Wherefore I aryse not gretely agrevyd
And besawght god of hys espesyall grace
That he wolde be my socowre in this cace,   45
Prayng as yt folowyth wyth hert and wyll;
Arysyng full lyghtely mysylfe dyd I mase,
Makyng my prayowre vndyr this skyll:

33   so ms.; probably a phrase like "I hadde" has dropped out after "And."
43   aryse ms. (for arose)

"**O R**eformer(e) of mankynde, one ij. & iij.,   f. iii
Eternall kynge and prynce moste emperyall,   50
Veray god and man, o blessyd trynyté
Which from owre mortall enemye redemyst vs all
And madest vs fre where afore we were thrall,
Thorowgh dyvyne consayle of thy godhede
Me to thy grace reconsyle and call,   55
Whome thow haste formyd to the fygure of thy manhed.

"And syth thy godhed hathe endewed me
Wyth vertues ij. or iij. full resonable,
Wyth wyt, mynde, resone, and volunté
And othyr mo full delectable,   60
Yet I confesse mysylf moste vnable
Wyth anythynge to medle that groundyd ys on prudens,
Of eloquens but symple my cunnynge ys vnstable.
Therefore in me there ys no grete influence.

"But o gode lorde, syth I knowe hyt ys thy wyll,   65
As I conseyve by the voyce that thow dydest sende,
Thy degre and comaundeme(n)t trwly to fullfylle
Wyth mynde, hert, and body sewe and entend.
Me from all errowre kepe and defend
In thys matyre to the whych thow haste wyllyd me,   70
As thowe frome erth to hevyn dydest assende,
Veray god and man, o blessyd t(ri)nyte."

Incepc(i)o materie cum p(ro)prietatib(us) Veer &c.

All thyng ys ordeynyd by goddys provysyon —
Man and beste, ayre, wedre and wynde,
Wat(er) and land wyth ther(e) dysposyon,   75
And eche in apparens schewyth theyre kynde.
The ȝere ys deuyded, as I wryttyn fynde,
In monethes, wokes, and seasounes iij.,
In which wyth xij. sygnes, vij. planetys ther be.

75   dysposyon ms. (for dysposysyon)

Of all tymes or seasounes w^towte comparysoun   80
None ys found so gode ne so precyous
Ne none so prophetable as ys the seasoun
Of lusty veer, whos tarrage so oderous
Comfortyth euery creature and maketh them corragyus,
Avoydeth all dulnes and makyth them lusty   85
In hert and body gladde, proude, and mery.

Whan passyd ys all clowdy derknesse,
All stormy schowr(es) ferre fledde fro syght,
Than lusty veer schewyth hys swetnesse.
The wedyr cleryth and by nature ys bryght;   90
The mone full plesauntly gyfyth hyr lyght.
Than veer co(m)maundyth Apryll wyth hys schowrys
That May brynge forth erbys and flowrys.

All trees than buddyth, aftyr(e) fruyte bryngyth;
All sedys and cornys flowryth in prosperyté.   95
The nyghtyngale, the thrystekok merely syngyth;   f. iii^v
All fowlis and bestys ioyeth in ther(e) degre.
He cawsyth all thynge full Iocounde to be.
Who than ys so precyous or may do more
Than lusty Veer, whom I lyken to a bor(e)?   100

To thys bore he ys not lykenyd in condicion onely
But \in/ properté, for prop(er)té gyfen mor(e) fructuous.
And the bore in that seasoune approchyth naturally
To luste and to lykynge enforsyd maruelo(us);
He walkyth ioyyng, whettyng hys tuskes,   105
Thynkyng as longe as contynuyth veere
Neuyr to obey hys enemyes for feere.

He houyth ne he wanyth for wynde ne blaste;
He dredyth no mystys, ne stormys ne schowrys,
But standyth styfe in tryeuth stronge as a maste   110
And to the lyons obeys(a)unt in all howrys,
Redy w^t hys power(e) to helpe in all stowrys —

111 lyons ms. (for lyon)

The lyon hys lorde wher(e) he standyth in dystresse,
Hys natyf attend(a)unt on the lyonnesse.

Thys bore may well be callyd the bore of grace,   115
Of whom prophesyes of antiquite makyth mencion,
Which as hyt is sayde wythyn schorte space
Schall in grete nede socowr(e) the lyoune
And in that batell gete hym grete renoun,
Confounde hys mortall fone, ellys were grete ruyth.   120
That day schall be knowen hys p(er)manent trwth.

In hys p(er)sone ys founde so pur(e) verité
And standyth so clene wythowte transgresse
That all England may ioy hys natiuité.
Of contynewyng trwth he standyth pereles,   125
Hys progenie neu(er) distayned w^t falsenes.
Syth hys fyrst day he hathe contynwyd so demur(e)
Vnto now that he \is/ her(e) colowred w^t azur(e).

Now vnto thys blew bor(e) hono(ur) and grace,
Ioy, laude, and praysyng, fortune and magnyfycens.   130
Criste graunt hym of grace suche ioy to purchace
As may be worthy vnto hys reuerence.
Foreuyr(e) in feyfull trouth hathe ben hys p(er)manence;
Wher(e)for(e) now of all England he hathe avauntage,
Owte excepte the blode ryall the moste trwyste lynage.   135

Betwyxt veer and thys I put no diuisioun;
They standyth as one, who vndyrstondyth ary3th.
Veer wan thys blew bore throwgh grete renoun,
At that tyme standyng aventuro(us) knyght,
Sechyng aventur(e)s and provynge hys myght.   140
In hethenesse 3et thy sey that Aubray the Gryme
Benome the blewe bor(e) hys chyefe lymme.

140   ms. provy(n)nge?
141   thy ms. (for they)

Lo for the proves of thys wurschippfull knygh
That slewe thys bore thorowth strengyth of chyualry,   f. iv
All hys auncestr(e)s euyr syth of veray dyew ryght   145
Beryth hym azure enarmyd w^t gold dependynge by
The worschyppfull armys of the olde auncestrye:
Quartely goull(es) and goolde, and in the chyef quart(er)
A molet v. poynte syluer(e), as I schall tell her(e)after.

      Beholde nowe the ma(n)hode, proves, and chyualry,   150
Trowth, fortune, grace, and parfyte stedfastnes
That euyr(e) hath contynued in thys progenie.
Lo wher(e) hyt fortuned to stande in dystresse
The kynge of Englande in the land of hethynes,
A knyght of thys auncestery, gou(er)no(ur) of hys puysh(a)unce, 155
For(e) hys kynge thys he dydde of hys grete afyaunce:

      Reme(m)bryng hys manhode, confortyd w^t the holy goste,
Consyderyng hys feyth, he drede no woo;
At mydnyght iuste, he sembled the kyng(es) ooste.   160
The nyght so derke, not knowyng hys foo,
To the kynge vnwyttyng that hit scholde be soo,
Prayng full hertlye he fyll to the grounde
That god wolde sende hym lyght hys enemye to co(n)founde.

      To thys prayowr(e) so devoute god gaue exaudicion,   165
Not wyllyng hys cristened fygur(e) vttr(e)ly to be spylt.
Euery man than knelyng devowtely sayde their(e) orysoun,
"Lorde for thy pyté, haue mercy on owr(e) gylt;
Saue vs or spyll vs, do as thou wylt."
Thys prayo(ur) fynyshed, ther(e) sprange into hys schelde   170
A v. poynte mollet which lyghnyd all hys felde.

148 Quartely ms. (for -rly)

Thys he was inspyred w^t the grace of the holy goste,
Hys enemyes were obscuryd and voyde of all myght,
God comfortyd and chered hym and all hys oste
And endewyd thys mollet w^t a plentuous lyght;　　　　175
The hethyn were obscuryd and hadde no syght.
So he put hys enemyes to vtter confusyoun,
Dystressyd the felde, and gate hym grete renoun.

O thow roiall bore fullfyllyd wyth grace,
That of suche a mollet nowe hathe d(omi)nacion,　　　　180
Cryste graunt the contynewyng tyme and space
That the mollet may resplende ou(er) eu(er)y region,
Worthely and knyghtely as a lorde of renown.
And for the encr(e)ce of thy lyght that h(y)t fall not derke,
All England owyth to p(ra)y w^t entyer(e) deuocion,　　　　185
Man, chylde, and wyfe, bothe preste and clerke.　Amen
　　　　　　　　　　　　　　P(er) Rotheley

Go lytell balade, full rude of composicion,
Softe and mekely, nothynge to bolde;
Pray all that of the schall haue inspexion　　　fortune be
Thy derke ygnoraunce that they pardon wolde.　frendely &c.　190
Sey that thow were made in a prysone colde,
Thy maker(e) standyng in dyssete and greu(au)nce
Which cawsed hym the so symply to avaunce.

172　Thys ms. (for Thus)
186　P(er) Rotheley: in ms., opposite this line

Proverbial Chaucer and the Chaucer Canon

JULIA BOFFEY

The history of the Chaucer canon begins with fifteenth-century manuscripts and the variety of ways in which they have preserved information
about Chaucer's authorship of particular texts. Most obviously, this
information takes the form of scribal attribution, although it also includes testimony offered by other authors (Lydgate and Gower, for example), or internal evidence such as the eagle's identification of Chaucer in *The House of Fame*, or the
revealing biographical details of the Prologue to *The Legend of Good Women*.[1]
These categories of information are not wholly unproblematical: considerable
skepticism has been expressed, for example, about the validity of the scribal notes
that attach Chaucer's name to the short poems *Womanly Noblesse* and *To
Rosemounde*[2] and about the nature of Chaucer's connection with the various fragments of *The Romaunt of the Rose;*[3] and recent studies have begun to demonstrate
that a variety of powerful factors were at work on even the very early processes of
canon formation.[4] The influential roles of early Chaucer promoters such as the
fifteenth-century scribe John Shirley or the sixteenth-century antiquary John
Stow are also currently under investigation that seems likely to question or at least
to expose for consideration the weight of their authority.[5] The construction, over

1. On the history of the Chaucer canon see W. W. Skeat, *The Chaucer Canon* (Oxford, 1900); Paul G. Ruggiers,
   ed., *Editing Chaucer: The Great Tradition* (Norman, Okla., 1984); Ruth Morse and Barry Windeatt, eds.,
   Chaucer Traditions: Studies in Honour of Derek Brewer (Cambridge, 1990); and Tim William Machan,
   Textual Criticism and Middle English Texts (Charlottesville, Va., and London, 1994).
2. For a summary of views on these scribal notes, see George B. Pace and Alfred David, eds., *Geoffrey Chaucer:
   The Minor Poems, Part One*, vol. 5 of *The Variorum Chaucer* (Norman, Okla., 1982), 179–86, 161–70.
3. The fragments of the *Romaunt* survive in Hunterian Library, Glasgow, MS. V. 3. 7 and in William Thynne's
   printed edition of 1532. The first leaf of the manuscript, which may have contained details of authorship, is
   now lost. See further Larry D. Benson, ed., *The Riverside Chaucer*, 3d ed. (Boston, 1987), 1103–4, 1198–99.
4. See, for example, John M. Bowers, "The House of Chaucer and Son: The Business of Lancastrian Canon-
   Formation," *Medieval Perspectives (Southeastern Medieval Association)* 6 (1991): 135–43; and Seth Lerer,
   Chaucer and His Readers: Imagining the Author in Late-Medieval England (Princeton, N.J., 1993).
5. On Shirley see, most recently, Lerer, *Chaucer and His Readers*, 117–46; and A. S. G. Edwards, "John Shirley
   and the Emulation of Courtly Culture," forthcoming in the proceedings of the Eighth Triennial Congress
   of the International Courtly Literature Society, held in Belfast in 1995. Stow's activities are considered by
   Anne Hudson in Ruggiers, *The Great Tradition*, 53–70.

some five centuries, of a body of writing considered to be a "Chaucer apocrypha" is in itself worthy of study.[6] According to what criteria have different ages deemed particular works to be either especially "Chaucerian" or, alternatively, especially inadmissable to the canon? In the construction of a number of rather different Chaucers, how are these criteria themselves subject to historical (or conceivably to social or local) change?

In the case of a canon that has been so thoroughly and extensively explored, it may seem that there is little prospect of adjustments based on new evidence: most of the ground has been exhaustively, if not repetitively, covered. But serendipitous findings in manuscripts with no obvious connection to Chaucer's works can sometimes refine and clarify our understanding of his reputation among his earliest readers and extend our comprehension of the means by which his works were transmitted. Undertakings such as the current revision of *The Index of Middle English Verse* and its *Supplement*, which involve looking afresh at a number of manuscripts, are uncovering hidden or overlooked information— particularly in the area of attribution—that can build up a more comprehensive picture of the early reception of Chaucer's writings and suggest some of the channels of transmission that were crucial to the construction of influential "Chaucers" of different aspects.[7]

An attribution to Chaucer found in British Library, MS. Cotton Vitellius E. xi provides a scrap of information that may form a part of this picture. The unindexed item attributed to Chaucer is an eight-line ballade stanza copied on a small slip of paper (fol. 4ᵛ) that has been bound with other damaged fragments into the front of the manuscript, a copy of John of Fordun's *Chronica gentis Scotorum* and related material.[8] The three other fragments are a torn frontispiece from a printed book (fol. 1); a fragment of parchment on which a later hand has copied what

6. See F. W. Bonner, "The Genesis of the Chaucerian Apocrypha," *Studies in Philology* 48 (1951): 461–81; R. H. Robbins, "The Chaucerian Apocrypha," in Albert E. Hartung, gen. ed., *A Manual of the Writings in Middle English, 1050–1500*, vol. 4 (New Haven, Conn., 1967).
7. The existing *Index of Middle English Verse* was prepared by Carleton Brown and Rossell Hope Robbins (New York, 1943); and the *Supplement to the Index of Middle English Verse* by Robbins and John L. Cutler (Lexington, Ky., 1965). The revision of *IMEV* and *SIMEV*, funded jointly by the National Endowment for the Humanities, the British Academy, and the Social Sciences and Humanities Research Council of Canada, is being undertaken by Linne R. Mooney, A. S. G. Edwards, and Julia Boffey, and will generate not only hard copy but also an electronic version of a capacity that will make possible the inclusion of manuscript attributions.
8. For a description of Cotton Vitellius E. xi, see William F. Skene, *The Historians of Scotland*, vol. 1, *Johannis de Fordun, Chronica gentis Scotorum* (Edinburgh, 1871), xxvii–viii.

appears to be a list of the contents of the volume (fol. 2); and a paper leaf, on which the first hand of *Chronica* has copied a table of chapter headings to part of that text (fol. 3). On folio 4^v what looks to be a less polished form of this same hand has written the eight-line stanza:

> Right as pouert causis sobirnes
> and febilnes enforsis continence
> Right so prosperite and riches
> þe modir is of vice and negligence
> And power alswa causis insolence
> and honours oft sis changis thewis
> þar is no more p*er*olous pestilence
> than hye estat yeuyn onto schrewis[9]

Consulting the existing *Index* and *Supplement* reveals that the lines are a further copy of item 2820, extant in at least nine other witnesses,[10] a one-stanza extract from the prologue to John Walton's early-fifteenth-century verse translation of Boethius, *De consolatione philosophiae* (stanza 11, translating part of the prologue to book 1 of the Latin); it has been given the conventional modern title of "Walton's Prosperity." In Cotton Vitellius E. xi, a connection with Chaucer is noted twice on the leaf, in the space to the right of the text: once by the hand that copied it and again, below, by another hand, the ink of which has become faint; both attributions appear to read "chauser geffrey." The only other of the copies to confirm the attribution—not noted in either *Index* or *Supplement*—is that in Bodleian Library, MS. Arch. Selden. B. 24, where the stanza (on folio 119) is followed by the words "Quod Chaucer." None of the other copies preserves information as clear as this, although the version in Huntington Library, MS. EL 26 A 13 concludes somewhat obscurely "To yowe Chaucier" (fol. 3). Furthermore, the version in John Rylands Library, MS. Lat. 201—which appears to have been added to a collection of fourteenth-century Latin treatises—is incorporated with other lines of verse that include the apocryphal "Chaucer's

9. The transcription of quotations is diplomatic. Expansions of abbreviations are represented in italics.
10. *IMEV* and *SIMEV* list seven manuscripts. Not hitherto noted are two further copies, brought to my attention by A. S. G. Edwards: an unascribed copy added to the Taylor MS of Gower's *Confessio Amantis*, in Princeton University Library (I am grateful to Kate Harris for information about this copy); and another in Huntington Library, MS. EL 26 A 13, a copy of Hoccleve's *De Regimine Principum* and some poems by Lydgate. The first of these (formerly Phillipps 8192 and subsequently Rosenbach 369) is described in David Anderson, ed., *Sixty Bokes Olde and Newe: Manuscripts and Early Printed Books from Libraries in and near Philadelphia* . . . (Norman, Okla., 1986), 101–3; on the second see C. W. Dutschke, *Guide to Medieval and Renaissance Manuscripts in the Huntington Library*, 2 vols. (San Marino, Calif., 1989), 1:35–39.

Prophecy" (*IMEV* 3943).[11] The fragments with which it occurs in the Taylor manuscript include some lines of Chaucer. Of the other copies, one occurs in the extensive "Wagstaff Miscellany" (Beinecke Library, MS. 163),[12] and another in the Scottish Bannatyne Manuscript (National Library of Scotland, Advocates' MS. 1. 1. 6), copied in 1568;[13] three are in manuscripts, like EL 26 A 13, somehow connected with John Shirley, and will be discussed below.[14]

Walton's translation of Boethius was completed in 1410, apparently undertaken for Elizabeth, daughter of Sir Thomas Berkeley and wife of the earl of Warwick.[15] Although most of the manuscripts preserve it in complete form, extracts of different portions were also in circulation. In addition to the stanza on prosperity, the *Index* and *Supplement* list two further independent extracts (and it is not impossible that more are waiting to be identified): a stanza on death (*IMEV* 1254; stanza 503, translating part of book 3, metrum 10, and surviving in British Library, MS. Royal 9. c. ii);[16] and another on common governance (*SIMEV* 856.5; stanza 77, translating part of book 1, prosa 4, now in Pierpont Morgan Library, Bühler MS. 17).[17]

11. The manuscript is briefly described by R. Fawtier, "Hand-List of Additions to the Collection of Latin Manuscripts in the John Rylands Library, 1908–20," *Bulletin of the John Rylands Library* 6 (1920): 186–208 at 193; the other added items are "Pees maketh plente" (*IMEV* 2742), the verse Ten Commandments from the *Speculum Christiani* (*IMEV* 3687), and "Erthe upon erth" (*IMEV* 3985).

12. See Barbara A. Shailor, *Catalogue of Medieval and Renaissance Manuscripts in the Beinecke Rare Book and Manuscript Library, Yale University,* vol. 1: MSS. 1–250 (Binghamton, N.Y., 1984), 216–23.

13. See Denton Fox and William Ringler, introduction to *The Bannatyne Manuscript: National Library of Scotland, Advocates' MS 1.1.6* (London, 1980).

14. British Library, MSS. Add. 29729, Harley 2251, and Royal 20. B. xv.

15. See Mark Science, ed., *Boethius: De Consolatione Philosophiae, Translated by John Walton*, Early English Text Society, original series, 170 (London, 1927); and Ralph Hanna III, "Sir Thomas Berkeley and His Patronage," *Speculum* 64 (1989): 878–916 at 899–903. R. R. Raymo, in "Works of Religious and Philosophical Instruction," Albert E. Hartung, gen. ed., *A Manual of the Writings in Middle English, 1050–1500*, vol. 7, (New Haven, Conn., 1986), lists twenty-two manuscripts of the complete translation (p. 2578). Another one, now MS. 615 in the Schøyen Collection, has recently come to light; see Jeremy Griffiths, "Thomas Hyngham, Monk of Bury and the Macro Plays Manuscript," *English Manuscript Studies* 5 (1995): 214–19.
I am grateful to A. S. G. Edwards for advice on these manuscripts.

16. Edited by Carleton Brown in *Religious Lyrics of the Fifteenth Century* (Oxford, 1939) as "Death, the Port of Peace" (p. 259); its source was identified by Richard L. Greene in "'The Port of Peace': Not Death But God," *MLN* 69 (1954): 307–9. For a description of the manuscript, a thirteenth-century copy of the Decretals of Gregory IX, see G. F. Warner and J. Gilson, *Catalogue of the Western Manuscripts in the Old Royal and King's Collections*, 4 vols. (London, 1921), 1:291.

17. Curt F. Bühler, "A Middle-English Stanza on 'The Commonwealth and the Need for Wisdom,'" *English Language Notes* 2 (1964–65): 4–5; the manuscript, a copy of Petrus de Crecentiis, *Liber ruralium commodorum*, is described in C. U. Faye and W. H. Bond, *Supplement to the Census of Medieval and Renaissance Manuscripts in the United States and Canada* (New York, 1962), 390. Bühler seems also to have been responsible for identifying the source of the stanza on prosperity.

These extracts share a quality of succinctness that makes their moral points easy to memorize: the first is a series of terse but alluring definitions of death ("refuge to wreches," "comforte of myschefe & mysese"), and the second expands an originally Platonic maxim to conclude with the reminder, "A blisful thynge were comyn gouernaunce / Yff onely wyse men shold haue itt on hand." Walton's decision to translate into stanzaic verse clearly made his version more inviting than Chaucer's prose *Boece* for those wishing to pillage neatly formulated extracts, and the form must account in some part for the evidence that his was the better known of the two English translations: Chaucer's prose *Boece* survives in ten manuscripts in comparison with the twenty-three of Walton's version.[18] Even so, the scribes of the extracts in Cotton Vitellius E. xi and Arch. Selden. B. 24 seem to have been ignorant of Walton's association with the stanza they copied or, even if they knew of it, to have preferred to associate the stanza with Chaucer's name.

$$\sim \quad \sim$$

On the recto of the fragmentary leaf in Cotton Vitellius E. xi are three lines of Latin verse in which the initial letters of each word spell out the name "iohannes de fordun":

> Incipies opus hoc adonay no*m*ine nostri
> Exceptu*m* scriptis dirigat emanuel
> fauces ornate ructent du*m* verbula nectant

The acrostic is written out in the space to the right of the text: "i. o. h. a. n. n. e. s / d. e. f. o. r. d. u. n," in a manner that perhaps inspired or replicated the placing of Chaucer's name alongside the Walton stanza. Although the hand that copied the Latin lines does not seem to be the same as any of the main hands responsible for the Latin text in the manuscript, it looks to be contemporary with them, and there are reasonable grounds to suppose that the damaged folio 4 survives from an early stage of the manuscript's compilation. The lines that include the Latin acrostic are customarily found, in conjunction with three further lines of Latin,[19] at the conclusion of the list of contents of the chapters of the first book of the *Chronica* (they

18. See I. R. Johnson, "Walton's Sapient Orpheus," in A. J. Minnis, ed., *The Medieval Boethius: Studies in the Vernacular Translations of the De Consolatione Philosophiae* (Cambridge, 1987), 139–68. Walton's version was also printed, in Tavistock, in 1525 (*STC* 3200); Chaucer's *Boece* first appeared in print in the context of Thynne's collected edition of 1532 (*STC* 5068).

19. In Cotton Vitellius E. xi these read as follows: "Compilatoris nomen superis elementis / Construe quem lector precor ora scandere celum, / Atque pater noster confer amore dei." Skene, in *Historians of Scotland*, notes that "there is every reason to think that the six lines annexed to the titles of the chapters of the first book were written by [John of Fordun]" (pp. xiii–xiv).

are copied twice on folios 1ʳ and 1ᵛ of British Library, MS. Harley 4764, for example), and are designed to draw attention to both the author's identity and the significance of the text with which he is associated.

John of Fordun's *Chronica gentis Scotorum*, which draws together stories and
legends about Scotland's early history up to 1153 and extends them to 1385 in a
further series of notes known as the *Gesta annalia*, has been described as "the first
attempt to write a comprehensive history of Scotland, . . . to give the Scots a sense
of national identity, to show that the Scottish people had a past more distinguished than the British or English and that Scotland was a historically independent kingdom over which the English had no claim."[20] Material from both the
formal chronicle and the annals made its way into later chronicles such as the
Scotichronicon and the revision of this known as *The Book of Cupar* (both attributed to Walter Bower), and into texts such as the *Liber Pluscardensis*.[21] One early
owner of Cotton Vitellius E. xi, William Schevez, Archbishop of St. Andrews
(d. 1497), was clearly interested in the different formulations of Scottish history
represented by these texts: apart from Cotton Vitellius E. xi (in which his name
is copied several times),[22] he also owned Bower's *Scotichronicon* (in what is now
British Library, MS. Harley 712) and the *Liber Pluscardensis* (now University
Library, Glasgow, MS. Gen. 333).[23]

The attachment of Chaucer's name to the Walton stanza in Cotton Vitellius E. xi,
a book that is otherwise concerned with Scottish national history, is not easy to com-

---

20. See Edward Donald Kennedy, "Chronicles and Other Historical Writing," in Albert E. Hartung, gen. ed.,
    A Manual of the Writings in Middle English, vol. 8 (New Haven, Conn., 1989), 2679–80; and Skene,
    Historians of Scotland, introduction. Skene also provided an English translation: *The Historians of Scotland*,
    vol. 4, *John of Fordun's Chronicle of the Scottish Nation* (Edinburgh, 1872). On the ideological aspects of the
    compiling of a Scottish national history, see R. James Goldstein, *The Matter of Scotland: Historical Narrative
    in Medieval Scotland* (Lincoln, Neb., 1993).
21. On the sequence of these redactions, see Skene, *Historians of Scotland*, introduction; D. E. R. Watt,
    "Editing Walter Bower's *Scotichronicon*," in Roderick J. Lyall and Felicity Riddy, eds., *Proceedings of the
    Third International Conference on Scottish Language and Literature (Medieval and Renaissance), University of
    Stirling, 2–7 July 1981* (Glasgow, 1981), 161–76; Marjorie Drexler, "The Extant Abridgments of Walter
    Bower's *Scotichronicon*," *Scottish Historical Review* 61 (1982): 62–74; and Kennedy, *Manual*. A full discus-
    sion of the manuscripts is promised in volume 9 of D. E. R. Watt, ed., *Scotichronicon, by Walter Bower, in
    Latin and English*, forthcoming from Aberdeen University Press.
22. See, for example, folios 3ʳ, 3ᵛ, 5ʳ.
23. George H. Bushnell, "Portrait of a Bibliophile, IV: William Schevez, Archbishop of St. Andrews, d. 1497,"
    Book Collector 9 (1960): 19–29. It is just about possible that the paper slip that now forms folio 4 of
    Cotton Vitellius E. xi made its way into this volume from another of Schevez's Fordun-related manuscripts,
    although on scribal evidence this seems unlikely.

prehend. Some explanation for it may be sought in the history of the other manuscript that contains the attribution, MS. Arch. Selden. B. 24. This is a very late fif-
teenth- or early-sixteenth-century anthology that unites *Troilus and Criseyde* and
some of Chaucer's dream poems with *The Kingis Quair* and a number of shorter
pieces.[24] Apart from a copy of Chaucer's lyric "Truth" that accompanies the
romance *Lancelot of the Laik* in Cambridge University Library, MS. Kk. 1. 5, and
some other scattered evidence,[25] its Chaucer texts offer the earliest extant written
testimony to a Scottish interest in Chaucer's writings (texts such as *The Kingis
Quair* or *The Buke of the Howlat,* which seem influenced by Chaucer's poems, constitute a different sort of evidence). Notable in Arch. Selden. B. 24 is a series of
spurious Chaucer attributions that claim for the canon not just the Walton extract
but also Lydgate's *Complaint of the Black Knight,* Hoccleve's *Mother of God,*[26] an
antifeminist lyric ("Deuise proues and eke humylitee," *IMEV* 679), and a lyric to
the Virgin ("O hie emperice and quene celestiall," *IMEV* 2461). One explanation
of these misattributions might read them as attempts to project some homogene-
ity onto otherwise arbitrarily assorted contents—inherited thus, perhaps, from
one or more exemplar(s)—and to make of the collection a comprehensive
Chaucer anthology. The attribution to Chaucer of a love vision such as Lydgate's
Complaint of the Black Knight is consonant with one well-known aspect of his reputation, represented elsewhere in the manuscript by the inclusion of
The Parliament of Fowls and *The Legend of Good Women,* and is unlikely to surprise. Even claiming an antifeminist poem or the two Marian lyrics for the canon
might be seen as a response to the multiple self-constructions of the Prologue to
The Legend of Good Women.[27]

Another explanation might seek to relate the Chaucer attributions more
specifically to the historical circumstances in which Arch. Selden. B. 24 was com-

24. A facsimile of this anthology, introduced by Julia Boffey and A. S. G. Edwards, is forthcoming from
   Boydell and Brewer. See the discussion of the contents in the introduction to J. Norton-Smith and
   I. Pravda, eds., *The Quare of Jelusy* (Heidelberg, 1976).
25. Margaret Muriel Gray, ed., *Lancelot of the Laik,* Scottish Text Society, n.s., 2 (Edinburgh, 1912); the other
   evidence is considered by A. S. G. Edwards, "Bodleian Library MS. Arch. Selden. B. 24: A 'Transitional'
   Collection," in Siegfried Wenzel and Stephen G. Nichols, eds., *The Whole Book: Cultural Perspectives on the
   Medieval Miscellany,* forthcoming from University of Michigan Press; and in an unpublished paper by
   David Parkinson, "Chaucer Apocrypha in Sixteenth-Century Scottish Manuscripts," given at the New
   Chaucer Society Biennial Congress, Seattle, 1992.
26. The only other manuscript to connect Chaucer with this is National Library of Scotland, Advocates'
   MS. 18. 2. 8 (John of Ireland's *Miroure of Wisdom*).
27. The construction of an antifeminist Chaucer seems to have been influential in Scotland: see, for example,
   the contents of the Bannatyne Manuscript, which alongside *IMEV* 679, ascribe to Chaucer a poem beginning "O wiket women wilful and variable" (*IMEV* 2580).

piled. Physical evidence concerning scribal stints, watermarks, and decoration suggests that the anthology as it now exists was the result of two distinct stages of production. The first involved the copying of Chaucer's *Troilus and Criseyde;* the second the upgrading of this with decoration and the addition of an anthology of further texts including *The Kingis Quair* and poems both correctly and incorrectly attributed to Chaucer. One occasion that might have called for an amalgamation of these distinctly English and Scottish bodies of material was the marriage of James IV of Scotland (whose date of birth is noted in the manuscript, on folio 120) to Margaret Tudor in 1503.[28] While the contents of the extended anthology may give pride of place to the English Chaucer, both linguistically and contextually they also contrive to Scotticize him—an act of rhetorical appropriation that might have seemed temptingly analogous to the maneuvers that culminated in the royal marriage.

The conjunction of items in Cotton Vitellius E. xi constructs a sagacious Chaucer, perhaps with an English national standing set parallel to the Scottish reputation of John of Fordun. As "author" of Walton's Boethian stanza on prosperity he appears as a relentlessly if succinctly moralizing figure, cited as a fount of proverbial wisdom rather than as the source of eloquence, the more familiar portrayal. The manner in which the layout of the Walton stanza here is contrived to mirror that of the Latin lines of John of Fordun, with the words "chauser geffrey" replicating "i. o. h. a. n. n. e. s. d. e. f. o. r. d. u. n" may even suggest some perceived equivalence between the two figures—a learned pairing to match the rhetorical pairing of Chaucer with James I and the anonymous Scottish poets represented in Arch. Selden. B. 24.

Different though the two contexts of the Scottish stanza may be, there are grounds for suspecting that the compilers of the two manuscripts had access to common sources. The hand of the main scribe of Arch. Selden B. 24, who copied folios 1–209^v (including the Walton stanza), is very similar to (although not to be identified with) that of the scribe James Graye (d. ca. 1505), who was secretary to Archbishop Schevez—one-time owner of Cotton Vitellius E. xi—and who was connected with the production of at least two manuscripts of the *Scotichronicon*.[29]

---

28. This possibility has been explored by Louise Olga Fradenburg, *City, Marriage, Tournament: Arts of Rule in Late Medieval Scotland* (Madison, Wis., 1991), 129–30; and "The Wedding of Margaret Tudor and James IV," in *Women and Sovereignty, Cosmos* 7 (Edinburgh, 1992), 78–100. Although the manuscript seems generally apposite for the occasion, it is difficult to see how it could have been intended for presentation to James or Margaret.

29. On the identification of the Selden scribe as Graye, see George Neilson, "The Scribe of the 'Kingis Quair,'" *Athenaeum*, 16 December 1899, 835–36; and (for a refutation) Neil Ker, *Medieval Manuscripts in British Libraries II: Abbotsford-Keele* (Oxford, 1977), 1–2. More information on Graye is provided by John

The Selden scribe himself is known to have copied texts relating to Scottish history in at least one surviving volume, and he was clearly an experienced copyist with access to a wide range of material.[30] Because scribes of similar habit and probably of common training worked for Schevez and for members of the Sinclair family, with which Arch. Selden B. 24 can be associated,[31] it is easy to imagine that texts might have been passed between them.

The route by which the stanza reached the hands of these Scottish scribes remains largely obscure, but it is tempting to speculate that John Shirley, to whom four copies of it can be linked, may have played a role.[32] In Huntington Library EL 26 A 13, a copy of Hoccleve's *De Regimine Principum* and some poems by Lydgate, Shirley inserted the stanza with a small group of short pieces, including two extracts from *Troilus and Criseyde*. Another copy, in Shirley's own hand, occurs on folio 1ᵛ of British Library, MS. Royal 20. B. xv, a French translation of Vegetius' *De re militari;*[33] Shirley used the space on what was effectively a flyleaf for some personal inscriptions and this single stanza, which is attributed simply to "Boicius de *consolacione* &c." Another copy, in British Library, MS. Harley 2251, derived largely from Shirleian exemplars, is the work of the so-called Multon-scribe,[34] who here interestingly tacks the stanza on to Lydgate's *Wicked Tongue* (on fol. 152ᵛ), as if it forms a part of that poem. And in British Library, MS. Add. 29729—copied in 1558 by the antiquary John Stow, who again had

MacQueen, "The Literature of Fifteenth-Century Scotland," in Jennifer M. Brown, ed., *Scottish Society in the Fifteenth Century* (London, 1977), 201. Graye worked jointly with the scribe Magnus Mackulloch on the copy of the *Scotichronicon* that is now on deposit in the Scottish Record Office, MS. GD 45/26/48; Mackulloch also worked on the copy of the *Scotichronicon* that is now British Library, MS. Harley 712, owned by Archbishop Schevez; see Watt, "Editing the *Scotichronicon.*"

30. His hand has been identified in the Dalhousie MS, which contains texts relating to Scottish and Scottish-Scandinavian history; see Michael Chesnutt, "The Dalhousie Manuscript of the *Historia Norvegiae,*" *Opuscula* 8, Bibliotheca Arnamagnaeana, 38 (Copenhagen, 1986): 54–95; in National Library of Scotland, MS. Acc. 9253, translations of French texts on knighthood and governance made by Gilbert Haye; and in St. John's College, Cambridge, MS. G. 19, a copy of a printed edition of Mirk's *Festial* and the *Quatuor sermones*. See further the introduction to the forthcoming facsimile.

31. The arms of Henry, Lord Sinclair, appear on folio 118ᵛ, and the note "liber Henrici domini Sinclar" on folio 230ᵛ.

32. Shirley had reason to be interested in Walton's translation, since he was secretary to Richard Beauchamp, earl of Warwick, whose wife Elizabeth apparently commissioned the undertaking. He also copied Chaucer's *Boece,* in British Library, MS. Add. 16165. See Hanna, "Sir Thomas Berkeley."

33. See Warner and Gilson, *Catalogue of Royal MSS,* 2:367.

34. For a description and discussion of the manuscript's reliance on Shirleian exemplars, see E. P. Hammond, "Two British Museum Manuscripts: A Contribution to the Bibliography of John Lydgate," *Anglia* 28 (1905): 1–28. The work of the scribe has been most recently surveyed in Margaret Lucille Kekewich et al., *The Politics of Fifteenth-Century England: John Vale's Book* (Stroud, England, 1995), 107–12.

access to Shirley's anthologies[35]—the stanza is written on the final leaf (fol. 288^V),
beneath Stow's own ownership note, with the Boethian association signaled in a
heading, "boecius de consolatio philosophie." As inherited from Shirley, it seems,
the stanza carried Boethian associations and a wise authority that made it appropriate in the role of an epigraph.

Shirley's many interests also included Scottish history, or at least that portion
of it concerned with the death of James I (presumed author of *The Kingis Quair*)
in 1437. Two British Library manuscripts, Add. 5467 and 38690, contain copies
of his translation, from a Latin source that is now lost, of an account of the mur-
der.[36] It is possible that the routes that offered Shirley access to Scottish material
served for traffic in the other direction, and made his own collections (or parts of
them) available to Scottish scribes and readers. Shirley's reference to Boethius, in
his own copy of the stanza in Royal 20. B. xv, may in the end explain its mistak-
en and uniquely Scottish attribution to Chaucer rather than to Walton. Scribes
or readers whose understanding of Chaucer's relationship to Boethius was impre-
cise—prompted, for instance, by a reading of *The Kingis Quair*, which begins
with the reading of Boethius and ends with an invocation of Chaucer—might
easily infer that a stanza of English that concluded "Boicius de consolacione &c."
could not be other than Chaucer's work.[37]

Inference is not the prerogative of fifteenth-century readers, and much of this
discussion is based on inference or on hypothesis: manuscript study offers suggestions more often than answers, and its allure for those in search of hard facts
is often specious. But a case study of this sort highlights certain features of the
late-fifteenth-century reception of Chaucer and can suggest some new aspects to
it. In addition to the association of Chaucer with Boethius, there are hints of a
more general tendency to regard Chaucer as a source of wisdom: an inclination
reflected elsewhere in the attribution to Chaucer of proverbs and *sententiae* of dif-

35. On Stow's manuscripts, see *John Stow: A Survey of London*, ed. Charles Lethbridge Kingsford, 2 vols. (Oxford, 1908), 1:lxxxvi; see also Aage Brusendorff, *The Chaucer Tradition* (Oxford, 1925), 224–28.
36. See, most recently, Margaret Connolly, "*The Dethe of the Kynge of Scotis*: A New Edition," *Scottish Historical Review* 71 (1992): 46–69.
37. It has been argued that James I knew Walton's translation of Boethius and made reference to it in *The Kingis Quair* (see, for example, M. McDiarmid, ed., *The Kingis Quair of James Stewart* [London, 1973], 118, note to stanza 3; and Johnson, "Walton's Sapient Orpheus"), although the evidence is not especially compelling. An implied association between Boethius and Chaucer is in line with the overall range of Chaucerian reference in the poem; see further Lois A. Ebin, "Boethius, Chaucer, and *The Kingis Quair*," *Philological Quarterly* 53 (1974): 324–41.

ferent sorts.[38] The pairing of Chaucer with John of Fordun anticipates the nation-alistic adoption of Chaucer evident in Sir Brian Tuke's preface to Thynne's print-ed edition of 1532, where he is hailed as "that noble & famous clerke Geffray Chaucer . . . suche an excellent poete in our tonge" to rival Homer and Cicero.[39] These Chaucers could coexist, of course, with constructions of different sorts: the antifeminist Chaucer of the Scottish Bannatyne manuscript (derived in part, per-haps, from the prompting of Arch. Selden. B. 24); Protestant Chaucer;[40] the alchemical Chaucer of later-sixteenth-century antiquarian scholarship.[41] To iden-tify and to trace some of the processes that brought these constructions into being contributes a little toward that "historicizing understanding of literary works as products of their transmission" that is a part of informed historical reading.[42]

Queen Mary and Westfield College

38. Starting with the *Proverbs* (*IMEV* 3914; Benson, ed., *Riverside Chaucer*, 657), and continuing with attribu-tions by association, such as the proverbial sayings used as makeweights in Caxton's 1477 printed edition of *Anelida and Arcite*, which came to be known as "Chaucer's Prophecy" (*IMEV* 3943), and the "Eight Goodly Questions and Their Answers" (*IMEV* 3183) incorporated into the introductory pages of Thynne's printed Chaucer of 1532.
39. *The Workes of Geffray Chaucer newly printed* (*STC* 5068); for a facsimile see Derek S. Brewer, introduction to *The Works, 1532* (Menston, England, 1969).
40. See Felix Swart, "Chaucer and the English Reformation," *Neophilologus* 62 (1978): 616–19; Andrew N. Wawn, "Chaucer, *The Plowman's Tale,* and Reformation Propaganda: The Testimonies of Thomas Godfray and *I Playne Piers*," *Bulletin of the John Rylands Library* 56 (1973–74): 174–92.
41. See Robert M. Schuler, "The Renaissance Chaucer as Alchemist," *Viator* 15 (1984): 305–33.
42. Lerer, *Chaucer and His Readers*, 9.

Mise-en-page in the *Troilus* Manuscripts: Chaucer and French Manuscript Culture

ARDIS BUTTERFIELD

The scribes of the *Troilus* manuscripts stand implicitly accused of a *trahison des clercs*. Their view of the poem, firmly fixed in the fifteenth century or even later, pushes the authorial version back into historical opacity. Despite (or perhaps because of) the fact that Chaucer's *Troilus and Criseyde* is the text that represents our notion of the English medieval author in its most culturally prestigious guise, scholars have typically regarded the manuscripts as witnesses of a lost history—secondary rather than primary evidence of the authentic cultural moment of the poem.

This essay is part of an effort by a number of scholars to reconstitute the page of the scribal manuscript as an authentic object in its own right. We are beginning to recognize that it is not a mere transparency through which the author's "original" is to be viewed but rather an artifact of independent visual interest. We must, too, credit the scribe—indeed all of those involved in turning the text into a written, and painted, material object—with certain "reproductive rights," for each text is idiosyncratically shaped and formed by the unique physical act of writing it out.[1] This is not to abandon the notion of authorship but to broaden it. The more we concentrate on the physical characteristics of medieval manuscripts, the more closely we can perceive notions of authorship in the making.

What we see on a manuscript page is more than a record of the words of the text. It is more even—in the case of glossed manuscripts—than a record of early readers' verbalized responses, in the margins, to the central text. The process of glossing the text cannot be regarded as distinct from the visual structure of the whole manuscript page and, in turn, of the book or codex. Every decision of layout—indeed, every material fact of the text's existence—not only reflects the

---

1. See Bernard Cerquiglini, *Éloge de la variante: histoire critique de la philologie* (Paris, 1989); and David F. Hult, "Reading It Right: The Ideology of Text Editing," in Marina S. Brownlee, Kevin Brownlee, and Stephen G. Nichols, eds., *The New Medievalism* (Baltimore and London, 1991), 113–30.

assumptions and cultural habits of medieval readers but also forms assumptions and habits that govern the way in which the text is received.[2]

Modern discussion of how a medieval author may have been involved in any aspect of his or her contemporary reception is required by this logic to depend on a secure knowledge about the manuscripts and their transmission and circulation.[3] But if we credit medieval scribes with a major role in the production of texts, we may well ask how such security of knowledge is to be gained. What were the models for a scribe in the making and dissemination of vernacular fiction? What expectations about the nature and format of copying particular kinds of text (for example, lyrics, narratives, songs, or letters) were brought to bear on scribes and illuminators, and by whom? Constructing responses to such questions is a slow and often piecemeal process, and this essay cannot pretend to offer definitive answers. Rather, I hope to ask these questions both more broadly and more precisely than before: to stress the importance of seeking wider cultural perspectives on manuscript production, and in particular to reexamine the nature of scribal transmission in vernacular poetry.

We often place considerable constraints on the kinds of connections that we make between one manuscript and another: the notion of a source—in one sense quite a loose and imaginary model for the process of acquiring assumptions or concepts—takes on a fierce, and perhaps false, strictness. The metaphor of inheritance is similarly unhelpful if we try to use it to posit single and definable moments of transference between a reader and his or her reading matter. My concern here is not so much with finding specific moments of "influence" from one scribe to another. Instead, I seek to fill in the traces of a much larger network of relationships, the consequences of which constitute, in Pierre Bourdieu's terms,

2. See the studies by Michael Camille, *Image on the Edge: The Margins of Medieval Art* (London, 1992); Sylvia Huot, *From Song to Book: The Poetics of Writing in Old French Lyric and Lyrical Narrative Poetry* (Ithaca, N.Y., and London, 1987), and *The Roman de la Rose and Its Medieval Readers* (Cambridge, 1994); and Martin Irvine, *The Making of Textual Culture: "Grammatica" and Literary Theory 350–1100* (Cambridge, 1994). Although the attention to manuscripts as primary artifacts is a recent emphasis in the much-heralded "New Philology" of medieval studies, it is salutary to be reminded by L. D. Reynolds and N. G. Wilson (*Scribes and Scholars: A Guide to the Transmission of Greek and Latin Literature*, 3d ed. [Oxford, 1991], 192) that the argument that manuscripts "can be treated as documents illustrating the history of medieval culture" was first put forward by Ludwig Traube (1861–1907).
3. As Judson Allen trenchantly warns, "we must seek, not to establish texts, but to understand surviving codices"; see "Eleven Unpublished Commentaries on Ovid's *Metamorphoses* and Two Other Texts of Mythographic Interest: Some Comments on a Bibliography," in Jane Chance, ed., *The Mythographic Art: Classical Fable and the Rise of the Vernacular in Early France and England* (Gainesville, Fl., 1990), 281–89 at 286.

cultural habits.[4] Such a model is useful when we try to grasp the intangible processes by which a set of cultural habits passes from one culture to another—in this case the habits of French manuscript production passing into English reading and writing.

Although sustained attention to the details of the manuscript page is widespread among those who study French and Latin culture, the Chaucer manuscripts have only recently begun to attract the same kind of attention.[5] Only gradually has the kind of manuscript feature normally ignored by editors as *hors du texte* come to be described and published. Marginal glosses have been newly presented as clues to the reactions of medieval readers to the central text.[6] However, these glosses form only one element in the *ordinatio* of the *Troilus* manuscripts, which comprises a network of interpretive features.[7] As yet there is no assessment of how we are to see the connections between, say, a space for a picture, the heading "Cantus," and the insertion of Latin verses into the body of the narrative. Even more wanting is an account of the cultural history of these features.[8]

---

4. Pierre Bourdieu, *Le sens pratique* (Paris, 1980); trans. R. Nice as *The Logic of Practice* (Stanford, Calif., 1990). On the genesis of the term *habitus* in Bourdieu's work, see Pierre Bourdieu, *The Field of Cultural Production*, trans. Randal Johnson (Oxford, 1993), 4, nn. 16–21.

5. Cf. Martin Irvine, "'Bothe text and gloss': Manuscript Form, the Textuality of Commentary, and Chaucer's Dream Poems," in Charlotte Cook Morse et al., eds., *The Uses of Manuscripts in Literary Studies: Essays in Memory of Judson Boyce Allen* (Kalamazoo, Mich., 1992), 81–120. See Christopher Baswell, "Talking Back to the Text: Marginal Voices in Medieval Secular Literature," in Morse, *The Uses of Manuscripts,* 121–60; Robert W. Hanning, "'I Shal Finde It in a Maner Glose': Versions of Textual Harassment in Medieval Literature," in Laurie A. Finke and Martin B. Schichtman, eds., *Medieval Texts and Contemporary Readers* (Ithaca, N.Y., and London, 1987); Robert F. Yeager, "English, Latin, and the Text as 'Other': The Page as Sign in the Work of John Gower," in Stephanie Trigg, ed., *Medieval English Poetry* (London, 1993), 203–16; and Daniel J. Pinti, "The Vernacular Gloss(ed) in Gavin Douglas's *Eneados," Exemplaria* 7 (1995): 443–64.

6. See C. David Benson and Barry A. Windeatt, "The Manuscript Glosses to Chaucer's *Troilus and Criseyde," Chaucer Review* 25 (1990): 33–53.

7. Benson and Windeatt make certain puzzling distinctions in their transcription of the glosses: they include "decorated oversized initial letters" as "glosses" because they are "designed to call attention to special passages" but not *incipits* and *explicits,* which "are different from comment on the text itself" (p. 33). It is not clear, however, why initials constitute more of a comment on the text than the *incipits;* and if initials, then why not the illustrations, too? In fact, not all the initials are included. As well as generally omitting the initials alongside *incipits* and *explicits,* they also omit those in S1 at V.1422 and V.1590, and in S2 at III.1744 and V.1632. The grounds for omitting the sign manuals—"le vostre T" and "la vostre C"—present in many of the manuscripts after V.1421 and V.1631, might also be queried.

8. Julia Boffey ("Annotation in Some Manuscripts of *Troilus and Criseyde," English Manuscript Studies 1110–1700* 5 [1995]: 1–17), does, however, make some reference to Scottish connections. Elizabeth Salter's work is another important exception; see especially D. Pearsall and N. Zeeman, eds., *English and International: Studies in the Literature, Art, and Patronage of Medieval England* (Cambridge, 1988).

Chaucer's *Troilus and Criseyde* thus offers a test case for a new approach to manuscript study. My purpose here is to look at the *Troilus* manuscripts as primary artifacts, to describe the principal features of their *ordinatio*, and to investigate the ways in which they interconnect by situating them within a larger context: the manuscript culture of thirteenth- and fourteenth-century French secular writing. The grounds for doing so are various. First, by setting the *Troilus* manuscripts within a broad scribal practice, it becomes easier to determine whether they are the product of late, idiosyncratic readers or whether they register earlier scribal habits. Such a comparison may help in the particularly difficult task of establishing the sequence in which different elements of *ordinatio* were added to the manuscript tradition. Manuscripts that are both near in date to the composition of the work(s) they contain and contemporary with the *Troilus* manuscripts offer an important point of reference. Second, the large tradition in French of composing and copying works in which song and narrative are juxtaposed and interleaved, as they are in *Troilus and Criseyde*, constitutes a rich resource of information about the practice of copying works of mixed genre. Finally, although much remains to be done in establishing the lines of circulation and distribution of French manuscripts in England during this period, it is clear that the connections with France, and with Northern French and Burgundian copyists and artists in particular, are of first importance to the production of English manuscripts in the same period.[9]

MISE-EN-PAGE IN THE TROILUS MANUSCRIPTS

It may be helpful to begin with a general outline of the *mise-en-page* among the sixteen surviving *Troilus* manuscripts.[10] At first sight the manuscripts seem rather disparate in their characteristics. Some are heavily glossed with marginal annotations, others are sparse and bare. Some are expensively produced, others are plain and monochrome, usually in inverse relationship to the extent of the glossing. Three manuscripts in particular constitute the largest source of marginalia:

9. Salter, "The *Troilus* Frontispiece," *English and International*, 267–71; see also V. J. Scattergood and J. W. Sherborne, eds., *English Court Culture in the Later Middle Ages* (London, 1983). The production of manuscripts by Herman Scheere's London-based workshop (with which the *Troilus* Campsall manuscript may possibly be associated) is one such connection. See also Julia Boffey, "English Dream Poems of the Fifteenth Century and Their French Connections," in Donald and Sara Sturm-Maddox, eds., *Literary Aspects of Courtly Culture: Selected Papers from ICLS, Seventh Triennial Congress* (Cambridge, 1994), 113–21.
10. For descriptions, see R. K. Root, *The Manuscripts of Chaucer's Troilus*, Chaucer Society, 1st ser., no. 98 (London, 1914); and B. A. Windeatt, ed., *Geoffrey Chaucer: Troilus and Criseyde* (London, 1984).

British Library, Harley 2392 (H4), a fifteenth-century manuscript; Bodleian Library, MS. Rawlinson Poet. 163 (R), in four fifteenth-century hands; and Bodleian Library, Arch. Selden MS. B. 24 (S1, dated between 1488 and 1513).[11] The numerous glosses in the Harley copy are mostly in Latin, carefully and intelligently marking out rhetorical passages, for example: *verba cressaid* (fol. 27^r), *Cantus Antigon* (fol. 35^r), *recapitulacio* (fol. 68^r), and classical allusions, *Dares/ auctor nobilitatis troili* (fol. 144^r). The annotation in both R and S1 is mostly English, detailed and lengthy, and often idiosyncratic (note the crisply inventive phrasing of the summary "Creseid in hir self at argument" that the sribe of S1 puts beside her soliloquy in II.715).

Of the rest, most have very few marginal glosses. Four more—British Library, Harley 2280 (H1); Harley 4912 (H5); St. John's College, Cambridge, MS. L.1 (J); and Bodleian Library, Arch. Selden MS. Supra 56 (S2)—have a fair sprinkling, but the remaining nine have only the odd brief explanatory note. What else characterizes the layout of this large group? First it should be made plain that despite the paucity of marginalia in the majority of manuscripts, nearly all of them have various forms of heading or colophon, usually set within the narrative columns (though these are also sometimes presented marginally). The most consistent and visually arresting of these headings are the *incipits* and *explicits* that divide the poem into books and proems. Only one copy (H2) lacks these;[12] nearly all of the others have (or have had, in the case of the mutilated Gg) a full program of headings marking the beginning and ending of each proem and book (though not all copies agree on where these divisions occur). These are often highly emphatic, such as the *explicit* after the first book in Dg (fol. 68^r), which is written in a large script in the center of the text with small penwork drawings on either side. S1 also has running titles (several have been cropped). Other forms of visual emphasis include red script (Cp), underlining in red (J), boxing (Dg), and the liberal (and carefully graded) use of line spacing to set off one book from another and the proems from the books (Cp).

The most direct and widespread means of providing visual support to the structural outline of the poem, however, is the use of large initials. In the richer

11. Sigla follow Windeatt, *Troilus and Criseyde* (34–35): C1 (Campsall MS, Pierpont Morgan Library, M. 817); Cp (Corpus Christi College, Cambridge, MS. 61); Dg (Bodleian Library, MS. Digby 181); Gg (Cambridge University Library, MS. Gg.4.27); H4 (British Library, MS. Harley 2392); H5 (British Library, MS. Harley 4912); J (St. John's College, Cambridge, MS L1); R (Bodleian Library, MS. Rawlinson Poet. 163); S1 (Bodleian Library, MS. Arch. Selden B.24); S2 (Bodleian Library, MS. Arch. Selden, Supra 56).

12. H2 has just one *explicit*, after IV.1701.

copies, such as C1, Cp, and Gg, not only are there elaborately painted and gilded initials, but borders have been added also. In Cp there is the famous frontispiece painting followed by spaces for a possible further ninety pictures. But
even in the plainer copies, where the initials simply alternate in red and blue or
are not colored at all (S2), a hierarchical relation is routinely (though not always
consistently) set up between different textual elements, most obviously between
the books and the proems. J, for instance, has two degrees of blue initials with red
pen flourishes, one larger, one smaller, for the start of each book and proem. In a
manuscript containing very few verbal glosses, the initials take on a more significant role in articulating the text. In Dg, for example, although the initials have
not been completed, the spaces allocated give them a large and prominent position on the page: the whole of a stanza is indented for the start of each book, and
five or six lines are indented for each prohemium.

Initials are also used in some of the copies to mark out the division between
stanzas. R has a *littera notabilior* for the first letter of each stanza, as does Cp;
other manuscripts rely on paraphs by the first line of each stanza (J, Gg, S2, and
Dg). The paraphs in S2 are very sporadic (there is only one, for instance, on fol.
13^r), even though here and in Gg they have an important function since the stanzas are run together on the page.[13] In Gg the paraphs alternate regularly in red
and blue (the blue ones are not filled in). J has the most striking (if not the most
elegant) visual display for its stanzas of any of the manuscripts: the alternating red
and blue paraphs extend the whole length of each stanza and are complemented
in the earlier pages by red brackets on the right-hand side joining the first and last
lines of each stanza, often including roughly drawn pen squiggles. Scribes 2 and
3 in R also add, respectively, sweeping zigzag and red interlaced brackets to each
stanza. In general, most of the manuscripts make a clear visual distinction
between the stanzas, either by leaving a line spacing (Dg, S1, J, CP, R) or a horizontal dash (various occasions in R).

Another role for initials emerges suddenly when, toward the end of Book IV
and at the start of Book V in Gg, pen-flourished initials mark the changes in
speaker and, on occasion, changes of topic in the dialogue.[14] It is evident that

---

13. The fourth scribe in R also runs stanzas together.
14. In M. B. Parkes and Richard Beadle, eds., *The Poetical Works of Geoffrey Chaucer: A Facsimile of Cambridge
University Library MS GG.4.27*, 3 vols. (Cambridge, 1979–80), the reference to an initial at IV.661 (on 89^v)
should read IV.659; the error is reiterated in Windeatt, *Troilus and Criseyde*, 70. For an instance of an initial
used to mark a point where Pandarus changes direction in the midst of a speech, see fol. 92^r (IV.848).

these are not later additions, because spaces have been left for them by the textual scribe. A related practice is found in S1 and H5 where, rather than initials, the names of the characters are written in the margins. In a particularly dense cluster of names on folios 6–14 of S1, the name "Pandar" is written directly in the middle of a stanza to indicate a switch in the dialogue (I.829).

The visual emphasis given to the structure of speech in the poem is confirmed by a further pattern in the use of initials. We have already noted in some manuscripts the use of initials to mark book and proem divisions, and in some of these copies, initials are also used to draw visual attention to the songs and letters. S1 provides a particularly emphatic example. The end of Troilus's letter in Book V (fol. 111^V) is marked out not just with a large illuminated initial but also with a whole border decoration. Criseyde's answering letter has a large colored initial (fol. 114^V). What is remarkable is that the scribe employs illuminated initials and borders elsewhere in this manuscript only for the book divisions, and large colored initials elsewhere only for proems. In other words, he makes a bold visual alignment between an inset formal type and the proems and book divisions. The Dg manuscript makes a similar connection. We recall that this scribe leaves spaces for large-size initials alongside each divisional heading (a whole stanza is indented for a book colophon, five lines for a prohemium). Only one other space for an initial is left: this occurs alongside the rubric "Cantus Troili" at I.400, where five lines of the song's first stanza are indented. Here, it is significant not just that the rubric is emphasized by an initial but also that the size and exclusive positioning of the initial equate the song with the prohemiums in the visual and rhetorical hierarchy of the work. A third example, Cp, makes (at least potentially) an even bolder visual statement: of the twenty-five or so songs, complaints, and letters presented in the narrative, some twenty correspond with gaps for illustrations.

This visual equation of the songs and letters with the major book divisions of the poem is confirmed by the patterns of rubrication and annotation.[15] Excepting only the book colophons, the songs and letters receive more consistent attention from the scribes than any other parts of the poem. The headings range from Latin titles such as "Cantus" (V.1317)—written (in S2) on a separate line within the columns of narrative—to an anglicized marginal heading such as "The Song of Troilus" (in R), which is underlined. It is notable not merely that so many

---

15. For a list of the songs, complaints, and letters in *Troilus* (nearly all of which are given some form of scribal annotation), see A. Butterfield, "Interpolated Lyric in Medieval Narrative Poetry" (Ph.D. diss., University of Cambridge, 1988), appendix B (271–72); see also 170–78.

manuscripts pick out the songs in this way but also that even those that have lit-tle or no marginal annotation (such as Cp) nonetheless include song headings. The Dg copy (which breaks off after III.532) is another case in point: it has just three marginal headings (in addition to the book *incipits*), of which one is "Cantus Troili" (fol. 59^r), and the second "invocacio" (fol. 68^r).[16] S2, similarly, has relatively few glosses, but nearly all of them relate to the songs and letters.[17]

This feature of the layout prompts questions about the chronology of the *ordinatio*. Is it possible to distinguish between those elements belonging to the ear-liest stages of the layout of the poem and those added subsequently by fifteenth-century interpreters? At issue is a delicate archaeological problem, for although the general assumption that the earliest manuscripts of any work will be the most authoritative is usually a fair one, this need not imply that later copies are neces-sarily "inauthentic." In the case of the *Troilus* copies, it has been well observed that an especially "early" characteristic is the division of the poem into books.[18] This can be deduced from both the near-unanimity of all the witnesses and the presence of these divisions in the four earliest manuscripts (C1, Cp, Gg and Ph, all from the first quarter of the fifteenth century). A similar case can be made for the early sta-tus of the song headings, present in three out of four of the early manuscripts and featured in a wide cross-section of all the manuscripts, regardless of date or prove-nance. Their absence in C1 (the earliest copy) might be thought to be significant, but only, I think, if one takes a ruthlessly evolutionary view of the annotation. What seems a more accurate reflection on the group as a whole is that different manuscripts register a varying number of layers of interpretation, ranging from the minimal to the verbose. C1 is not so much a representation of the primal state of readers' reactions to *Troilus* as an exception that proves the rule. This rule, as attest-ed in all the other early copies, shows the bare minimum of *ordinatio* to comprise not only the division of the poem into books but also formal rubrics marking out the songs and letters:[19] either the *only* headings are of the *incipit/explicit* and *can-*

16. The third is the gloss "Cato" at III.294.
17. Compare also H5 (Harley 4912), which, after a fair sprinkling of formal headings and name glosses in Books I and II, offers only the single heading "Cantus trolle" in Book III (as well as three "Nota" glosses).
18. See Parkes and Beadle, *Facsimile of GG.4.27,* III.41.
19. There are five headings in Cp (the *Cantica Troili* in Books I, III, V; and the two letters in Book V), and five in Ph (misses out the song in III, but adds headings for *Cantus Antigone* in II and Criseyde's complaint in IV). Gg has just one heading (the song in I) but also has large initials for the predestination soliloquy and Criseyde's letter in V.

tus/littera type; *or* these two types of heading are privileged within a more elaborate pattern of annotation and decoration.[20]

Even in later copies, where the *ordinatio* is more elaborate, there are reasons for thinking that the *cantus* and *littera* rubrics continued to be associated with the earliest layer of *ordinatio*, that is, with the colophons and headings to the books and proems. This can be seen in S1, for instance, where the scribe distinguishes visually among different types of gloss: formal or generic headings, rhetorical terms, references to *auctores* and classical allusions, the names of characters, narrative summaries, and, finally, instances of personal commentary. Not all of these types are consistently differentiated, but certain decisions of layout are clear, in particular the way in which the *cantus* rubrics (such as "Cantus Troili" on fol. 6[v] and "Cantus Oenonee" on fol. 10[v]) are boxed and written in a larger, firmer script—more like the *incipits* in style—than the other more informally written glosses. There is a large gap in the glosses throughout most of Book III, and only a scrappy gloss alongside the song at III.1744. But the gloss "Here maketh troylus his compleynt vpon fortune" at IV.260 is again in a clearer, larger script; and in Book V, Troilus's "Testament," the songs and the letters are all given particular visual prominence, including, as we noted above, a full illuminated border and initial to mark the end of Troilus's letter, and a large colophon "Le vostre Troil" inserted into the body of the text.

J offers further—though not fully decipherable—clues to the history of glossing *Troilus*.[21] It is clear that the initials and paraphs were added after the colophons and headings because the red flourishes run over the brown ink of the headings in several places (see fol. 17[r]), and also over the glosses (see fols. 16[v], 104[v]). This reflects not only the sequence of the features but also mutual support among the different features of *ordinatio* in the manuscripts. S2, which, like J, contains only the *Troilus*, conducts its presentation of the text without the help of any color. Nonetheless, out of twenty-six glosses ten refer to songs or letters,

---

20. It is interesting to note that the song and letter headings were also singled out by Thynne, Stowe, and Speght: Thynne's first edition (1532) includes "The song of Troilus" (Book I) between stanzas, with a paraph for both the heading and the first line of the song, and "The copy of the letter" printed in the bottom margin (left-hand side) for Troilus's letter in Book V, together with "Le Vostre T" in between stanzas. Criseyde's letter has a paraph and signature but no heading. His 1542 edition repeats this layout but with greater visual emphasis: the initials are more flamboyant, and the headings are set off by line spaces before and after. Stowe (1561) follows a practice similar to that in Thynne's first edition, as does Speght (1598).

21. See Richard Beadle and Jeremy Griffiths, eds., *St John's College, Cambridge, Manuscript L.1: A Facsimile*, Facsimile Series of the Works of Geoffrey Chaucer, gen. ed. Paul G. Ruggiers, no. 3 (Norman, Okla., and Woodbridge, England, 1983), xxi–xxiii.

and many of these are written out particularly clearly, or boxed, or—in the case of "Cantus Troyli versus Criseide" at V.1317—inserted into the body of the text with a space left before and after.[22]

In general terms, we can conclude that it was the practice of the fifteenth-century scribes to divide the text of *Troilus* to register not only large formal sections but also categories of text. This they did through a system of headings together with a hierarchical use of initials. The *canticus* and *littera* rubrics—despite the greater emphasis with which they are generally treated—should be understood as part of the overall logic of rhetorical division taken for granted by the scribes in their presentation of the poem. While the example of J confirms this, it also shows that even within single manuscripts, the different elements of the *ordinatio* were added in a complex and not always predictable sequence of layers. This reminds us that it is difficult to disentangle elements of the *mise-en-page* that might represent an "authentic," even authorial, perception of the poem—a view of the poem from within, as it were—from later attempts to impose an external structural logic that perhaps reflects new criteria of critical appreciation.

One way of responding to this problem is to look harder at the structural logic itself in terms of the relationship of generic types. It may not be entirely clear to a modern reader why the *Troilus* scribes appear to treat songs and letters as formally connected, or even, in some cases, directly equivalent.[23] However, in two cases a scribe even gives a letter the title of "cantus." The first of these occurs at I.659, where Pandarus quotes to Troilus the letter written by Oenone to Paris "of hir heuynesse." Three scribes comment here in the margin on the form and character of the set piece. The scribe in R explains "How Pandar told Troylus the sorowe of Oenonee"; S2 writes "littera Oenone"; but S1 writes "Cantus Oenonee" (fol. 10ᵛ). In the first instance, they are probably responding independently to Pandarus's own double terminology in the narrative. He explains to Troilus:

> I woot wel that it fareth thus by me
> As to thi brother, Paris, an herdesse,
> Which that i-cleped was Oenone,

22. "Versus in latino" (fol. 101ᵛ) and "La voustre Criseide" (fol. 103ᵛ) are each given a similar layout. It is a measure of this scribe's preoccupation with song that he should call this letter a *cantus*.

23. An instance of modern editorial discrimination against the letters in *Troilus* is seen in Windeatt's edition, in that over and above the headings given in his base text he chooses to include "Cantus Antigone" at I.827, but not the "littera" heading at II.1065, even though it has similarly broad manuscript support.

> Wrote in a compleynte of hir heuynesse;
> ʒee say the lettre that she wrote, I gesse?
>
> (I.652–56)

For Pandarus, Oenone's letter is as much a "compleynte" as a "lettre." The second example is the one mentioned earlier, where S2 describes Troilus's letter to Criseyde in V.1317–1421 as "Cantus Troyli versus Criseide," instead of "Litera Troili" as it is labeled by most of the other scribes. There are sure signs here that the scribes (along with Chaucer himself) saw "littera," "cantus," and "compleynte" as closely related formal types.[24]

The scribes are assiduous in marking out the letters in *Troilus*. Among them, they give titles to five altogether: to Oenone's letter in Book I (659–65), to the two fully quoted letters in Book V (1317–1421 and 1590–1631) by Troilus and Criseyde respectively, and also to their first letters to each other in Book II (1065–85 and 1219–25), which Chaucer (unlike Boccaccio) summarizes in the third person rather than quoting them directly. The scribes usually mark not only the start but also the end of the letters, by finishing them either with a French-style sign manual ("Le vostre T" [Cp, J, Th, S1], V.1421; and "La vostre C" [D, H, Th, S2], V.1631) or, as in H4, by the rubric "Finis littere Troili . . . Finis littere Cress." This has the effect of marking the letter as a discrete unit in the narrative. The scribes respond as readily to a description of a letter as to a quoted letter, for no fewer than seven of them note the summary of Troilus's letter, and the scribe of S1 even marks out the end of the three-stanza description by writing "Her endes Troylus his first lettyr" (II.1085). Criseyde's letter takes only one stanza to summarize, so it is not surprising that fewer scribes think it worth recording, namely those of H4, H5, S1, and R. But this shows that the scribes commented not only on the quoted set pieces but also on any reference to a known form or type, and it implies that the scribe of S1, at least, viewed the three-stanza summary of Troilus's letter as a set piece in its own right. That the scribe of H4 has a special interest in marking out the boundaries of the poem's set pieces is further shown by his careful marking of an *explicit* at the end of Antigone's song and a *nota* at the end of Troilus's letter in Book II.[25]

---

24. This scribal perception finds interesting corroboration in the way in which Antigone's song was anthologized. It was not copied out as a discrete song but instead pillaged for the purposes of letter-writing. A love letter in nine rhyme royal stanzas takes three stanzas from it (lines 841–47, 869–82), and a love complaint takes one (lines 855–61).

25. See also "Nota" in R by V.645 (the end of the "Canticus Troili"), fol. 97ʳ (not included by Benson and Windeatt, "Manuscript Glosses to *Troilus and Criseyde*").

If we consider this instance of visual annotation on its own terms, we find that the scribal view of the letters as formally distinct from the narrative corresponds to their view of other kinds of interpolation. In Gg, one of the early copies, Criseyde's letter at V.1590 has a large flourished initial, whereas Troilus's letter has a small paraph (in brown ink) to mark the start (at V.1317, fol. 121^r) and a tilde at the end of the final line (at V.1421, fol. 122^v). The only other tilde signs in the manuscript occur by some lines of interpolated Latin verse at V.819–24 (fol. 114^r). These lines are further set off with a "verso" abbreviation in the left-hand margin and bracketing on the right.[26] Once again, we can see from such details of *mise-en-page* how keen the scribe is on highlighting inset material, and how he draws an equivalence in this regard between Latin interpolations and Troilus's letter. In S2 similarly, "Versus in latino" (fol. 101^v) is given the same layout as "Cantus Troyli versus Criseide" at V.1317 and "La voustre Criseide" (fol. 103^v). It has been argued, on the analogy of the Latin glosses in copies of *The Canterbury Tales*, that these sections of Latin are likely to be part of the earliest stages of the poem's construction. The association of a letter with such material in the *ordinatio* of Gg (an association that resurfaces in S2) reinforces our sense that the perception of the songs and letters as distinct formal elements in the poem is one that runs deep in its compositional make-up.

Perhaps because some of the song and letter headings take the form of marginal glosses, their relation to the *incipits* and *explicits* has not been fully grasped. Although Benson and Windeatt specifically exclude the *incipits* and *explicits* from their list of glosses, their decision points to a larger need to clarify the kind of distinction we think there to be between glosses that appear in the margin and those that are written within the text columns. Benson and Windeatt state in their description of the manuscripts that Gg has no glosses, but go on to note in the main list of glosses the "cantus" at I.400, which in fact appears in the margin. This problem probably arises from inadequate attention to the whole visual structure of the manuscript page: if we look too narrowly at certain textual elements without appreciating that they form part of the larger critical perception implied by the interconnected decisions of layout in a manuscript, we will miss their significance or worry over categories of our own making.

The book division of *Troilus and Criseyde* has long since been accepted into the *textus receptus* of the poem. Subsequent literary history makes such a division

---

26. The Statius summary also has a "verso" abbreviation by each of the five lines (fol. 123^v).

appear completely natural, although it should be noted that Chaucer's work is in fact the first (completed) poem in English to use it. Much less familiar in the modern reception of *Troilus,* however, is the almost equal prominence given to the songs and letters in the visual articulation of the poem among the early witnesses.[28] It is particularly interesting, for instance, to find the scribe of H4 using the same kind of formal Latin terminology ("explicit") to mark the end of a song as of a book. Modern editors have transcribed some (though not all) of the song and letter headings but without much understanding or contextual familiarity with this tradition. As headings, they remain merely formal and hence rather opaque. Yet if we are concerned to re-create the manuscript culture of the poem and through it the visual apprehension of the poem's early readers, it is this feature of the *ordinatio* that most requires commentary and annotation.

FOURTEENTH- AND FIFTEENTH-CENTURY ANGLO-FRENCH MANUSCRIPT CULTURE

For comparison with the practices of the *Troilus* scribes, we should perhaps turn first to manuscripts of other Chaucer narratives with inset songs: for example, *The Book of the Duchess* (with its two lyrics), the *Parliament of Fowls* (the closing roundel), and the Prologue to *The Legend of Good Women* (the ballade "Hyd Absalon thy gilte tresses clere"). As with the *Troilus* manuscripts, some of which in any case also contain other Chaucerian material, these are all of the fifteenth century or later, and they include such well-known compilations as Bodleian Library, MSS. Bodley 638, Tanner 346, Fairfax 16; and Trinity College, Cambridge, R.3.20. There is considerable agreement among the manuscripts about the visual attention given to the songs. Bodley 638, a paper manuscript, makes use of red horizontal lines to distinguish stanzas throughout, as well as red paraphs (it also has running titles in red).[29] The ballade in the Prologue to *The Legend of Good Women* has a red horizontal line drawn right across the page after

---

27. Strictly speaking, as John Burrow remarks, *The House of Fame* is the first to have book divisions (signaled in the text); see *Ricardian Poetry* (London, 1971), 59. However, these divisions were first put in by Caxton; the three manuscripts indicate them only by large capitals.

28. One might add that the Statius argument is equally and wrongfully neglected by modern editors, despite the fact that it occurs in all the manuscripts except H4 and R.

29. Examples of works in which the stanzas are separated in this way include *The Parliament of Fowls, The Temple of Glass,* and *Anelida.* The markings (though not their color) can be seen in Pamela Robinson, ed., *Bodley 638: A Facsimile,* Facsimile Series of the Works of Geoffrey Chaucer, gen. ed. Paul G. Ruggiers (Norman, Okla., and Woodbridge, England, 1982).

the final refrain (fol. 51^v), and a red paraph marks the line immediately follow-ing the ballade. The first song in *The Book of the Duchess* is singled out with a black ink paraph alongside each "stanza" (that is, by "Allas deth" and "Whan he had," fol. 119^v); the line introducing the second ("Algatys songys thus I made," fol. 137^r)—though not the song itself—has a further paraph.[30] Bodley 638 also contains a copy of *The Parliament of Fowls*: here, as in Trinity College, Cambridge, MS. R.3.19 and Fairfax 16, the French refrain "Qui ben ayme a tard oblye" is written into the space where the roundel would be (fol. 110^r), with red lettering, flanked above and below by two horizontal red lines.[31]

The same French refrain is written out in red, with a paraph, in the Fairfax copy of the *Parliament* (as it is also in John Shirley's copy in Trinity R.3.19). Paraphs again mark out the songs in *The Book of the Duchess* and the Prologue.[32] Song headings are used in this manuscript only for independent lyric pieces such as *The Compleynt of Mars* and *The Compleynt of Venus* (both have full titles and *nota* in the margin at the start, and "compleynt" and *nota* written again when the set piece itself begins). In Tanner 346, however, "balade" is written in the margin alongside the song in the Prologue, together with the first line of the song in the right-hand margin and a paraph. Paraphs mark the start of each stanza, and "Explicit cantus" at the end. Paraphs again mark out the "stanzas" of the first song in the *Duchess*. A "littera" heading is given to a passage from "The Legend of Phyllis." This may be compared with the widespread use of headings, titles, and summaries underlined in red for the material in the Lydgate manuscript, Harley 2251. The copy of the *Kingis Quair* in the *Troilus* manuscript S1 has "cantus" in the margin alongside the song on folio 195^r in the same clear, bold style charac-teristic of the "cantus" headings earlier in the manuscript.

Altogether, the songs are consistently marked out, often stanza by stanza. Without a detailed comparison of the layout of independent lyrics, or indeed a full analysis of the general patterns of paraph and *nota* markings in each of these texts, conclusions can only be provisional, but it seems safe to say that these fifteenth-century scribes were assiduous in their attention to a poem's structure and formal division. In particular, we may compare the way in which stanza divisions are marked by a horizontal red line in Bodley 638 with the horizontal dashes used in

30. The only other paraph in the poem occurs at line 711.
31. Caxton also prints the refrain.
32. Paraphs also mark out each stanza of the ballade (with one extra at the resumption of the narrative) in the Prologue to *The Legend of Good Women* in the Pepys 2006 copy; see A. S. G. Edwards, ed., *Manuscript Pepys 2006, Magdalen College Cambridge* (Norman, Okla., 1985), 59.

Troilus manuscript R. Both sets of scribes, it seems, are pointing to Chaucer's use of a lyric stanza as a means of composing love narratives. The French connection here, given that rhyme royal was the form most commonly used in the French ballade, is noticed by a scribe in Cp who, in a place where six stanzas are missing (IV.491, fol. 100^v), remarks in the margin "deficuit vi balettes."

Seen from this perspective, *Troilus* appears as a lyric compilation, and in these terms it has no direct English comparison, except perhaps Lydgate's *The Temple of Glass.* Significantly, the only contemporary compilations that concentrate exclusively on lyrics are French, namely the manuscripts of Charles d'Orléans's poetry.[33] The designation "French" here requires a certain elasticity. One manuscript, personally owned by Charles and now f.fr. 25458, represents the earliest working collection of his French ballades, chansons, complaintes, and caroles, to which he continued to add throughout his life.[34] Several further copies, some of them highly sumptuous, were made from this personal edition. One of them, however, British Library, MS. Royal 16. F. ii, was prepared under English direction and carries the arms of Henry VII, Elizabeth of York, and the Prince of Wales in a gorgeously decorated heraldic border on the frontispiece.[35] A far more humble copy, British Library, MS. Harley 682, contains Charles's ballades and chansons in English. Dated 1440, it is closely contemporary with several of the *Troilus* manuscripts.

Royal 16. F. ii, a magnificently produced volume, is meticulously provided with a hierarchical scheme of initials, decorated line-fillers, and flourished titles and headings in alternating red and blue. Each song is given a generic title ("Balade," "chancon," "carole") that, with the flourishes, can take up as many as five lines. One title in particular ("Lettre en balade," fol. 62^r) concisely sums up the hybrid relation between song and letter that occurs in *Troilus.* Descriptive headings are also included, such as "Sen suit balade ou lamant parle a son cuer" (fol. 15^v) or "Le dessoubz de la letre" (fol. 63^r). The versified letter to which the latter rubric refers is the last element in a dramatized lyric sequence, entitled in Champion's edition "Songe en Complainte." It ends with a signature like those of the letters of Troilus and Criseyde:

33. See J. Boffey, "The Manuscripts of English Courtly Love Lyrics in the Fifteenth Century," in D. Pearsall, ed., *Manuscripts and Readers in Fifteenth-Century England: The Literary Implications of Manuscript Study* (Cambridge, 1983), 3–14 at 4–5.

34. All manuscripts of French writing are from Paris, Bibliothèque Nationale, unless otherwise stated.

35. For the argument that the volume was prepared in the 1480s for Edward IV, perhaps by the scribe Hugues de Lembourg, an employee of Thomas Thwayte, sometime Chancellor of the Exchequer and Chancellor of the Duchy of Lancaster under Edward, see Janet Backhouse, "Founders of the Royal Library: Edward IV and Henry VII as Collectors of Illuminated Manuscripts," in D. Williams, ed., *England in the Fifteenth Century: Proceedings of the 1986 Harlaxton Symposium* (Woodbridge, England, 1987), 23–41 at 36–38.

> Le bien vostre, Charles, duc d'Orlians
> Qui jadis fut l'un de voz vrais servans.
>
> (Lines 549–50)[36]

This last pair of lines is here set off from the rest of the letter by the rubric, giving a specific near-contemporary parallel to the French signatures put in by Chaucer's scribes.

The Charles d'Orléans manuscripts represent an interesting point of connection between English and French scribal practices in the fifteenth century.[37] A likely line of contact with Chaucer's poetry can be traced through Charles's enforced stay from 1432 with William de la Pole, later duke of Suffolk, whose wife Alice was Chaucer's granddaughter. Charles's twenty-five-year period of exile in England suggests that he acted as a living instance of naturalization between English and French poetic expectations and practice. As has often been remarked, the circulation of French manuscripts was not only high but also highly valued in the English aristocratic community. Some of the most expensive and beautifully crafted copies of vernacular writing in the period include copies of French poetry written in England, or commissioned by or presented to English patrons (often by means of a French spouse). Christine de Pisan's *Le Livre du duc des vrais amants* and *Cent balades d'amant et de dame* are part of British Library, MS. Harley 4431, a manuscript that was owned by John, duke of Bedford (husband to Jacquetta of Luxembourg) and then by Richard Woodville.[38] Froissart's collected love poetry (in f.fr. 831) was owned by Richard Beauchamp, earl of Warwick; and a compilation of Machaut's oeuvres (f.fr. 9221) was presented to Thomas, duke of Clarence, by Jean, duc de Berry, in 1412.[39]

Fifteenth-century English knowledge and appreciation of French love poetry itself built on a wide network of connections—social, political, and literary—established during the preceding century. These contacts, arising partly out of the constraints of war and the exchange of royal hostages, have been well documented elsewhere.[40] As Elizabeth Salter has suggested, "these were the cosmopolitan

---

36. P. Champion, ed., *Charles d'Orléans: Poésies*, 2 vols. (1923; Paris, 1982), 1:118.
37. Fairfax 16, a major Chaucer compendium, contains many of the English versions of Charles's poetry.
38. Both Jacquetta's signature and that of Richard's eldest son Anthony appear on the manuscript cover.
39. BN, f.fr. 831, completed on 12 May 1394, has a note on the inside cover stating that it belonged to "Richart le gentil fauls conte de Waryewyck." Richard held this title from 1401 to his death in 1439. See A. Fourrier, ed., *Jean Froissart: L'Espinette amoureuse* (Paris, 1972), 10–11.
40. See for instance, Elizabeth Salter, "Chaucer and Internationalism," Pearsall and Zeeman, *English and International*, 239–44; Scattergood and Sherborne, *English Court Culture*; and James I. Wimsatt, *Chaucer and His French Contemporaries: Natural Music in the Fourteenth Century* (Toronto, 1991).

years which saw the translation of leading members of the French court to England."[41] But also part of this cultural exchange were French scribes and painters (such as Girard d'Orléans, a member of Jean le Bon's retinue), and poets such as Jehan de la Mote and Froissart, and some of them stayed for long periods working for both French and English patrons. French books were readily purchased in England at this time. It is important to remember, furthermore, the dominant international reputation of French artistic production in the fields of painting, music, poetry, and vernacular translation.

It is in this context that it may be valuable to consider the *mise-en-page* of the Machaut and Froissart manuscripts. It is not possible to confirm that the *Troilus* scribes would have been familiar with a specific copy, but it is likely that some of the *Troilus* scribes saw these manuscripts. The patterns of layout in manuscripts that Chaucer would have seen, furthermore, in the works of poets that had so powerful an effect on his literary imagination, would certainly have had a direct and lasting influence on the expectations of his own readers and copyists.

There are twelve surviving manuscripts that contain a more or less complete collection of Machaut's works, nine from the fourteenth century and three from the fifteenth. Several of his works were also copied out individually in many other compilations.[42] The observations here are drawn from eight of the "complete" manuscripts, including two compilations that Machaut himself probably oversaw, now f.fr. 1586 and 1584.[43] Recent research by James Wimsatt and William Kibler on the manuscript tradition of two of his narrative "dits," *Le Jugement dou Roy de Behaingne* and *Le Remede de Fortune,* has encouraged them to speculate, perhaps overenthusiastically, that Chaucer may have known the beautifully illuminated f.fr. 1586. The hypothesized connection with Chaucer starts with a link between the artist and someone who worked on several manuscripts for Jean le Bon between 1350 and 1356.[44] Jean, captured at the Battle of Poitiers and imprisoned in England, may have taken the manuscript with

---

41. Salter, "Chaucer and Internationalism," 241.
42. See *Guillaume de Machaut: Poésies lyriques*, ed. V. Chichmaref, 2 vols. (Paris, 1909), lxxii–cxvi; Lawrence Earp, "Scribal Practice, Manuscript Production, and the Transmission of Music in Late Medieval France: The Manuscripts of Guillaume de Machaut" (Ph.D diss., Princeton University, 1983); and Earp, "Machaut's Role in the Production of Manuscripts of His Works," *Journal of the American Musicological Society* 42 (1989): 461–503. The preponderance of "complete oeuvres" compilations is an innovation: no French author before Machaut had such a large-scale, carefully orchestrated production of his poetic works, and hence of himself as a poet.
43. See Huot, *From Song to Book*, 246ff. and 274–75.
44. François Avril, "Les Manuscrits enluminés de Guillaume de Machaut: essai de chronologie," in *Guillaume de Machaut, poète et compositeur*, Actes et colloques, no. 23 (Paris, 1982), 117–33.

him, the story continues, whereupon "the further probability that young Chaucer saw it appears strong."[45] Unfortunately, there are many key assumptions in this tempting hypothesis that gloss over our lack of knowledge of the precise means by which Chaucer gained access to Machaut's poetry. He evidently knew much of it intimately, but how he acquired this intimacy is uncertain. Would he have required a personal copy? Did he memorize the material? What kind of access could he have had to this particular volume, expensive and no doubt carefully guarded? Wimsatt and Kibler go on in similar vein to comment that f.fr. 1586 "suggests, perhaps as well as any manuscript extant, how early elaborate court manuscripts of Chaucer's works might have been arranged and illuminated." This is the kind of speculation that we cannot entertain without a much more detailed understanding of the relationship between French and English manuscript culture. What we can conclude is that some, at least, of these surviving Machaut manuscripts (or copies derived from them) would have been seen by Chaucer and the influence of their *mise-en-page* felt and experienced by both the poet and his contemporary scribes.

The works of Machaut that invite the most direct structural comparison with *Troilus* are the *Remede de Fortune* and *Le Voir Dit*, both substantial narratives with inset songs, and, in the case of the *Voir Dit*, inset letters as well. Frequent rubrics are characteristic of all the manuscripts: lyrics (both those set into narrative and in separate groups) are given generic titles ("balade," "rondeau," "chanson royal"), usually set on a separate line within a column and sometimes in the margin as well (as in f.fr. 881); and there are frequent summarizing headings in the narrative *dits*. Standard practice with lyrics, taken over from thirteenth- and fourteenth-century chansonniers, was to mark the start with a larger initial, and subsequent strophes with smaller blue or red initials. Those *formes fixes* with music (again following chansonnier practice) are given with the text of the first strophe set underneath the notation, and remaining strophes set out in columns below.[46]

45. James J. Wimsatt and William W. Kibler, *Guillaume de Machaut: Le Jugement du roy de Behaigne and Remede de Fortune* (Athens, Ga., and London, 1988), 53. See my review in *Review of English Studies* 42 (1991): 246–48.
46. Layout for polyphony or for the more complex musical genres such as the lay or *complainte* makes far greater demands on the scribes: each page is designed as a whole or rather, as a double opening. According to Earp, "Scribal Practice," chap. 2, it is a general rule in the Machaut manuscripts that the voices of a polyphonic composition—those that sound together—"are never split across a recto-verso page turn by the scribe."

When we turn to the lyrics set within narrative, such as the copy of the *Remede* in f.fr. 9221 (MS. E), we find a careful juxtaposition and alternation of columnar format, the width of the text columns being expanded where necessary to incorporate the music. The *Remede* contains seven lyric pieces set to music (as well as a spoken *priere* and a refrain), in decreasing order of formal complexity: lai, complainte, chant royal, baladelle, ballade, chanson balladee, and rondelet. (Three of these, the two ballades and the rondeau, are given polyphonic settings.) It has often been remarked that this very precise range of inset songs, one of each kind, gives the *Remede* the function of a kind of *summa* of all the current lyric genres favored by Machaut and his contemporaries. It may be added that the presentation of these songs all within a single narrative frame creates for the copyist the design challenge of producing a model set of layouts, varied according to the demands of each genre.[47]

In terms of the practice of the *Troilus* scribes, what is of interest is that Machaut's poetry was copied with a keen eye to differentiating between lyric and narrative and among lyric genres. The presence of musical notation itself of course creates the greatest visual distinction between song and narrative, with the abrupt use of the whole width of a page, red staves and notes possessing their own calligraphic features, longs, breves, and semi-breves. The more luxurious manuscripts, such as f.fr. 9221, 1584 and 1586, interweave with the musical passages an elaborate scheme of miniatures, each with their own rubrics. In copies of the *Voir Dit* there is further variation in the prose layout of the forty-six letters (the totals vary among individual manuscripts).

The complexity of the overall design is further increased by the widespread use of rubrics to indicate different speakers/performers. The section of the *Remede* in which there is a dialogue between "L'Amant" and "Esperance" thus looks like a play text in f.fr. 9221 and 22545, for instance, with the lines divided between each speaker under their respective names. Where appropriate, the rubrics interrupt a line of text:

> l amant
> Nenil ma dame esperance Tu dis voir
> (Fol. 30^r, f.fr. 9221)

---

47. Not all scribes were equal to the challenge: for instance, as Rebecca Baltzer notes, in the copy of the *Remede* in MS. K the top voice of the baladelle has been missed out by the musical scribe, even though the text scribe had left sufficient space for it (see Wimsatt and Kibler, *Guillaume de Machaut,* 414).

All the narrative *dits,* such as *Le Jugement dou Roy de Behaingne* and *Le Jugement dou Roy de Navarre,* receive this kind of layout. The names in f.fr. 1587 assigned to the *Navarre* speakers include la dame, le roy, Foy, lacteur, Guillaume, Franchise, and so on. The distinction between "guillaume" and "L'acteur" is particularly interesting, in the way that it recognizes the persona of the poet as a separate voice within the poet's own text. Machaut scribes are drawing on the practice of the *Roman de la Rose* copyists, who consistently distinguish between "L'acteur" and "L'Amant" in their rubrication.[48] Given the very wide circulation of the *Roman de la Rose* it is clear that this way of dividing up narrative according to the number and type of first-person speakers would have exercised a great deal of influence on scribes, readers, and authors of vernacular court poetry. The *Troilus* scribes, particularly those in Gg, S1, and H5, where initials and rubrics are used to mark changes of speaker, are clearly participating in this well-established practice.

Two manuscripts that were deeply influenced by the arrangement and disposition of the Machaut anthologies are f.fr. 830 and 831, the two surviving versions of Froissart's collected love poetry. The probability that Froissart's work circulated in England, and these copies of it in particular, is great. Not only did he spend some six years in England in the employ of Queen Philippa, but it has also been plausibly argued that f.fr. 831 is the very manuscript that Froissart, in his *Chroniques,* describes himself presenting to Richard II in July 1394.[49] Although none of Froissart's lyrics is provided with music, both of these manuscripts imitate the patterns of rubrication in the Machaut manuscripts extensively, just as so many of the individual works are themselves modeled on Machaut's. The particularly close structural correspondence between Froissart's *La Prison Amoureuse* and Machaut's *Voir Dit* is thus reflected in the layout of the two works:[50] the inset songs in Froissart (eight virelais, six ballades, one lai, and one

---

48. See David F. Hult, *Self-Fulfilling Prophecies: Readership and Authority in the First* Roman de la Rose (Cambridge, 1986), 74–93; and Huot, *From Song to Book,* 91 n. 18, and appendix A. Huot reports finding "Aucteur-Amant" rubrication in 53 out of 72 manuscripts (there are around 150 altogether surviving today from before 1400). On the use of author portraits to mark the transition between authors, see Lori Walters, "Appendix: Author Portraits, and Textual Demarcation in Manuscripts of the *Romance of the Rose,*" in Kevin Brownlee and Sylvia Huot, eds., *Rethinking the* Romance of the Rose: *Text, Image, Reception* (Philadelphia, 1992), 359–73.

49. See Peter F. Dembowski, ed., *Le Paradis d'Amour; L'Orloge Amoureus,* Textes littéraires français (Geneva, 1986), 3–4; f.fr. 831 has certain texts edited out that might have been unflattering to English king, and one edited in, a ballade about King Brut that is not included in f.fr. 830 (see pp. 8–12).

50. See A. Butterfield, "Froissart, Machaut, Chaucer, and the Genres of Imagination," in André Crépin, ed., *L'Imagination médiévale: Chaucer et ses contemporains,* Actes du colloque en Sorbonne, Publications de l'Association des Médiévistes Anglicistes de l'Enseignement Supérieur, no. 16 (Paris, 1991), 53–69.

complainte), like those in Machaut, receive generic titles, with the twelve letters written out in prose across the width of the whole page, starting with an enlarged initial. *Meliador,* a long romance with seventy-nine inset songs (eleven ballades, sixteen virelais, and fifty-two rondeaux), which Froissart began while he was in Queen Philippa's household, is similarly punctuated in f.fr. 12557 with generic rubrics and enlarged, gilded initials for the songs.

Perhaps the most interesting layout among the Froissart manuscripts occurs in a Brussels copy (1410–15) of the *Trésor amoureux* (Bibl. Royale 11140), the first few folios of which are richly illuminated.[51] The *Trésor* (a work only tentatively ascribed to Froissart) is a large lyric anthology interspersed with blocks of narrative couplets, rather like some of the sequences by Charles d'Orléans.[52] A notable feature of the manuscript is the extent to which glossing, in the form of frequent summaries *within* the narrative sections, is incorporated by the poet into the structure of the *dit,* suggesting heightened self-consciousness on the part of the poet about his own activity in relation to scribal practice. Furthermore, the miniatures are often accompanied by lengthy rubrics that seem poised in a transitional stage, part instructions to the artist, part glosses for the reader.[53]

A similar role for rubrics can be found in a fourteenth-century copy of *Le Romans de la dame a la licorne et du biau chevalier* (f.fr. 12562), a narrative with numerous inset ballades and rondeaux. The two kinds of rubric (for the illuminator and for the reader) are written out separately for many of the miniatures. It is unusual to find both kinds of annotation together. The reader sees both the intention that the producer of the manuscript expressed for the picture and the comment on the result—before and after—with the picture itself literally occupying the intervening conceptual space. For instance, on folio 12^V, before the third song (a ballade), there is a marginal instruction that says "faites .i. *chlr* tout droit tenant .i. rolle en sa main." Next to this is a picture of the knight standing with his right finger pointing upward and a scroll in his left hand, and the rubric

51. C. Gaspar and F. Lyna, *Les Principaux manuscrits à peintures de la Bibliothèque Royale de Belgique,* 2 vols. (1984; reprint, Brussels, 1937), 1:453–54, Notice 191.
52. Other works constructed on related formal principles include *Le Livre des cent balades,* Christine de Pisan's *Cent balades d'amant et de dame,* and her *Le Livre des duc des vrais amants,* and René d'Anjou's *Le Livre du cueur d'amours espris.* See *Le Livre des Cent Balades,* ed. G. Raynaud (Paris, 1905); Christine de Pisan, *Cent balades d'amant et de dame,* ed. J. Cerquiglini (Paris, 1982); *Le Livre des duc des vrais amants,* ed. M. Roy, vol. 3 of *Oeuvres poétiques de Christine de Pisan,* 3 vols. (Paris, 1886–96), 59–208; and René d'Anjou, *Le Livre du cueur d'amours espris,* ed. S. Wharton (Paris, 1980).
53. See J. J. G. Alexander, *Medieval Illuminators and Their Methods of Work* (New Haven, Conn., and London, 1992), chap. 3 and 117–18.

"Comment li biaus chlr chante le lyon."[54] All of this gives us a surprisingly explicit account of the process by which a song is rendered into visual form by a medieval scribe.

To return to the *Trésor* manuscript: a series of three pictures goes even further to suggest the poet's heightened self-consciousness about literary production. In an illustration on folio 9 Amour is shown on the left with a company of people on the right, two of whom (a man and a woman) are holding scrolls with writing on them.[55] In the margin is the heading "Comment Amours fait nouvelles ordonnances sur ses gens et dit." On folio 13 the marginal heading "Comment amour deuise a l'auteur la maniere de faire son livre" appears next to a picture. Finally, on folio 15ᵛ, a picture surrounded by very elaborate decorations over the whole page shows Amour sitting on a throne with his hands in a gesture of instruction, the poet kneeling before him, holding an open book and a quill pen in his right hand and looking up at Amour expectantly. The phrase "nouvelles ordonnances" has a double significance in this context: Amour not only inspires the poet but also advises him about how to turn his poetry into a book ("la maniere de faire son livre"). The picture illustrates a passage in the work where highly detailed formal instructions on the composition of his book are given to the poet: the number of rhyming couplets it should have, the precise arrangement and number of ballades and rondeaux. Amour even tells him to incorporate a table of refrains and a first-line index.[56]

Ordonner is a key word for Froissart:[57] he repeats the word three times in the rubrics that open and close the anthologies in f.fr. 831 and 830. These rubrics are emphatic forms of self-announcement, in which he both names himself as the author and fully explains the date and circumstance of the production of each volume:

> Vous devés sçavoir que dedens ce livre sont contenu pluisour dittié et traitié amourous et de moralité, les quels sire Jehans Froissars, prestres, . . . a fais, dittés et ordonnés. . . . Et vous ensagnera ceste table comment il sont escript ou dit livre par ordenance.[58]

---

54. Ibid., 60.
55. This picture is reproduced in Gaspar and Lyna, *Les Principaux manuscrits à peintures,* vol. 2.
56. *Le Trésor amoureux,* ed. A. Scheler, vol. 3 of *Oeuvres de Froissart: Poésies* (Brussels, 1870–72), 52–305, lines 712–96.
57. L. Foulet, "Etude sur le vocabulaire abstrait de Froissart: Ordonnance," *Romania* 67 (1942–43): 145–216.
58. Dembowski, *Le Paradis d'Amour,* 2.

For Froissart, the art of *ordinatio* is part of the process of creative composition.[59] The art of exerting control over the *ordinatio* of one's own poetry stimulates and indeed begins to define for Froissart and for Machaut the public role of authorship.

The *Mise-en-Page* of Lyrics in French Narrative

The overwhelming visual impression made by the Machaut and Froissart manuscripts is the emphasis given to the element of song—by music, by generic titles, by pictures of scrolls and performers, by large initials. All of these elements combine to give visual prominence to the structural outline of each work and genre in the codex, including the *dits*, and the different lyric genres in the lyric sections. This kind of visual pointing extends over the codex as a whole, thereby displaying it in turn as a single structurally complex entity. The vivid red headings, in particular, especially in the plainer copies, make verbally as well as visually explicit the shifts in genre from page to page, as the eye moves from ballade to verse narrative to rondeau, lai, complainte, and prose letter. This emphatic form of structural articulation gives a specific context to our sense of the particular pains being taken in the *Troilus* manuscripts to outline the structural and generic divisions in *Troilus and Criseyde*. It suggests that the instinct to mark out the generic shifts in *Troilus* was an early one, embedded as it was in the practice of Chaucer's French contemporaries.[60]

Machaut and Froissart tend to be viewed by Chaucerians from a misleading or at any rate parochial perspective, as precursors to Chaucer. From the perspective of French writing, however, their poetry (and in Machaut's case, music too) is situated at the far end of artistic practices that had been explored with sophistication throughout the previous century. While we must be as attentive as possible to the precise paths of particular manuscripts, it is important also to be alive to the *longue durée* of influence, contact, circumstance, and habit in a manuscript culture. Not everything is visible within a strictly circumscribed view of scribal relationships.

It is worth looking at headings and rubrics in the manuscripts of French narratives to develop a broader notion of the scribal role in transmission. Headings and rubrics are extensively used in these manuscripts, varying from marginal notes that simply comment informally on the presence of a song to a more systematic allocation of generic headings. Those in lat. 11331 and Munich lat. 4660

---

59. See Huot, *From Song to Book*, 239.
60. Similar conclusions, though from a different perspective, are drawn by Boffey in "Annotation."

serve as examples of informal comment: in the former, a French refrain is written out in the margin next to a Latin song, and in the latter, "refr" (for *refractus*) is written next to the refrain. It seems likely that the use of headings developed (at least in part) from the scribe's need to be aware of a change of layout. "Chant" occurs in black ink in the margin on folio 3^v in Brussels, Bibliothèque Royale, Albert 1er 10747, a copy of Gautier de Coinci's *Les Miracles de Notre Dame*; similarly, in one of the manuscripts of the *Roman du Castelain de Couci,* f.fr. 15098, "chancon" is written in the extreme top margin of each page on which a song is written (fol. 116^{r-v}, for example) in the same brown ink used for the ruled lines. The latter, especially, indicates that the location of the songs was not some kind of afterthought but an intrinsic part of the planning of the whole manuscript. Otherwise, rubrics and headings for the songs (usually "Canchon," sometimes, more specifically, "balade," "rondel," and so on) tend to be written into the body of the text, as in manuscripts of the *Castelain de Couci, Cleomadés, Meliacin,* the prose *Violette, La Prise amoureuse,* and *Le Parfait du Paon.* The presence of "chanson," as well as the name of the author alongside each song in Vatican Reg. 1725 (Renart's *Rose*), seems to have more of a labeling function, as does the writing of "chanson," "prouerbe," and so on alongside the large number of interpolated refrains and proverbs in the glossing text of the *Traduction et commentaire de l'Ars amatoria d'Ovide.* These forms recognizing refrains and other song genres act as examples not just of simple visual highlighting but also of an incipient kind of commentary, or rhetorical description, one that comes to be more fully articulated in the Machaut and Froissart manuscripts.

In these manuscripts the songs are indicated by a remarkably extensive range of textual markers. Clearly the physical activity of writing involved the scribes in many decisions about how to place the songs, which they carried out with recourse to various framing, signaling, and labeling devices. The context for the type of sign chosen varies, presumably according to the training and background of the individual scribe and his perception of the kind of work he is copying, so that at times the decisions owe more to *chansonnier* layout, and at others to the writing of sermons. As we saw in the *Troilus* manuscripts, verbal headings are supplemented by various kinds of visual markers, including red used for either the lettering of song headings or for underlining—which we have also noticed in fifteenth-century English compilations. In several manuscripts of the *Parliament of Fowls,* for example, as we noted, the French refrain is picked out in red. Songs and refrains are similarly highlighted in red in f.fr. 1374 (a copy of Gerbert de Montreuil's *Le Roman de la Violette*), f.fr. 14968 (a *fatrasie* by Watriquet de Couvin), and Paris Ars. 3142 (a copy of a "Bele Aelis" sermon). They are underlined in red in f.fr. 1455 (*Meliacin*) and f.fr. 1554 (*Restor de Paon*).[61] The *Meliacin* manuscript also gives a few of the twenty-four inset songs the heading "chançon" in red. Such colorful pointing of songs is paralleled by various other signs. The final word of a refrain may be followed by a tilde, or longer flourish (for example, *Le Roman de la Poire*, f.fr. 2186, fol. 34^v, 69 and 72; and the sermon in Vienna 2621, fol. 52^v); or else by a distinctive form of punctuation, such as an extended "tick" (a form of *punctus elevatus*) in Jacquemart Giélée's *Renart le Nouvel* and Adam de la Halle's *Robin et Marion*, both copied in f.fr. 25566.[62] There are also manuscripts where song and "narrative" are distinguished by the size of the script, such as Paris, Arsenal 2741 of the *Traduction d'Ovide*, and Besançon, Bibl. Mun. 4816 of Gautier de Coinci's *Miracles*.

By far the most widespread and consistent sign to register the presence of a song in thirteenth- and fourteenth-century French manuscripts—confirming the practice among the *Troilus* scribes—is the use of initials. In several manuscripts this usage is supplemented by paraphs: if both visual signs are used then they are placed in a hierarchical relation. Thus three stanzaic works copied in f.fr 837—*La Chastelaine de Saint Gille*, *Li Confrere d'Amours*, and *Salut d'Amours (I)*— all have initials by every stanza and paraphs by every chanson and refrain.[63] Similarly, the copy of *La Prise amoreuse* of Jehan Acart de Hesdin, in f.fr. 24391—which has initials for every stanza of its nine rondeaux and nine balades—picks out the refrains within each balade with paraphs.[64] This kind of hierarchy demonstrates, first, a desire to divide up songs (and narratives) stanzaically, and second, a particular focus on the unit of the refrain, even when it forms part of a larger song division.[65]

Many of these features in the *ordinatio* of inset songs and refrains find their place in the larger history of the development of layout and punctuation in medieval academic books. As M. B. Parkes has argued, developments in the organization of manuscripts from the twelfth century onward work in harmony with

---

61. BN, f.fr. 1802 (*Paradis*) has black lead/faint pen underlining for the refrains (of an uncertain date).
62. Line decoration at the end of songs also occurs in Vatican Reg. 1725 (Renart's *Rose*) and f.fr. 24378 (*Roman de la Violette*, prose version).
63. A fourth, the fabliau *Le Lai d'Aristote*, has paraphs for every refrain and an initial for just one of its three *rondets*.
64. BN f.fr. 817 and 1533 (Gautier de Coinci) have large initials for the start of a chanson, smaller ones for the stanzas.
65. Eglal Doss-Quinby (after Spanke) has pointed out that upper-case initials are regularly given to refrains in the manuscripts of *chansons-avec-des-refrains*; see *Les Refrains chez les trouvères du XIIe siècle au début du XIVe* (New York, 1984), 107–8 and n. 18.

developments in "the structure of reasoning."[66] The analogies between the layout of songs and that of scholastic texts reveal the kinds of assumptions scribes were making about the role and function of embedded songs. Songs that are written or underlined in red recall the practice in the commentaries of Peter Lombard on the Psalter and Epistles of Paul of underlining *lemmata* in red. The *auctores* cited in the commentary were also named in red in the margin.[67] A parallel practice is found in the single surviving manuscript of Renart's *Rose* (Vatican Reg. 1725), where the names of the authors of the chansons cited by Renart are written in the margin next to each song. Not surprisingly, the sermon contexts for *rondets* offer the closest analogy to scholastic practice: in Paris Arsenal 3142 the "Bele Aelis" *rondet* is given in red at the start with a large initial, and then each line is written out singly in red as a *lemma* followed by individual commentary. The use of a hierarchy of script in copies of the *Traduction d'Ovide* and the *Miracles* is another standard means by which *lemmata* and commentary were distinguished in academic theological books.[68] In the *Traduction,* "Texte" and "Glose" are laid out alternately with headings, the gloss (of which the refrains and other song and proverbial citations form a part) in a smaller script than the text (Paris, Arsenal 2741). In the Besançon copy of the *Miracles,* as I remarked earlier, the chansons are again in a smaller module than the text, but in a sermon copied in Vatican Borghese 200, on folio 3, the rondeau is written in larger script than the following sermon. The hierarchy does not always privilege the same elements, for sometimes the refrains and songs are represented as commentary, sometimes as text. Together these manuscripts offer interestingly varied examples of vernacular appropriation of academic systems of textual organization.

The whole practice of marking the beginning of songs with initials (in varying degrees of decoration) and paraphs again finds an analogy in the use of *litterae notabiliores* to indicate the beginnings of *sententiae,* and in the proliferation of paraphs in manuscripts from the thirteenth century onward, "used increasingly to indicate the beginning of a new *propositio,* or of a new stage in the development of an argument."[69] In this context we see refrains and songs treated as authoritative texts, as the object and the source of commentary. The ancient asso-

---

66. See M. B. Parkes, "The Influence of the Concepts of *Ordinatio* and *Compilatio* on the Development of the Book," in J. J. G. Alexander and M. T. Gibson, eds., *Medieval Learning and Literature: Essays Presented to Richard William Hunt* (Oxford, 1976), 115–41 at 121. See also M. B. Parkes, *Pause and Effect: An Introduction to the History of Punctuation in the West* (Aldershot, England, 1992).
67. See Parkes, "*Ordinatio* and *Compilatio,*" 116.
68. See Parkes, *Pause and Effect,* 27.
69. Ibid., 43–44.

ciation of authoritative texts with special scripts, which began in Western culture with Anglo-Saxon scribes, seems to pass into Continental vernacular culture with these song-embedded texts. The particular form of their visual emphasis seems to indicate that many thirteenth- and fourteenth-century scribes saw the songs not only as special points of progress in the structural development of a work but also as examples of authoritative and sententious observation that demanded attention and comment.[70]

The ways in which scribes marked off the end of a song have a further implication. It would be a mistake to think of them, even in their more decorated versions, as mere space-fillers. More likely they are forms of *positurae,* or "end-of-section" marks, used in the twelfth and thirteenth centuries to show the completion of a gloss at the end of a column. As Parkes notes, these appear "sporadically throughout the later Middle Ages to indicate the end of a division (usually a Book) within a work" and can also be found "at the ends of headings."[71] I suggest that we consider them alongside the very common practice in our group of manuscripts of giving initials to the section of narrative that immediately *follows* a song. In some cases these are the only parts of a work that are initialed (as in *Renart le Nouvel,* f.fr. 372, f.fr. 1593; *Paradis,* f.fr. 1802; *Poire,* f.fr. 24431; Hesdin, *La Prise amoureuse,* f.fr. 24432); but more often they supplement the initials given to the songs themselves (as in *Cleomadés,* Brussels, Bibliothèque Royale, Albert 1er II 7444; *Couci,* f.fr. 15098; *Escanor,* f.fr. 24374; *Violette,* f.fr. 1553). Such emphasis placed on the end of a song and on the start of the narrative suggests that the *positurae* and initials are functioning together as a generic marker. Like the shift between gloss and text, the end of a song is viewed as the end of one mode and the herald of another.[72]

---

70. Compare *Le Roman de la Poire,* 2793–96, in which a refrain is described as the *sentence* of a song:
      Dites moi del chant la sentence!
      – Si vos volez, tres bien le vueill:
      Amors ai a ma volenté
        teles con ge veill.

71. Parkes, *Pause and Effect,* 43.

72. In several *roman* manuscripts with music for the inset songs, initials (either historiated or with accompanying miniatures) are used to represent the performer of the song. The placing of staves is often made to coincide with such an initial or a separate picture. In this way, the initial acts as a performative marker, emphasizing the dramatic role of the songs within the narrative structure. See, for instance, the *Poire* manuscript, BN f.fr. 218; and Aix-en-provence, Bibliothèque de Méjanes, MS. 572 (*Robin et Marion*). Other manuscripts that mark out changes of speaker with initials include f.fr. 15098 (Couci) and f.fr. 1446 (Kanor). All three manuscripts bear interesting comparison with a Machaut manuscript such as f.fr. 1584. The presence of songs gives a formal manifestation to each shift in voice: scribes mark this out by inscribing the voices into the margins, in headings and pictures.

We have already noted that the clear formal distinction made between the letters and the narrative in the *Troilus* manuscripts is paralleled in the layout of the letters in Machaut's *Voir Dit* and Froissart's *La Prison Amoureuse*, as well as Charles d'Orléans's *Songe en complainte*. Several authors prior to Machaut and Froissart set letters alongside songs in narrative contexts, namely Jacquemart Giélée in *Renart le Nouvel*, Jakemés in *Le Roman du Castelain de Couci,* and the anonymous author of the prose *Tristan* and *Le Romans de la dame a la licorne*. In *Renart le Nouvel* and *La dame a la licorne* the letters are in prose. This does not automatically distinguish them from songs, since songs are also often lineated as prose in *roman* manuscripts. Visually they tend to be emphasized by pictures, often with additional rubrics. In the f.fr. 776 copy of the prose *Tristan*, a large initial on folio 246^r alongside a notated letter shows a lady standing with a piece of paper in her hand on which writing is clearly visible.

It is in this light that I suggest we see the special attention paid to the letters in the *Troilus* manuscript, S1, where Troilus's letter in Book V has the kind of large border decoration reserved elsewhere in the manuscript for book *incipits*. Letters in these French narratives have a structural and visual importance. Their equivalence with song is shown most clearly in the *Castelain de Couci*, where the letters are not in prose but in verse, and they are treated similarly in terms of layout in both f.fr. 15098 and n.a.fr. 7514, with a line spacing before and after an enlarged initial. The fifteenth-century paper copy of the prose version in Lille fonds Godefroy 50 (ancien 134) makes almost more of the letters than of the songs. One letter on page 98 is illustrated with a picture of the Castelain's servant waiting outside the lady's house, looking into the middle distance, while she, sitting down, holding the letter in front of her face, reads avidly. With the blue fleuronnée initial at the start, and a lengthy rubric ("Com*ment* la dame de fayel rechupt et lisy les *lettre*s que le varlet auoit apportees de par le chastellain de coucy"), this letter and its reply are presented as self-contained visual units, like separate chapters.

It is clear that the use of headings in the *Troilus* manuscripts has a wide frame of reference. For this very reason, we do not need to posit a scenario in which the *Troilus* scribes are presented as encountering headings for songs or letters for the first time. French practice suggests that scribes developed patterns of rubrication in vernacular narratives with inset songs and letters for a variety of reasons: to indicate a change of layout for a music scribe, to mark out changes of genre, to single out songs as authorial citations or as examples of singular sententiousness, to emphasize the character of a work in performance. The habits and assumptions formed by the copying of academic material were a constant shaping force.

Furthermore, we need to take account of the fact that the process of setting lyric against, or with, or through narrative was already, by the time of Chaucer's invention of *Troilus and Criseyde*, a complex, various, and subtle one.[73]

MANUSCRIPTS AND AUTHORSHIP

A central preoccupation among these French authors was the nature of authorship itself. In looking at late medieval manuscripts for evidence of a reliable distinction between "the scribal" and "the authorial," we need to be certain that we are not posing the question in terms simpler than those of the authors and scribes themselves. The single surviving copy of Jean Renart's *Roman de la Rose* (Vatican Reg. 1725) shows the scribal annotator responding to Renart's self-conscious, indeed rather convoluted, prologue, where he immediately admits that the songs are not composed by him, but (often) by famous trouvères such as Gace Brulé or the Châtelain de Couci. At the same time he tries to claim some kind of authorial credit for fitting them so artfully into his *roman* that people will think they are his own compositions after all:

> s'est avis a chascun et samble
> que cil qui a fet le romans
> qu'il trovast toz les moz des chans,
> si afierent a ceuls del conte.
>
> (Lines 26–29)

From the very earliest ventures by romance authors with the device of inset songs, it seems that the question of authorship comes to the fore. It could be argued that Renart is aware that to bring in songs by other authors is to behave as a scribe or compiler. Perhaps that is why he is so keen to claim the activity back as authorial.

There is an analogy here with Chaucer's presentation of the narrator in *Troilus*. Alastair Minnis has shown how consistently Chaucer uses the vocabulary of a compiler or translator rather than that of a poet.[74] One might also note how

---

73. Perhaps the best illustration of this is the extraordinary complexity of layout in Chaillou de Pesstain's expanded version (c. 1316–18) of Gervès du Bus's *Roman de Fauvel* (f.fr.146). I discuss this manuscript in some detail in "The Refrain and the Transformation of Genre in the *Roman de Fauvel*," in Margaret Bent and Andrew Wathey, eds., *The Roman de Fauvel: Chronicle, Allegory, Music, and Image in Paris BN f.fr. 146* (Oxford, forthcoming).

74. A. J. Minnis, *Medieval Theory of Authorship* (London, 1984).

consistently the moments at which Chaucer reflects most explicitly about the nature of his own authorship occur following the introduction of a song.[75] Perhaps the most celebrated of these analytic reflexes is the two-stanza introduction to the "Cantus Troili" of Book I, where the narrator slyly brings in the fake allusion to "myn auctour called Lollius." Another example is Criseyde's "compleynte" in IV.743–49, 757–98: here, the narrator raises the difficult problem of how to render Criseyde's sorrow adequately. In both passages Chaucer allows questions about authorship to rise to the surface of the poem by means of a lyric pause. Like Renart, he seems to feel that his status as an author needs to be proved, and chooses to present this need by shifting the mode of narration out of narrative and into lyric.

The example of Froissart speaks further to the delicacy of the distinction between author and scribe in the later fourteenth century. Froissart's appropriation of the medium of the scribal rubric for the purposes of claiming authority for both the content and presentation of his writing shows how far the scribe was usurping the author's position. It is as if the author can only truly emerge by in turn usurping the scribe's space and borrowing his mantle.

One of the most arresting signals of authorship in the *Troilus* manuscripts is, of course, the division of the poem into books and proems. The precedents for this in secular French manuscripts are few but significant. Many manuscripts of *Le Roman de la Rose* mark out with a rubric, and often a miniature as well, the point at which Jean de Meun takes over from Guillaume de Lorris. One of the more interestingly detailed of such scribal explanations occurs in f.fr. 378:

> Ci endroit fina maistre Guillaume de Loriz cest Roumanz. Que plus n'en fist. Ou pour ce qu'il ne vost; Ou pour ce qu'il ne pot. Et pour ce que la matere enbelissoit a plusors, il plot a Maistre Jehan Chopinel de Meun a parfaire le livre. Et a ensivre la matere. Et commence en tele maniere comme vous porroiz oïr ci après.[76]

Scribes seem particularly interested in this relationship between the two parts of the poem and the two authors. The *Rose* clearly stimulated a radical reappraisal among its scribal readers of the kind of authorial possession of a work that a continuator in Jean de Meun's position could have. Jean de Meun explicitly draws attention to his own authorial role later in his continuation, at the midpoint of

---

75. For other examples, see I: 505–7 and 540–44; 655–56; II: 522; 824–26 and 876–77; 1064 and 1085–92; III: 1699–1701; 1743; IV: 825–27; 1170–75; V: 631–37 and 645–46; 1312–16 and 1422.
76. Quoted in Huot, *From Song to Book*, 342; see also 90–95.

the conjoined narrative.[77] The f.fr. 146 copy of *Le Roman de Fauvel* makes sophisticated allusion both to this passage and to the division made in the *Rose* manuscripts between the two poems/two authors. The original *roman* was divided into two books: this is retained in f.fr. 146, with an *incipit* and *explicit* on folio 11 and an author portrait. However, in the lower half of the central column of folio 23^v—on one reckoning the physical midpoint of the book—another rubric announces the point at which Chaillou de Pesstain begins his principal narrative as well as lyric "additions" to the *roman*:

> "Ci s'ensivent les addicions que mesire Chaillou de Pesstain ha mises en
> ce livre, oultre les choses dessus dites qui sont en chant."

This is immediately preceded by eight lines newly set into the narrative, in which Gervès du Bus is named in a riddling anagram as the author of the first *roman*:

> <g> clerc le roy françois, deRues,
> Aus paroles qu'il a conceues
> En ce livret qu'il a trouvé
> Ha bien et clerement prouvé
> Son vif engin, son mouvement;
> Car il parle trop proprement:
> Ou livret ne querez ja men-
> çonge, Dieux le gart! Amen
> (Lines 41–48)[78]

What is interesting about this gloss on the structure of the work—and on the relationship between the old author and the new—is that it forms a division that is parallel to, and competes with, the division of the *roman* into books. Chaillou presents his readers with two kinds of structure: the first author's division into books, and his own partition of the work into two kinds of formal experimentation, with song and narrative. His decision to place this division at or near to the midpoint of the book suggests a desire to make the rhetorical and physical structures of the text coincide, so that the latter expresses the former.

    None of the *Troilus* manuscripts shows signs of this kind of sophistication in their layout, with the possible exception of the unfinished Corpus manuscript. Nonetheless, the example of the *Fauvel* book, along with the *Rose* manuscripts and the Machaut and Froissart codices, prompts us to think of *Troilus and*

---

77. *Le Roman de la Rose*, ed. F. Lecoy, *Classiques français du moyen âge*, 3 vols. (Paris, 1965–70), lines 10496ff.
78. Emilie Dahnk, *L'Hérésie de Fauvel* (Leipzig, 1935), 113–14.

Criseyde as also participating in a larger and European cultural enterprise, in which a vernacular author shapes and articulates his identity through the physical form of his writings. In this sense, *Troilus* is itself a kind of codex: a self-consciously authorial compilation of distinct modes of writing that shifts back and forth between narrative on the one hand, song and letter on the other.

Considering the Machaut and Froissart manuscripts alongside the *Troilus* copies involves a double process of comparison: first, to take account of forms of *mise-en-page* that would have shaped Chaucer's conception of the poem as he composed it; and second, to understand the practices that informed the work of the fifteenth-century scribes on the manuscripts we now possess. The fact that both kinds of comparison are possible reduces the gap we suspect to exist between authorial and scribal perceptions of the poem. Yet in any case, this is not a gap that we should worry over unduly. *Troilus* is part of a cultural process in which new concepts of authorship are closely aligned to the traditionally scribal prerogatives of dividing the text and subordinating certain features to a larger conceptual hierarchy. The very absence of an authorial copy of *Troilus*, and indeed of any of Chaucer's works, may even mean that he had not found the means to equal the ability of his French contemporaries to express their poetic thinking in the physical virtuosity of their books. It could be, in other words, that his fifteenth-century scribes were the first to find ways—in an English context—of articulating on the page aspects of codicological thinking that were latent rather than overt features of Chaucer's poetry. Paradoxically, though not unexpectedly, given the profound fascination with French lyric culture in fifteenth-century England, it seems that the fourteenth-century French context for *Troilus* is something that emerges more clearly in the later scribal renditions of the poem than in the earliest copies. The *Troilus* manuscripts persistently speak with a double voice: as fifteenth-century readings of *Troilus*, but also, in their breaking up of the text, as witnesses to features in the poem that have a marked Continental accent.

University College London

Social Texts: Bodley 686 and the Politics of the Cook's Tale

DAVID LORENZO BOYD

In the prologue to his second edition of *The Canterbury Tales* (c. 1484), William Caxton asserts that he has reproduced Chaucer's texts according to the poet's "owen makyng," eschewing those manuscripts "in whyche wryters have abrydgyd it and many thynges left out, and in somme place have sette certayn versys that he [Chaucer] never made ne sette in hys booke." Caxton goes on to confess, however, that his first edition of the *Tales* was based on just such an un-authorized text. Because his narrative has some important implications for a postmodern philology, I shall quote it at length:

> Of whyche bookes so incorrecte was one brought to me vi yere passyd, whyche I supposed had ben veray true and correcte. And accordyng to the same I dyde do enprynte a certayn nombre of them, whyche anon were sold to many and dyverse gentylmen. Of whome one gentylman cam to me and said that this book was not accordyng in many places unto the book that Gefferey Chaucer had made. To whom I answerd that I had make it accordyng to my copye, and by me was nothyng added ne mynusshyd. Thenne he sayd he knewe a book whyche hys fader had and moche lovyd that was very trewe and accordyng unto hys owen first book by hym made; and sayd more yf I wold enprynte it agayn, he wold gete me the same book for a copye, how be it he wyst wel that hys fader wold not gladly departe fro it. To whom I said in caas that he coude gete me such a book trewe and correcte, yet I wold ones endevoyre me to enprynte it agayn for to satysfye th'auctour, where as tofore by ygnouraunce I erryd in hurtyng and dyffamyng his book in dyverce places, in settyng in somme thynges that he never sayd ne made and levyng out many thynges that he made whyche ben requysite be sette in it.[1]

---

1.   Quoted in *Caxton's Own Prose*, ed. N. F. Blake (London, 1973), 62.

Apart from revealing the profit motive that Caxton might have had in issuing a "corrected" copy of the *Tales*—it would appeal to both new patrons and those already owning the now-problematic first edition—the prologue, with its appeal to the gentlemanly opinion of paternal authority, poignantly underscores two undisputed facts of medieval manuscript production and dissemination: variance and historicity. Because medieval texts were repeatedly recopied, reformatted, and misprisioned, the linguistic and bibliographical codes comprising them were radically unstable phenomena. Their variability challenges the scholarly notion of a transcendent literary work—at least one for which a transtemporal social existence is claimed—as the basis for a historicist critical practice.[2]

The reasons for such a challenge lie embedded in Caxton's mellifluous prose. Seeking the authorized book of *The Canterbury Tales*, Caxton examines extant imperfect books of the *Tales* in order to find it. The implicit distinction that he sets up—the platonic or transcendent Book that does not exist versus its extant manifestations in their particular, hence corrupt and mutable, material forms—results in the continual deferral of the authorized volume to yet another particular version: the first edition followed by the second, each considered "veray true" at some point, and each authorized not by Chaucer but, ironically, by Caxton (and later by Caxton and "one gentylman").

Regardless of their truthfulness to Chaucer's original words, the first edition and, for that matter, the second were purchased by "many and dyverse gentylmen" who in each instance had no doubt that they were reading Chaucer's "veray trew" work and not a particularized version of it. It is probably safe to assume that most readers and owners of the *Tales* manuscripts, remote from Caxton's editorial impulses or the collative opportunities of the printer's observant gentleman,

2. Several scholars have treated aspects of this issue. The concept of "linguistic and bibliographical codes"—here referring to the words written on a folio page as well as the other aspects of the book, such as parchment, binding, formatting, decoration, illumination, *mise-en-page*—is developed by Jerome McGann in *The Textual Condition* (Princeton, N.J., 1991), esp. 48–68. Although McGann is primarily concerned with postmedieval books, his statements apply to the verbal and codicological elements of medieval manuscripts as well. Cf. Stephen G. Nichols's use of the term "manuscript matrix" in his important "Introduction: Philology in a Manuscript Culture," *Speculum* 65 (1990): 6–7. On the manuscript as an object whose production and meaning were social, see another essay by Nichols, "On the Sociology of Medieval Manuscript Annotation," in Stephen Barney, ed., *Annotation and Its Texts* (New York, 1991), 43–73. On the significance of variance in medieval texts, see Bernard Cerquiglini's *Éloge de la variante: Histoire critique de la philologie* (Paris, 1989). The distinction between actual texts and the transcendental text is treated, in Shakespeare studies, by Margreta de Grazia, "The Essential Shakespeare and the Material Book: What Is This Quintessence of Dust?" *Textual Practice* 2 (1988): 69–86.

considered their versions to be Chaucer's, whether or not they had been altered in some way, and consumed them as such.[3] Caxton's second edition—the correction of the first edition against a manuscript—thus began a tradition of the primary means of rediscovering Chaucer's originality: the comparison of texts to produce the Text (or even the edition) that erases their particularities—a tradition that persists with respect to many other authors and texts.

For a "postmodern return to the origins of medieval studies" and to manuscript studies in particular,[4] the implications of Caxton's prologue are provocative. Each particular version of an authorial text—despite the extent to which it differs both bibliographically and linguistically from what the author(s) originally wrote or had formatted—exists socially and historically as the author's(s') work—that transcendental object that Caxton and subsequent editors have sought—to a particular group of readers and owners of particular versions. From this perspective, what matters is that the version functions socially as a representative (and, in practice, the equivalent) of the original authorial utterance. It is always already a re-presentation, and its authority, whatever its actual variance, is a social construction.[5] Both Caxton's attempt to "satysfye" his author and his earlier error in "hurtyng and dyffamyng" *The Canterbury Tales* are socially constructed and resolved affairs. His project, the discovery of originality, threatens to make irrelevant those imperfect texts preceding each printing, displacing them with another imperfect text. The threat, however, is an empty one, for each attempt to reproduce an ideal text, as recent textual theory has taught us, yields a simulacrum at best.

On both linguistic and bibliographical levels, an author's text simultaneously creates and is created by an interpretive and ideologically presupposed community; it is in the relationship between these two levels that interpretation

---

3. This is, of course, not to say that medieval readers and writers were ignorant of scribal intervention (as "Chaucers Wordes unto Adam, His Owne Scriveyn" attests), nor that medieval book owners would not have an author's text altered in some way (for example, the selections from *The Canterbury Tales* in manuscripts such as British Library, MS. Harley 1239; or the collaborative changes made by owner and scribe to the *Tales* in Bibliothèque nationale, Paris Anglais 39). Rather, the texts that were produced out of this collaborative process were still considered the author's, and were authorized as such. This reflects radically different—and much broader—notions of authorship than those current today. Cf. Michel Foucault, "What Is an Author?" in Josué Harari, ed., *Textual Strategies* (Ithaca, N.Y., 1979), 141–60.
4. See Nichols, "Philology in a Manuscript Culture," 7.
5. Cf. Gabrielle Spiegel, "History, Historicism, and the Social Logic of the Text," *Speculum* 65 (1990), esp. 78–86.

occurs.[6] Caxton's editions, like those following it, such as Thynne's, Speght's, or Benson's *Riverside Chaucer,* suppress this relationship in the very act of reproduction. Thus not just the author's reconstructed original but also every manuscript text of a work—whether it is *The Canterbury Tales,* the *Roman de la Rose,* or the *Historia regum britanniae*—should be considered a valid text worthy of analysis, even if traditional and positivistic editorial theory has marginalized it as corrupt or inferior, or has suppressed or relegated it to the apparatus of a critical edition.[7] By recognizing medieval texts as social documents whose variance is thoroughly grounded in modes of re-production, dissemination, and interpretive practice— a "radical" stance that is thoroughly traditional in many respects—we will have taken an important step toward refiguring the methodological basis of medieval literary studies.

Among *The Canterbury Tales,* the Cook's Tale illustrates these points well. Perhaps left unfinished (or perhaps canceled) by Chaucer, the Cook's Tale of riotous Perkyn Revelour has been considered a fragment by Caxton and many later editors.[8] Such a representation, however, suppresses many of the extant medieval forms of the tale in favor of a transcendent—and, ironically, unfinished—original form. The narrative was the focus of much fifteenth-century edi-

6. McGann, in *The Textual Condition,* provides a striking example of this process in his final analysis of "Reagan's Farewell" (pp. 126–28).
7. This is not to devalue critical editing or the attempt to recreate an author's original text—or something as close to it as we can get—but rather to point out what these processes can conceal. See Nichols, "Sociology of Medieval Manuscript Annotation," 48–49; and Fred C. Robinson, "Consider the Source," in Katharina Wilson, ed., *Medieval Perspectives* (Binghamton, N.Y., 1987), 7–8. Most Middle English scholars advocating the examination of "bad texts" do so not to acknowledge the value of such a text *en sui generis* but rather to argue its usefulness in understanding contemporary responses to an author's original text or the literary and interpretive tastes of scribes and readers. Thus they recommend a comparative, or relational, methodology privileging originality over particularity—a methodological problem, since the particular is itself original. See, for example, A. S. G. Edwards, "Lydgate Manuscripts: Some Directions for Future Research," in Derek Pearsall, ed., *Manuscripts and Readers in Fifteenth-Century England* (Cambridge, 1983), 15–26; Kate Harris, "John Gower's *Confessio Amantis*: The Virtues of Bad Texts," *Manuscripts and Readers,* 27–40; and Derek Pearsall, "Editing Medieval Texts: Some Developments and Some Problems," in Jerome J. McGann, ed., *Textual Criticism and Literary Interpretation* (Chicago, 1985), 92–106. Even the "best-text" method privileges one text while obscuring others.
8. The representation of its fragmentary nature differs from edition to edition, and in effectiveness. Many editors punctuate the final couplet with a period and then move on, with or without an *explicit,* to the Man of Law's Prologue and note elsewhere that the narrative is unfinished. The effect is a linguistic acknowledgment (but a bibliographical concealment). For the most recent example, see *The Riverside Chaucer,* ed. Larry Benson (Boston, 1987), where the blank space following the tale indicates not the tale's incompleteness but rather the end of Fragment I of *The Canterbury Tales.* W. W. Skeat, however, in *The Student's Chaucer* (Oxford, 1894), employed both asterisks and the Hengwrt colophon, "Of this cokes tale maked Chaucer na moore."

torial creativity, for it presented a gap, an irresistible challenge, with which the book industry then had to contend. Many of the manuscripts containing the tale veer from the Hengwrt colophon and either provide the tale with some sort of closure or add the spurious *Gamelyn* to finish off the Cook's turn.[9] Hence, the Cook's little story provides a convenient site for considering the importance of the critical return to manuscripts and of the politics underwriting their linguistic and bibliographical codes. Because it is beyond the scope of this essay to examine all of these versions and their manuscript contexts, I shall instead focus on Bodleian Library, MS. Bodley 686, and its unique Cook's Tale.

❧ ❧

Produced in the second quarter of the fifteenth century (1420–40) for a member of the nobility or perhaps the merchant patriciate, Bodley 686 is a fine vellum manuscript written in several hands, containing *The Canterbury Tales* and selections from Lydgate's writings. The manuscript's extrawide margins, blue paragraph marks, letters touched in yellow, elaborate violet rulings, *mise-en-page*, careful correction, clear hands, elegant initials, and other beautiful decoration— all comprising its bibliographic codes—disclose the costly, collaborative effort that went into the volume's construction.[10] Even a cursory glance makes clear that the manuscript serves the socially symbolic function of making manifest the wealth and power of its owners. It calls attention to the material abundance out of which it was fashioned, underscoring both the commodification of the medieval book and the fifteenth-century fetishization of poetry.[11] Through its bibliographic codes, Bodley 686 at once reinforces and is inscribed in the social nexus of power and book production and ownership in the later Middle Ages.

---

9.   For a fuller discussion, see John M. Manly and Edith Rickert, *The Text of* The Canterbury Tales, 8 vols. (Chicago, 1940), 2:165, 169–72, 437. See also the individual manuscripts discussed in William McCormick, *The Manuscripts of* The Canterbury Tales (Oxford, 1933).

10. For a fuller description, and a folio in facsimile, see Manly and Rickert, *Text of the* Canterbury Tales, 1:64–70, and plate 4. Manly and Rickert date the manuscript 1430–40, but after paleographical examination I believe that it could have been written as early as 1420. As they point out, the manuscript might well have been made for a member of the Beauchamp family, and perhaps was owned at one point by Margaret, daughter of Richard, earl of Warwick (pp. 69–70). Ruth Morse speculates that ownership should be ascribed to the merchant class; see "Chaucer's Man of Law Sequence," *Poetica* 28 (1988): 16–31. Both groups did own such expensive manuscripts, but the names scribbled in the codex would seem to make Manly and Rickert's hypothesis more likely. As I shall demonstrate below, the politics of the manuscript and its Cook's Tale would be appropriate to either group.

11. Carol M. Meale explores the social function of these features of manuscript production and construction; see "Patrons, Buyers, and Owners: Book Production and Social Status," in Jeremy Griffiths and Derek Pearsall, eds., *Book Production and Publishing in Britain, 1375–1475* (Cambridge, 1989), 201–38.

The manuscript's linguistic codes—the arrangement of *The Canterbury Tales* and the compilation with Lydgate's poetry—create a hermeneutic that ensures an ethically contained reading of Chaucer's narratives. Much as the Parson's Tale does in other manuscripts, Lydgate's poetry works to efface retrospectively the ambiguous and "unethical" meanings that the dialogism of the tales readily allows.[12] Furthermore, the peculiarly arranged *Canterbury* sequence ends with the tales of the Manciple—which questions the value of tale-telling and truth—and the Second Nun—which asserts the value of hagiographical and didactic literature over other types of narrative, treating literary production and interpretation as an act of ethical behavior and worship.[13] Bodley 686 never contained the more typical end of the *Tales,* the confusing confessional narrative of the Canon's Yeoman, followed by the authoritative closure that the Parson's Tale seems to provide. Rather, it supplements the tales with the Lydgatian ethical, satirical, and didactic pieces.[14] The addition of these poems following the Second Nun's story reinforces her ethical poetics and provides an interpretative context for reconsidering both the preceding tales and the General Prologue. For example, the final text from Lydgate, *The Dance of the Seven Deadly Sins*, represents a macabre terpsichorean panorama of sinful estates (many found in the General Prologue to *The Canterbury Tales*), with abundant confessions urging socioethical reform and religious redemption. The codex's ending is thus disarming: even the Chaucerian fabliaux are contained and made safe for readerly consumption. The manuscript's linguistic codes emphasize the interpretive positions of official (and some would argue Augustinian) culture: a text's "solaas" must always be underwritten by its "sentence."

If we consider the manuscript's significance as the working relationship between its bibliographical and linguistic codes, several important points emerge.

12. On the workings of such a hermeneutic, see Lee Patterson, *Negotiating the Past: The Historical Understanding of Medieval Literature* (Madison, Wis., 1987), 115–53; and on manuscript compilation specifically, see David Lorenzo Boyd, "Compilation as Commentary: Controlling Chaucer's *Parliament of Fowls,*" *South Atlantic Quarterly* 91 (1992): 387–98.
13. Following the General Prologue the order is as follows: Knight, Miller, Reeve, Cook, Man of Law, Wife of Bath, Friar, Summoner, Clerk, Merchant, Squire, Franklin, Physician, Pardoner, Shipman, Prioress, Chaucer's "Thopas," Manciple, and Second Nun. The tales of the Monk, Nun's Priest, and Chaucer's "Melibee" never appeared, despite their appropriateness to the aims of the compilation as a whole. It is possible that they were not part of the exemplar.
14. The poems, as recorded by Manly and Rickert, *Text of* The Canterbury Tales (1:64), are "A lytel tretis of alle þe Kynges," "The godely tretis of þe Norture atte þe table," "a neadful Tretis for mannes helthe of his body," "Tretis of þe Crabbe," "Of þe Rammeshornes," "Reson de fallacia mundi," "þe prologe of þe holy seynt seyn Margarete," "þe lyfe of the glorious martir Seint George," "XV Joyes of oure ladye," "XV heuenesse of oure Ladye," and "A tretis of the daunce of Poulys otherweyes called Makabre."

First, there is remarkably little concern to maintain distinctions between individual authors' writings or to ascribe authorship correctly. Indeed, the collaborative effort of compiling and juxtaposing texts displaces authorial control over interpretation—a strategy consistent with the poststructuralist decentering of authorship. This "deauthorization" occurs most clearly after the Thopas-Melibee link. In most extant versions of the sequence Chaucer himself tells the two tales, connected by a link that seems to privilege meaning over authorship.[15] In Bodley 686 Chaucer's second tale is not "Melibee" but rather that of the Manciple, *ascribed to Lydgate.* The juxtaposition of the misattributed Manciple's Tale, concerned in its themes with the value of story telling and truth, to the "Melibee" link doubly questions an author's status as maker and controller of meaning.

The Lydgatian assignment suggests the variety of socioethical functions that authorial ascription might serve.[16] Through compilation and ascription, the manuscript's codes merge *The Canterbury Tales* with the ascribed Lydgatian poems, implying that a text's "received meaning" is precisely that—not necessarily in its authorship or original authorial form but rather in its "sociality," in its collaborative creation and use.[17]

The manuscript's bibliographical and linguistic codes also work together to valorize the interconnectedness between power, meaning, and ethico-didactic

15.   As thus: yet woot that every Evaungelist
That telleth us the peyne of Jhesu Crist
Ne seith nat alle thyng as his felawe dooth;
But nathelees hir sentence is al sooth,
And alle acorden as in hire sentence,
Al be ther in hir tellyng difference.
For somme of hem seyn moore, and somme
      seyn lesse,
What they his pitous passioun expresse—
I meene of Mark, Mathew, Luc, and John—
But doutelees hir sentence is al oon.
                (*Riverside Chaucer,* VII.943–55)

16. Manly and Rickert's theory of "interruption" (see *Text of* The Canterbury Tales, 1:68) ignores the effects that such attribution might have at this important textual juncture. Although there was no doubt much medieval concern over collecting an author's *ouevre*—Cambridge University Library, MS. GG 4.27 is an important example—the connection between author and text was not always firm, nor did it seem to be of much concern. Other manuscripts never assign authorship to texts at all. It seems likely that an authorial ascription authorizes the *later* use of a text by attaching to it a name validating its use in specific contexts for specific reasons. For an examination of one aspect of this topic, see Seth Lerer, *Chaucer and His Readers: Imagining the Author in Late-Medieval England* (Princeton, N.J., 1993).

17. See H. Marshall Leicester, "Oure Tonges Differance: Textuality and Deconstruction in Chaucer," in Laurie A. Finke and Martin B. Schichtman, eds., *Medieval Texts and Contemporary Readers.* (Ithaca, N.Y., 1987), 15–26.

imperatives. Just as the manuscript book suggests the status of its owner(s), so too does the compilation suggest a connection between the arrangement and ascription of these poems and the privileged status of the intended audience.[18] The strongly perceived link between class, status, behavior, and morality—whether among the merchant patriciate or the nobility, each group to benefit from proper behavior, both materially here on earth and in the afterlife—makes this connection all the more likely.[19] Arranged, contained, and compiled to meet class-specific ethical and social precepts, the poems of Chaucer and Lydgate—from the estates satire of the General Prologue to the admonitions of the *Dance*—not only reinforce these social codes but also justify them. Connecting a value-laden reading of Chaucer to luxury and power, the manuscript explicitly entrusts the guardianship of these values to empowered groups and implicitly reinforces their status. Both bibliographical and linguistic codes are enmeshed in a self-confirming, self-perpetuating hegemonic web.

One must also consider the reciprocal relationship of the codes to the sociocultural context of which they are a part, what Gabrielle Spiegel has called the "social logic of the text."[20] Looking briefly at the manuscript's "moment of inscription"—in this case the 1420s to the 1440s—it is possible to discern the relationship between Bodley 686 and the general outlines of a larger English cultural project. As the feudal system weakened and incipient capitalism suffered from labor shortages and other disruptions, rising violence and the fear of political and social instability haunted the imagination of empowered groups. Economic difficulties and the continued rumblings and revolt among the lower classes weighed uncertainly upon those who had previously profited. Religious heresy challenged traditional doctrine, and the perceived decline of morals, manners, and social conditions only seemed to offer proof of the broader instability of metaphysical and

18. For several examples of this connection, see Meale, "Patrons, Buyers, and Owners," 213–15.
19. Sylvia Thrupp, in *The Merchant Class of Medieval London* (Chicago, 1948), demonstrates this relationship at length for the merchants (pp. 155–90). On the nobility, one can turn to manuscripts of poems such as Hoccleve's *Regiment of Princes*, which serves such a function and, incidentally, was read not just by princes and kings but by other nobility and merchants as well, thus firmly reflecting and connecting their similar interests in such issues. On noble readership, see Lester K. Born, "The Perfect Prince: A Study in a Thirteenth- and Fourteenth-Century Ideal," *Speculum* 3 (1928), esp. 470–71. On wider readership, see M. C. Seymour, "The Manuscripts of Hoccleve's *Regiment of Princes*," *Edinburgh Bibliographical Society Transactions* 4 (1974): 198–255.
20. See Spiegel, "Social Logic of the Text," 77–78 and 84–85.

religions systems.[21] It is little wonder that much fifteenth-century literature, patronized largely by empowered groups, would have addressed social instability in terms of enhancing their authority.[22] Bodley 686 is a product of the very problems, potential and actual, that it sought to redress. From this perspective, even the seemingly insignificant actions of a wayward apprentice such as Perkyn Revelour must have conjured up for the hegemony a thickly textured and anxious image of cultural collapse and the fear of loss.[23] It is within this general but pervasive concern, and within the attempt to contain the threat while instructing readers, that we can now locate this unique version of the Cook's Tale.[24]

The Cook's Tale in Bodley 686—whatever implicit ethical or political significance the original may have had[25]—is not the fragmentary and somewhat celebratory narrative of the wild-boy apprentice Perkyn Revelour familiar in other, more "standard," versions. This text, connected firmly by bibliographical codes with those tales preceding and following it, is greatly "amended"—to use the editorial

21. A bibliography of recent work on this subject would be an article itself. A sampling includes see J. R. Lander, *Conflict and Stability in Fifteenth-Century England* (London, 1969); J. M. W. Bean, *The Decline of English Feudalism, 1215–1540* (Manchester, 1968); J. Hatcher, *Plague, Population, and the English Economy, 1348–1550* (London, 1977); John Bellamy, *Crime and Public Order in the Later Middle Ages* (London: 1973), esp. chap. 1; Gordon Leff, *The Dissolution of the Medieval Outlook* (New York, 1976), which is applicable for the early part of the fifteenth century; and Rodney Hilton, *Class Conflict and the Crisis of Feudalism* (London, 1985), especially "Ideology and Social Order in Late Medieval England," 246–52.

22. Again, an example is the *Regiment of Princes*. For an analysis of how political, economic, and moral authority is maintained and shared by groups, see Larry Scanlon, *Narrative, Authority, and Power: The Medieval Exemplum and the Chaucerian Tradition* (Cambridge, 1994). Thrupp, in *The Merchant Class of Medieval London*, discusses the importance of issues of control and authority for that class. See pp. 155–90, esp. 162–63, on literary patronage. See also Hilton, *Class Conflict,* the chapter "Ideology and Social Order."

23. The widespread problems with apprentices and with the apprenticeship system in the fifteenth century no doubt made this image seem all the more malevolent, just as the image, conversely, probably deepened the perceived significance of each individual problem. See the entries under "apprentices" in the volumes of the *Calendar of Plea and Memoranda Rolls,* 1413–1437, ed. A. H. Thomas (Cambridge, 1943); and 1437–57, ed. Philip E. Jones (Cambridge, 1954). See also A. Abram, *Social England in the Fifteenth Century: A Study of the Effects of Economic Conditions* (London, 1909), 121–22.

24. An easily accessible diplomatic transcription, with a number of minor errors, is available in Morse, "Man of Law Sequence," 29–31.

25. For various accounts of this significance, see Lee Patterson, *Chaucer and the Subject of History* (Madison, Wis., 1991), 278; V. A. Kolve, *Chaucer and the Imagery of Narrative* (Stanford, Calif., 1984), 257–79; V. J. Scattergood, "Perkyn Revelour and the Cook's Tale," *Chaucer Review* 19 (1984): 14–23; and E. G. Stanley, "Of This Cokes Tale Maked Chaucer Na Moore," *Poetica* 5 (1976): 36–59. This manuscript of the Cook's Tale intensifies many aspects of the fragmentary version, especially those concerning control and authority, explored from different perspectives by Kolve and Patterson.

term—and given a politically charged expansion grounded in the ideology at work in the rest of the manuscript.[26] In other versions, the tale ends when Perkyn lodges with a friend and his prostitute wife; here, in lines either completely neglected or designated "spurious" by editors, both Perkyn and his friend are punished for their transgressions:

> What thorowe hym selfe and his felawe þat sought
> Vnto a myschefe bothe þey were broght
> The tone y dampned to presonn perpetually
> The tother to deth for he couthe not of clergye
>
> (Fol. 55v, lines 28–31)

Perkyn's reprobate life of rioting, reveling, stealing, dancing, dicing, and wenching amounts to the discursive inversion of the good Londinium subject and victualler's apprentice. He is explicitly shown to have transgressed all boundaries of proper behavior. Dissent—in the form of carnivalesque subversion of hegemonic societal norms as well as the specific duties of apprenticeship—is here physically punished by life imprisonment or death. His friend fares no better. Although the ambiguously constructed passage leaves the reader to decide the recipient of each penalty and the specific cause of the "myschefe," the severity of the punishments reflects the extent to which the body must be penalized for deeds threatening society and the social order—the "body" politic. The intensity of this punishment—even the vague "myschefe" finally generalizes the text's exemplary applicability to all transgression—underscores the severity with which this text of the poem treats anarchic behavior.

By means of this conclusion, Chaucer's tale—and it probably was considered *his* for all intents and purposes by most of the manuscript's readers—is explicitly ethicized into a text valorizing proper private and public governance. The threat of death or life imprisonment has negatively reinforced the maintenance of a

---

26. The formatting, *mise-en-page*, rubrics, and beautiful *demivinet* border originating at the initial with which the tale begins on fol. 54v follow the same pattern as those preceding and following the Cook's Tale, although the ruling differs in color slightly in five lines on fol. 55v, where the tale ends. Two contemporary hands have transcribed the tale, the first having copied the preceding tales and the second (with a different ink) beginning on fol. 55r, finishing the tale and its additions. It seems that the second hand also corrects the rest of the manuscript in places, and it is probable that the tale from fol. 55r to the end was written during the correction process, blank space having been left for the expanded version. See Manly and Rickert, 1:68 and 571–74 for a discussion. Thus not only the bibliographical codes but also the association between the "corrected" manuscript and the unique completion of the Cook's Tale argue strongly for the tale's present form as being thoroughly integrated into the concerns of the manuscript as a whole.

hierarchical social order; the text goes on immediately to the terms and social rewards of an upright life:

> And therfore yonge men lerne while ye may
> That with mony dyuers thoghtes beth prycked al þe day
> Remembre you what myschefe cometh of mysgouernaunce
> Thus mowe ye lerne worschep & come to substaunce
> Thenke how grace and governaunce hath broght hem a boune
> Many pore mannys sonn chese state of þe towne
> Euer rewle the after þe beste man of name
> And god may grace þe to come to þe same
>
> (Fol. 55v, lines 32–39)

Signaling with a decisive "therfore" the lessons to be learned, the text provides a methodology for "yonge men," offered too many subject positions, to engage in a process of self-fashioning that at the same time reinforces and perpetuates the hegemony. The emphasis on proper governance—learning proper worship and imitating one's betters—stipulates both the social and pedagogical importance of subservience. The promise of wealth and power not only makes obedience—for which "governance" is a more palatable substitute—seem more desirable; it also makes clear that those who retain material control define obedience: the hierarchical structure is one and the same. Hence, the preservation of traditional social systems and the obedience that they entail are completely naturalized and justified in the closure that the Bodley 686 Cook's Tale offers its readers.[27]

But this version of the tale reinforces its hegemonic values in other ways as well, for it disrupts its own narrative focus with self-commentary and self-interpretation, anticipating and preempting oppositional readings. Although the first eighteen lines celebrate Perkyn's transgressive play with his fellows, the text counters with personification allegory to specify these "pley ferys": among others, Rechneuer, Recheles, Waste, Wranglere, Lyctghonde, Lykorouse Mowth, Vnschamfast, Malaperte, and Mysse Avysed (fol. 55r, lines 1-6). This allegorization disrupts the tale's spatiotemporal context, London lowlife and small shops, and helps to generalize the text to a wide group of readers accustomed to making relevant to themselves such exemplary material. By connecting Perkyn Revelour

---

27. Cf. Morse, "Man of Law Sequence," 21; and Kolve, *Imagery of Narrative*, 275–77. Kolve's use of Thrupp's work in his discussion of the unfinished version of the tale reveals the extent to which Perkyn breaches the norms of expected behavior and the importance assigned to containing such disruption.

(whose own name of course works in this way) with such an unsavory and feckless crew, this version of the tale not only disparages this reveling but also marginalizes it as existing outside the realm of sanctioned forms.[28] Revel and play are to be reserved for those with sufficient wealth, moral standing, and self-control to conduct themselves properly (fol. 55r, lines 33-36). The text holds out the prospect of correctly pursued pleasure to justify the present restraint required of subordinates, simultaneously justifying the leisurely pursuits of superiors and suggesting that it is a model that will compel appropriate behavior: material wealth acquires moral authority. Both pain and pleasure are thus the tools of social control.

Much of the self-commentary in the text exists in the form of proverbial expressions that might justify the power exercised in any hierarchically devised relationship or social system. After Perkyn's master finds his money box empty, the text offers directive interpretive commentary: "An vnthryfty begynnyng for yong or for olde / A prentyse to be a reveloure & paramours to holde / That bargeyn no man so sore shalle abye / As his maister þat hath no parte of his melodye" (fol. 55r, lines 23-26). In the apprenticeship system, the master, in return for instruction and nurture, was to profit from an apprentice's labor; the profit gained validated and perpetuated the relationship. When this "trickle-up" system failed, profit was lost and the master suffered. The text's homespun advice lays bare the equation between profit and the need to control subversive, because unprofitable, behavior:

> Euen as a scabbed schepe in þe folde
> Alle flocke wolle defyle both yonge & olde
> Ryght euen so a febel seruaunt may
> Sistruye [Distruye] fourty of his felaws in a day

And

> Better ys betyme to voyde such a clerke
> The lenger he abydeth þe worse is his werke
> He þat his Maister no profite wolle wynne
> Y holde hym better out of þe hous þan with ynne
> (Fol. 55v, lines 8–11, 14–17)

---

28. See Morse, "Man of Law Sequence," 21.

The slippage between the terms *apprentice, clerk,* and *servant* illustrates the general use to which the text's politics can be put: the inferior's function is to profit the superior. Otherwise, force and punishment are justified to maintain the system. Here, the punishment is only expulsion; at the tale's end it is imprisonment and death. The sheep/flock simile in lines 8–10—which not only compares servants to sheep but furthermore a "febel" servant to a sick animal—naturalizes both their subservience and their use for profit: they require the subservience that the system finds useful.

⚜ ⚜

Although the tale's signifiers for male subservience slide effortlessly from one level to another of the sociopolitical matrix I briefly outlined, its conclusion emphatically excludes women from blame, even those committing wrongdoing in the narrative. The unfinished versions of the tale conclude abruptly (and some would argue felicitously) with a "a wyf that heeld for contenance / a Shoppe, and swyved for hir sustenance" (*Riverside Chaucer,* I.4421–22). Despite formal inconclusion, moral closure is decisively presented, concentrating all attention on female transgression and on the female body as the source of societal dysfunction. Prostitution, sexuality, and deceit, furthermore, provide economic support to Perkyn's friend (and perhaps later Perkyn as well). In the Bodley 686 version, however, the denunciation of women is replaced by an emphatic denunciation of transgressive "yonge men." This deflection is useful, and it is consistent with the interpretive matrix we have outlined, for it attempts to preclude any specific readings, especially those based in gender politics, that would displace the text's more general socioethical impulse.[29] The woman's "swyving" and the financial support that it offers can easily displace—or at least dilute—attention to male misdeeds, violence, and sexuality as the source of societal chaos.

It takes little medieval-patriarchal interpretive skill to read not only most versions of the Cook's Tale but also, retrospectively, all of the preceding tales in this text in a similar light: the desire that females elicit in men is at the center of male wrongdoing—as Chauntecleer puts it, *mulier est hominis confusio.* In most of the tales, blame is subtly, though decidedly, shifted onto Woman and her sexuality, especially when uncontrolled. In various forms of course, this agenda lay at the

29. Since male desire incited through female sexuality, along with "herbergage" and deceit, is emphasized in all of the previous tales of Fragment I, readings based on gender politics would have been likely to interfere with the social function of this version of the Cook's Tale. Stanley, in "Of This Cokes Tale," hints at the possibilities of such a gendered reading in the famous sequence: "Though the lodger be a thief, no loss if a thief in

heart of medieval misogyny and gender politics, ultimately justifying female sub-servience to male authority.[30]

The Bodley 686 text precludes such a reading, however, and substitutes for these gender politics more generalized relations of power and social maintenance. This gesture is consistent with its bibliographical codes and other proverbial interventions; it may furthermore suggest that the volume was produced for or would be read by a woman.[31] The wife who "swyved" is here replaced by one whose enterprise of sexual supply and demand is described in less vulgar, almost euphemistic terms: "A wyf he hadde that helde her contenaunce / A schoppe and ever sche *pleyed* for *his* sustenaunce" (fol. 55v, lines 26–27; italics added). Despite the negative contemporary connotation of "play"—and the sexual *double enten-dre*—the passage, through diction and allowance of ambiguity, however failed, attenuates the opprobrium attached to her activity. The shock value is reduced, and a more polite interpretive stance becomes available.

But more importantly, the text extenuates her "play" as necessitated by *her husband's* upkeep alone—"his sustenance." The use of the masculine possessive adjective here calls attention to the fact that her prostitution supports him, com-peer of Perkyn. It is *his* failure that he does not provide for her as the social order ordains—much as other additions to the tale have indicated that Perkyn, and not the behavior of his paramours, however questionable, is to blame for his wrong-doing. This text's final twelve lines—as noted above, an attempt to instill in young men proper work ethics, self-governance, and the emulation of authority through both exhortation and threats—directly follow the phrase "for his suste-naunce." The Bodley 686 tale thus explicitly places all blame for societal difficul-ties on the masculine subject. Women are represented as instruments, not as agents primarily responsible for transgressive social behavior, although they too could no doubt profit from the more general lesson of governance emphasized in the tale as a whole. Such a shift precludes a specifically misogynist interpretation

cahoots with him puts him up; though the lodger be a swiver, no danger if the landlady is a whore, and no honour to lose if the pimping landlord is her husband" (p. 59).

30. Primary sources are too abundant and well known to require citation. One fascinating recent treatment of this topic is Laura Kendrick, "Transgression, Contamination, and Woman," *Stanford French Review* 14 (1990): 211–30. For an influential rethinking of the discourse of misogyny, see R. Howard Bloch, "Medieval Misogyny," *Representations* 20 (1987): 1–24.

31. Manly and Rickert, in *Text of* The Canterbury Tales, note that the selection of Lydgatian materials also suggests female patronage (1:69).

of the preceding tales and focuses squarely on the politics of male behavior. It is
by maintaining this focus that the tale can more readily contain the political sub-
versiveness of the Miller's Tale and the sexual antics of the Reeve's Tale. More generally, it can reaffirm the hierarchical social order and the subaltern's passive
acceptance of authority—whether aristocratic, mercantile, or moral—that the
Knight's Tale ostensibly recommends.[32]

✑ ✑

For groups who saw themselves and their positions threatened in an unstable
world, the Bodley 686 Cook's Tale would have vindicated the maintenance of
power relations and authority that also underwrote the codice's construction.
Although it concerns apprentices (clerks and servants secondarily) and masters,
the tale encompasses the merchant patriciate and the nobility in specific ways. As
a type of the easily generalized exemplary piece, the tale warns against disobedi-
ence—whatever the form—much as the compilation of the *Tales* with Lydgate's
poetry does. For those groups prevailing not only through their participation in
hierarchical relationships but also through the assurance that each level can control that below it, down to the lowliest peasant, the Cook's Tale potentially
implied the large-scale crisis that anarchy can ultimately provoke.[33] But in this
expensively produced codex linking the maintenance of the social order and
moral precepts to the wealth, power, and status of its owners, Perkyn's anarchic
threat becomes instead an important opportunity for containing the transgressive
and justifying the social order.

Chaucer's "original" tale and the end he may have envisioned for it are of little concern in this codex; the tale as it stands here was, to owners and readers,
Chaucer's; and its inclusion in his *Canterbury Tales* authorizes both its form and
its message, much as the Lydgatian ascriptions function at other points in the
codex. Social ideologies and their preservation of power relations and order over-
rode the need to identify or preserve an author's original text, with all of its attendant ambiguity. Although the names of Chaucer and Lydgate, poets known
among fifteenth-century readers as moralists, authorized the manuscript generally, too much concern for the transmission of authorial originality would have
resulted in an ambiguous Cook's Tale potentially detracting from the manuscript's overarching concerns. Like the Hengwrt manuscript's *explicit* ("Of this

---

32. For a succinct explanation of such a sociopolitical function in the fragmentary Cook's Tale, both alone and in
    Fragment I, see Patterson, *Chaucer and the Subject of History*, 278.
33. Ibid.

cokes tale maked Chaucer na moore"), the narrative's lack of closure would have allowed the Cook's Tale to remain a readerly text, and radically so, for in that form it would invite its consumers to finish the poem themselves. Here, the tale is complete, textually and ideologically, and it both shapes and is shaped by the matrices—manuscript and social—preserving and sustaining it. Its use ultimately authorizes its interpretation, and its construction and consumption provide both a literal and symbolic bulwark against the perceived dissolution of early-fifteenth-century society. It is a larger historical irony, perhaps, that many of those workers involved in the manuscript's construction would have been among those over whom this version of the Cook's Tale sought to preserve control.

In "The Work of Art in the Age of Mechanical Reproduction," Walter Benjamin notes that "even the most perfect reproduction of a work of art is lacking in one element: its presence in time and space, its unique existence at the place where it happens to be."[34] Although Benjamin was not concerned with a work of art that already existed in multiple forms, his observations have important implications for medieval manuscripts, which partake of aspects of both the "copy" and the "original."[35] Each codex—and the textual versions that it contains—has a "unique existence" and a "presence in time and space." When modern editors and scholars, like Caxton before them, concern themselves *only* with recovering what an author really said and producing this original utterance, they attempt to create "the most perfect reproduction of a work of art." Although this is without doubt a worthy task, an exclusive concern for this originality and for a critical practice limited to it comes at a price, for it ignores the historicity of medieval texts—their mutable forms of social existence and their powerful social logic—and erases the uniqueness of each individual bibliographic and linguistic form in which a text exists, each a work of art in itself. The author's original words—if they are recoverable—should be sought precisely because that original is a key part of the local and particular. But we must have the critical and intellectual flexibility to recognize that

34. Walter Benjamin, *Illuminations* (New York, 1968), 220.
35. On originality, see Gerald L. Bruns, "The Originality of Texts in a Manuscript Culture," *Comparative Literature* 32 (1980): 113–29. Stephen Nichols, in "Sociology of Medieval Manuscript Annotation," first noted the importance of this part of Benjamin's essay for the New Philology (p. 47). The ultimate point of "The Work of Art" is to examine the way in which mechanical reproduction can destroy a work's "aura" in a politically useful fashion. Deconstruction of a work may have some of the same functions, I would argue, although it would demystify both work and "aura."

the predominance of the ideal of original utterance—the wish to discover it in order to reproduce it exactly and mechanically, in terms of the technologies of our own age—can hinder a full elaboration of the historicist project.

Taking Benjamin another step: we cannot separate the processes of medieval book production, construction, and transmission from our study of medieval texts or from issues of ideology, politics, and power, all of which are naturalized and may become invisible in the specific manuscript matrices within which and through which they operate. Each work of art called the Cook's Tale, each with its unique set of bibliographical and linguistic codes, supplies a different text for analysis, and from a recognition of this fact should follow a willingness to turn from the platonic ideology of the text that editorial theory has constructed and toward a study of the particular and the local. Each manuscript, its individuality suppressed and marginalized by the mechanical reproduction of later editorial endeavor, can serve as both subject and object of scholarly study and debate. A "postmodern return to the origins of medieval studies" can then undertake its study of where each text "happens to be."

University of Pennsylvania

Phylum-Tree-Rhizome

David Greetham

I have yet to see any problem, however complicated, which, when you look at it the right way, did not become still more complicated.
— Poul Anderson

My great-aunt Florence Ada [Greetham] had always looked like a dead end. There she sat in the records of the family Bible and on the family genealogy: fruitless, without issue, "given away to be looked after by Aunt Eliza in Sefton Park." And then, just two years ago, there came a letter from someone claiming to be her great-granddaughter. With the letter was an elaborate and detailed *Stammbaum,* a family tree bearing several recent branches of whose existence I had known nothing. The mysterious Florence Ada had apparently married one William Whittle Barton and, far from being without issue, had provided me with more than fifty newly discovered blood relations. Since then my newfound Barton "cousin" and I have been corresponding with news of one another's research into our different parts of this tree. I will probably never meet most of these new relations (we are, after all, separated by an ocean as well as three generations of ignorance), but their massive presence on my personal map of who I am is disturbing: it changes the balance, disorients my sense of place and filiation, even though none of the relationships I had previously been aware of has been changed by the discovery. My *patrilinear* descent is still intact.

For a (quondam) medievalist and a student of the genealogical descent of witnesses, this cautionary tale of that which was lost being found is cautionary precisely because there was no loss involved. The fact that my patrilinear descent remained unmoved was exemplary of our still-patriarchal culture: my new female cousin had "found" the link to my great-aunt and thus to me only as an offshoot of her research into her own patrilinear inheritance. She is a Barton for whom Greethams are just a parallel but unauthoritative set of witnesses. To me as a Greetham, the Bartons have the same function.

If G. Thomas Tanselle is right that "ancient" editors (biblicists, classicists, and medievalists) have been obsessed by classification, taxonomy, stemmatics, genealogy,[1] call it what you will, then my familial fable should strike an immediate chord for editors of Middle English. The heroic failures of J. M. Manly and Edith Rickert in pursuit of the grail of the archetype[2] are emblems of our history of class-consciousness. While recension has taken some knocks subsequently, particularly from George Kane and E. Talbot Donaldson in their editions of *Piers Plowman,*[3] I think it is still accurate to say that one of the first tasks that an editor of a multiple-witness medieval work will undertake is to distinguish the Bartons from the Greethams and to reduce the Florence Adas to collateral but inherently contaminated witnesses to the patriarchal name: to classify the witnesses according to their putative position on a patrilinear *Stammbaum.*[4] After all, it was only the *failure* of recension and stemmatics to plot adequately and consistently the "shape" of the descent of the A-manuscripts of Piers that led Kane to endorse "deep editing"—the individual scrutiny of every lection as it bore witness to the poetic of Langland—as the only proper method for adjudicating among the witnesses.[5] As Paul Maas readily admitted in his ideological and procedural brief for stemmatics, there was no "cure" for "contamination," since contamina-

---

1. G. Thomas Tanselle, "Classical, Biblical, and Medieval Textual Criticism and Modern Editing," *Studies in Bibliography* 36 (1983): 21–68, esp. 23–24.
2. J. M. Manly and Edith Rickert, *The Text of* The Canterbury Tales, 8 vols. (Chicago, 1940).
3. George Kane, ed., *Piers Plowman: The A Version* (London, 1960); and George Kane and E. Talbot Donaldson, eds., *Piers Plowman: The B Version* (London, 1975).
4. In both of my editorial projects, on Trevisa in the late '60s and early '70s, and on Hoccleve a decade later, this was the first editorial problem to be confronted; and both manuals of textual criticism and the textual introductions to medieval works usually mandate a discussion of descent and filiation. See, for example, Alfred Foulet and Mary B. Speer, *On Editing Old French Texts* (Lawrence, Kans., 1979); Alberto Blecua, *Manual de crítica textual* (Madrid, 1983); Charles Moorman, *Editing the Middle English Manuscript* (Jackson, Miss., 1975); and Dmitrij Sergeevič Lixačev, *Tekstologija russkoj literatury X–XVII vekov* (Leningrad, 1983).
5. See, for example, Kane's conviction that the "descent of hypothetical genetic groups from their respective exclusive common ancestors thus bears no relation to the various shapes of the manuscripts" (p. 20); his discussion of the "effects of manipulation of an A copy by a scribe imperfectly familiar with the poem and ignorant of the purposes behind the revisions which he was conflating with their unrevised originals" (p. 32); and his decision to sacrifice genetics to shape in the cause of "authenticity" (p. 40). See Anne Hudson on what she calls "authoritative conflation" in the transmission of the Wycliffite Bible ("Middle English," in *Editing Medieval Texts: English, French, and Latin Written in England* [New York, 1977], 48). Hudson cites Kane and Donaldson's attack on the circular logic of genealogical editing ("to employ [recension] the editor must have a stemma; to draw the stemma he must first edit his texts by other methods. If he has not done this efficiently his stemma will be inaccurate or obscure, and his results correspondingly deficient; if he has been a successful editor he does not need a stemma, or recension, for his editing"

tion[6] (or what W. W. Greg more delicately refers to as "cross-fertilisation"[7]) was the equivalent of introducing females into family trees. Stemmatics assumes a nonsexual, parthenogenetic biology of descent, for its two-dimensional space cannot adequately map a sexual system that combines features from different parents. Rather, it turns the conventional biological schema on its head, with single parents having multiple offspring. It was in this sense of downward divergence and patrilinear origins that my cousin and I did not need one another's set of female-derived witnesses to establish the basic topography of our life-lines. The witnesses added by the female (that is, sexual) interposition on the stemma might have given each of us a greater sense of placement, of belonging to an enlarged tribe, but they were not necessary to that basic, monogenous tribal identity. To the stemmaticist such female witnesses are evidence of the breakdown of the system.[8]

[*B Version*, 17–18, n. 10]); but she then argues that the *Piers* editors have allowed their enthusiasm for deep editing and the editorial empowerment it promotes to run away with their critical judgment: "Emendation is carried beyond that warranted by manuscript collation or the necessity of sense, to include alterations based on the editors' view of the total textual history of the poem in all its versions, and on their conception of Langland's poetic habits" (p. 42). Quite so, and it is precisely this freedom—and responsibility—to adjudicate the poetic of an author that is the major rationale in deep editing for sacrificing the genetics of recension. For a very lucid and convincing account of these conflicts, see Robert Adams, "Editing *Piers Plowman B:* The Imperative of an Intermittently Critical Edition," *Studies in Bibliography* 45 (1992): 31–68. For further references in this discussion of recension versus deep editing, see D. C. Greetham, "Reading in and around *Piers Plowman*," in Philip Cohen, ed., *Texts and Textualities* (New York, 1996); A. S. G. Edwards, "Middle English Literature," in D. C. Greetham, ed., *Scholarly Editing: A Guide to Research* (New York, 1995); and Derek Pearsall, "Theory and Practice in Middle English Editing," *TEXT* 7 (1994): 107–26 .

6. Paul Maas, *Textual Criticism,* trans. Barbara Flower (Oxford, 1958), esp. 49 ("No specific has yet been discovered against contamination"). As R. J. Tarrant notes ("Classical Latin Literature," in Greetham, *Scholarly Editing*, 108–9), this "despairing final sentence" in Maas's handbook on stemmatics is "even starker in the original: 'Gegen die Kontamination ist noch kein Kraut gewachsen'" (*Textkritik,* rev. ed. [Leipzig, 1950], 31). See the "Stemmatics Past and Present" section of Tarrant's essay (pp. 103–15) for a concise and illuminating account of the theory of genealogical editing; and see Michael Weitzman's "The Analysis of OpenTraditions," *Studies in Bibliography* 38 (1985): 82–120, for a sophisticated typology of stemmatic (or at least *spatial*) models in contaminated or conflated transmission, using such tools as lattice algebra, cluster analysis, and enchainment to map out the trees and tangles of filiation.

7. W. W. Greg, *The Calculus of Variants* (Oxford, 1927): 11ff.

8. See, for example, James Willis's attack on both stemmatics and scribal transmission in *Latin Textual Criticism* (Urbana, Ill., 1972): "to impute rationality to scribes is dangerous" (p. 22); "a stemma can sometimes tell us which is the reading best attested, never which is the best" (p. 32). Finding that the "breakdown" of the monogenous system is virtually the norm in (medieval) transmission of classical texts, Willis polemically argues that "in defending all readings that cannot be proved wrong, the conservative critic must necessarily defend many that are in fact wrong, but cannot be proved so" and that "the professedly conservative critic is a professed patron of error" (p. 11). These are more or less the terms under which Kane and Donaldson reject stemmatics in favor of deep editing.

My discovery was different in kind, therefore, from the sudden appearance of *Symbion pandora,* that wonderful creature that inhabits the mouthparts of a lobster, eating its table-spills.[9] My newfound witnesses enriched and confirmed the biological plan without changing its fundamental shape, but *Symbion pandora* dislocated it. Unable to place the new creature on any of the current grids of classification, its discoverers were forced to construct a new phylum, *Cycliophora,* for the lobster's guest, of which it was the only exemplar. That is, the difference of *Symbion pandora* from any other inhabitant of the Linnean system at the level of species, genus, family, or class was greater than its possible similarities. It had therefore to be moved up into the level of phylum (of which there are only thirty-five or so in biological classification) and just missed making it to the top level of all, the kingdom (plants, animals). Whether the phylum of *Cycliophora* will survive further research into its "differences,"or whether *Symbion pandora* will continue to be its sole witness, the importance of the rhetorical and taxonomic move made by its discoverers can hardly be overstated, nor the epistemological implications of the rhetoric for other systems of classification, like the filiation of manuscripts.

The status of a textual witness as phylum, genus, and so on within a map of difference is an indication of its level of authority. Under the dictum "Witnesses must be weighed, not counted," a *single* exemplar of one branch of a family tree of descent has the authority of a hundred or even a thousand witnesses to a collateral branch. But this is so only if the purpose of the weighing and evaluation is a quest for origins rather than a demonstration of dissemination.[10] If medieval textual editing is still primarily driven by a desire to reconstitute the singularity of authorial intention (admittedly a very fraught issue these days[11]), then the status of a newly discovered witness on the level of phylum is inevitably greater than one designated a new genus, and so on down the levels of the tree. If, with respect to all other parts of the classificatory system, the differences are greater than the similarities, we have a new and unique insight into the quest for origins. Adding another few *codices descriptes* to an already blooming branch of a tree is not going

---

9. "A Whole New Animal," *New York Times,* 17 December 1995, sec. 4, p. 2.
10. The metaphor of "dissemination" is of course a particularly charged one, given the gendered discriminations that stemmatics and manuscript genealogy endorse. That seminal engendering should be the operative figure for the tree organization confirms the parthenogenic, nonsexual model we have intuitively privileged in the mechanics of textual devolution.
11. See the general coverage of this complex issue in the "Intention in the Text" chapter of D. C. Greetham, *Theories of the Text* (Oxford, 1996). The basic document remains G. Thomas Tanselle's "The Editorial Problem of Authorial Final Intention," *Studies in Bibliography* 29 (1976): 167–211.

to set the textual world of intentionality on fire. Discovering a hyparchetype or an undreamed-of parallel text with a new and independent access to the Big Bang of authorial composition may merit a textual Nobel.[12]

But if the grail of intention and origins is not the focus of our editorial ministrations, then ironically it may well be that the lower, better-attested, even more "corrupt" witnesses (as measured in terms of the putative distance from the archetype or fair copy or in terms of the adaptability and cross-fertilized state of the text) could become more culturally significant than the single, lone exemplar with no relatives and no descendants. That is, ants, spiders, and cockroaches, because they are virtually ubiquitous and adaptable to so many different contexts, become more interesting than *Symbion pandora,* precisely because of their "contaminated" or "corrupt" condition, their ability to change their features in order to survive. Under such a socialized view of descent and survival and authority, the more a document may show signs of its adaptation to new contexts—the more it departs from a putative originary form—the lower on the *Stammbaum* it is to be placed and the more iconic it becomes of the biological condition: adapt or die.[13]

The issues confronting the taxonomist of any living and therefore corruptible tradition of transmission (biological, racial, documentary, or linguistic) will include: How close and mappable do the similarities of classification need to be for a plausible genetics to be constructed? How different do the exemplars, live or without issue, have to be before a new phylum must be postulated? What sort of divergent and convergent evidence do we need to place an empirical witness to historical development (a fruit fly, a dialect, a script, a manuscript) securely within a specific niche of a "perfect phylogeny"?

12. Consider, for example, the cultural significance given to such discoveries as the Winchester manuscript of Malory, the "lost" first part of the manuscript of Twain's *Huckleberry Finn,* and the Leningrad Codex of the Bible. Compared to such phylum-like discoveries, an article on a "new" manuscript deriving from an already well-attested descent, published in a bibliographical or codicological journal, will usually be of interest only to specialists.

13. The iconic cultural status of filiation informs continued contention over questions such as the genealogical position of the Neanderthals in the development of the European tree of human life. Did they simply die off in the face of competition from Cro-Magnon, or are most of the current European stock just adaptations of this foreparent? Were they like my great-aunt Florence Ada *before* I heard from the collateral Bartons (a dead end) or like the enormously expanded tribal map that the unexpected letter from my unknown cousin created? That the question can still be debated, and regarded as an important element in a European's sense of self and place, is clearly an indication of the cultural value endowed on filiation. If the Neanderthals prove, like Florence Ada, to be not the dead ends we have thought them but an essential part of the breeding stock of Europe, then their status will undoubtedly rise on the biological roster. But if they remain as a collateral fruitless branch, then we can afford to continue our disdainful attitude, based on a teleological sense of progress, but progress by patrilineal rather than corrupted descent.

∾ ∾

The recent and ongoing struggle over the descent of the Germanic languages from Proto-Indo-European offers a particularly rich analogical model for observing these questions and their relation to theories of manuscript classification. Perfect phylogeny is a biological term, but one with "economic" ramifications. Just as Archibald Hill has argued for the "simplification" model in stemmatic analysis (the tree with the fewest branches possible to explain the bibliographical data),[14] and just as Vinton Dearing has demonstrated the similar "parsimony rule" in breaking an apparent "ring" of manuscript filiations,[15] so biologists need an algorithm that will produce a taxonomic chart that reduces the likelihood of mistaking "convergent evolution" (we textuists would call it "convergent variation") for linear descent. As George Johnson noted in a recent account of the descent of the Germanic languages from Proto-Indo-European, it might be tempting to regard the common traits of birds, insects, and bats (that is, that they all have wings) as demonstrating a common descent, but this would be mistaking the empirical datum—the specific trait—of convergent evolution for linear development, and if plotted on a taxonomic chart would produce "a tangle instead of a tree."[16]

This was exactly the problem that Kane saw in the manuscripts of the A-text of *Piers*: that the "hypothetical genetic groups" obscured the "shapes" of the mauuscripts.[17] And the algorithm he came up with in these complex circumstances of overlap and common trait was, of course, deep editing. Now, one can immediately see why, when faced with a tangle instead of a tree, there is a great temptation simply to cut the Gordian knot, or the manuscript kudzu, with the sword of a poetic of intention called deep editing. That is, one postulates the features of a common ancestor (the originary moment of composition) and then adjudicates the status of bastardized or legitimate readings by their genetic similarities to this postulated original: call it, as Joseph Grigely has done in a dif-

14. Archibald Hill, "Some Postulates for Distributional Study of Texts," *Studies in Bibliography* 3 (1950–51): 63–95, esp. 87–90.
15. Vinton A. Dearing, *Principles and Practice of Textual Analysis* (Berkeley, Calif., 1974), esp. 95, where he defines a ring as "a closed sequence in which all elements are intermediary." See the analysis of Dearing's filiation method in D. C. Greetham, *Textual Scholarship: An Introduction* (New York, 1992), 328–29; and the "Structure and Sign" chapter of Greetham, *Theories of the Text*.
16. George Johnson, "New Family Tree Is Constructed for Indo-European," *New York Times,* 2 January 1996, B15.
17. Kane, *A Version,* 20.

ferent context, "textual eugenics."[18] As Jay Jasanoff has argued, in criticizing the applicability of algorithmic analysis to linguistics, when constructing taxonomic charts there is always a danger that linguists (or biologists, or textuists) will unconsciously pick data that confirm their prejudices.[19] Well, yes, the perfect phylogeny preferred by Kane was not the perfect phylogeny advocated by T. A. Knott and David C. Fowler in their stemmatic analysis of the Piers manuscripts.[20] But given the exponential variability in complex traditions,[21] we can see the attractions of an algorithm that reduces the tangle and gives us a tree.

Indeed, the variation between the results of different algorithms (or the phylogenic variations produced during the implementation of a single algorithm) may be instructive. In this case, the algorithm resulting from the deselection of all possible features of "convergent evolution" still produced two different trees, with the Germanic languages in two different positions. Once the data for Germanic were removed from the algorithm, the number of anomalies was drastically reduced, down to a number that could be accounted for by "undetected borrowings." In using an algorithm to keep the perfect phylogeny chartable in two dimensions, the linguistic research thus came up with two different genetic descents for Germanic. According to this schema, the Germanic languages were initially an offshoot of Balto-Slavic (the root of Lithuanian, Latvian, Russian, Czech, and Polish), but then, migrating westward, the Germanic speakers came in the orbit of both Celtic (origin of Irish, Welsh, and Breton) and Italic (origin of Latin, French, Spanish, Portuguese, Romanian, and Romansch). By the lights of an idealist like Kane, Germanic becomes a doubly bastardized group of languages, the result of at least two stages of evidentiary conflation and/or contamination. For someone working back to that moment of originary speech, Germanic would therefore offer at best inferential and secondhand evidence for a prototypical "reading," because its combination of convergent evolution/variation and linguistic migration from one language affiliation to another would demonstrate its highly socialized, acculturated status rather than its value as a channel to an originary poetic. Germanic is, in stemmatic terms, unmappable with any consistency, since different features would place it in different positions: the duck-billed platypus of languages.

18. Joseph Grigely, "Textual Eugenics," in *Textualterity* (Ann Arbor, Mich., 1995).
19. Quoted by Johnson, "New Family Tree."
20. T. A. Knott and David C. Fowler, eds., *Piers the Plowman: A Critical Edition of the A Version* (Baltimore, 1952).
21. For example, it is estimated that there are 34,000,000 possible ways to draw the genealogical chart for the descent of the Germanic languages from Proto-Indo-European.

But that is so only if we determinedly remain in two dimensions and use an algorithm to sort the linguistic/textual sheep from the goats. There is another type of model available, as Johnson noted: "Some linguists have used Germanic's ambiguous position in the Indo-European family to argue that, in their early stages, these languages were more like a network than a tree; instead of neatly cleaving one from the other and developing in isolation, they hovered nearby, trading innovations back and forth."[22] The Barthesian overtones of the "network" rather than the "tree" hardly need to be spelled out here. I have elsewhere dealt with the direct *textual* (that is, "textile") function of both the etymology of *text* and Barthes's endorsement of the network, tissue, and weave over the solidity, fixedness, and determinedness of *work*.[23] In this study of phylogeny, I am more concerned with the taxonomic significance of the shift from tree to network, and with its implications for the possible production of editions (especially of Middle English) in the future. If the classical taxonomies of phylum and tree tried to produce unambiguous maps on which authority could be directly related to position and level, what sort of edition can come out of the tangle that is the alternative to the tree? Is there still a viable protocol of taxonomics in the biological realm of the rhizome and the network?

✌   ✌

Referring back to the epigraph for my essay, I could provide a quick answer to these questions: that is, no editions (at least in the conventional sense of critical and lexically stable editions) are possible under the figure of the tangle, and there are no stable taxonomics under the figure of the rhizome. But such an answer would be the equivalent of Michael Warren's coopting of Beckett's "rien à faire" as the motto for an anti-editing textuality in the face of what he has called the "theatricalization of text";[24] of Randall McLeod's declaration that "photography

---

22. Johnson, "New Family Tree."
23. See, for example, D. C. Greetham, "[Textual] Criticism and Deconstruction," *Studies in Bibliography* 44 (1991): 1–30 (reprinted in *Textual Transgressions: Essays toward a Biobibliography* [New York, 1996]); and the "Ontology" chapter of Greetham, *Theories of the Text*. Note that G. Thomas Tanselle, in such writings as "Textual Criticism and Deconstruction," *Studies in Bibliography* 43 (1990): 1–33, and *A Rationale of Textual Criticism* (Philadelphia, 1989), uses the text/work dichotomy with a significance exactly the *opposite* of that laid out in Barthes's famous essay, "From Work to Text," in *Image, Music, Text*, trans. Stephen Heath (New York, 1977).
24. Michael Warren, "The Theatricalization of Text: Beckett, Jonson, Shakespeare," in Dave Oliphant and Robin Bradford, eds., *New Directions in Textual Studies* (Austin, Tex., 1990). See my demurrals against Warren's prescription in "Enlarging the Text," *Review* 14 (1992): 1–33, esp. 10–12.

has killed editing. Period. *Someone* has to tell the editors";[25] of Derek Pearsall's rhetorical campaign against "critical editing";[26] of Lee Patterson's having offered the counsel of despair that all editing is circular reasoning;[27] finally, of Gary Taylor's messianic view of the "end of editing" for Renaissance texts.[28] I have argued that such contemporary rejections of taxonomically and lexically "strict and pure" textuality are the quite proper and predictable bibliographical conceits in the age of poststructuralism and postmodernism, but that they mistake the vehicle for the tenor. Editorial thinking can still go on in a fragmented, dissociative, and unstable cultural environment, but such thinking will not manifest its operations in critical, documentary, eclectic, ideal-text editions.[29]

In fact one might argue that because the rhizome figure—grass rather than tree—denies hierarchy of form and function, then editing under rhizome auspices might be not only much easier (because of the lack of "critical" decisions) but also a perfect exemplar of John L. Casti's program for the properties of the "simply complex" formal system. Casti's definition of such a system as having "[p]redictable behavior . . . . [f]ew interactions and feedback/feedforward loops. . . . centralized decision-making . . . . [and being] decomposable"[30] might seem to comport very well with McLeod's notion of the photograph (and singular reproduction) or Warren's "nothing to be done." But ironically, the very singularity of the rhizome and such simple systems may prevent our getting a firm and permanent grasp on their structure—despite attributes like centralization and predictability. Stephen Jay Gould has noted our cultural resistance to considering "root" or "rhizome" biological structure as anything but a primitive, headless pre-

25. Random Cloud (Randall McLeod), *"from* Tranceformations in the Text of 'Orlando Purioso,'" in Oliphant and Bradford, *New Directions.* See my cooption of McLeod's anti-editing argument, especially as it relates to the evaluation of textual evidence, in "Textual Forensics," *PMLA* 111 (1996): 32–51, esp. 37–38.

26. Derek Pearsall, "Editing Medieval Texts: Some Developments and Some Problems," in Jerome J. McGann, ed., *Textual Criticism and Literary Interpretation* (Chicago, 1985); and see my critique of Pearsall's case in "The Place of Fredson Bowers in Mediaeval Editing," *Papers of the Bibliographical Society of America* 82 (1988): 53–69.

27. Lee Patterson, "The Logic of Textual Criticism and the Way of Genius," in McGann, *Textual Criticism and Literary Interpretation;* and see my response to Patterson's argument in "Reading in and around *Piers.*"

28. Gary Taylor, "The Renaissance and the End of Editing," in George Bornstein and Ralph G. Williams, eds., *Palimpsest: Editorial Theory in the Humanities* (Ann Arbor, Mich., 1993).

29. See, for example, D. C. Greetham, "Editorial and Critical Theory: From Modernism to Postmodernism," in Bornstein and Williams, *Palimpsest;* and the "Forms of the Text" and "Deconstruction" chapters of Greetham, *Theories of the Text.*

30. John L. Casti, *Complexification: Explaining a Paradoxical World through the Science of Surprise* (New York, 1994): 271–72. Subsequent pages references are given in the text.

cursor of our more hierarchical notion of system.[31] If the symbolic representation
or theorem (F) for the structure of a rhizome (in Casti's diagram of the relations
between a "natural system" and a "formal system"; see figure 1) cannot take
advantage of, and indeed does not need, the encoding of a semantics into a syntax, then F ceases to function as the "formalization of the idea of complexity . . .
to mirror our informal ideas about what it is that makes a system complex"
(p. 275). There is a sort of self-reflexive essentialism about the natural system (N)
that *appears* to be irreducible according to conventional fractalization.[32] But
appearance is exactly the problem: the breakdown of fractal compression in the
case of the rhizome occurs because we can never find a ground from which to
perceive the structure at large (because it is incomprehensible, cannot be
"grasped"). In the epistemological darkness created by the rhizome, all cats are
indeed the same.

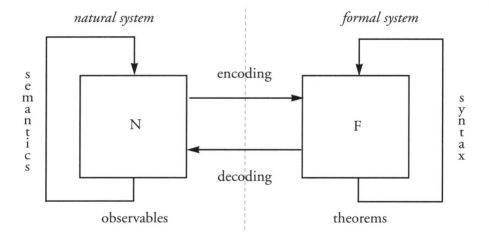

Fig. 1
The modeling relation

31. Stephen Jay Gould, "Triumph of the Root-Heads," *Natural History* 1/96: 10–17. I am grateful to Sealy
     Gilles for this reference.
32. See, for example, Casti's demonstration (via Kenneth Hsu) of the fractal "compression" of Bach's
     Invention 5 to a Bachian "essence" (pp. 248–49), a mathematical confirmation of Schencker's analyses of
     tonality to produce a refined basic structure for each composition.

Now this lack of a ground is obviously disturbing to textuists (they do like to know where great-aunt Florence Ada is to be found), and it might make us fall back on photography and "nothing to be done," because there's nothing to be *seen*. But that is because complexification is inherently counterintuitive, and is not a property of the system itself but of those "surprise-generating mechanisms."[33] And if complexification is counterintuitive, then, as Casti reports, there is an inevitable "problematic" in trying to "translate some of these informal notions about the complex and the commonplace into a more formal, stylized language, one in which intuition and meaning can be more or less faithfully captured in symbols and syntax. The problem is that an integral part of transforming complexity (or anything else) into a science involves making that which is fuzzy precise, not the other way around, an exercise we might more compactly express as 'formalizing the informal'" (p. 270). Within the tangle of the network, it is only to be expected that everything will look fuzzy, especially if the network's non-relating components appear to be headless rhizomes (Which way is up?). The challenge for the student of complexification—that is, the observer of the "textile" that is text—is to find a formal system (F) that can represent both the fractal and the semantic coding of the phenomena. For the last century and more this particular F has been the tree or *Stammbaum* of Lachmannian stemmatics. Now that we have seen the rhizome close up, what will the new F be for the dislocated, fragmentalized, textuality of our postmodernist moment?

While I recognize the justice of Casti's citation of the old adage "When you don't know what to do, apply what you do know" as a *warning* to taxonomists (the motto when put into practice may "translate into an attempt to decompose the hard problem into a collection of simpler subproblems that we understand" [p. 273]), I am still enough of an empiricist to argue that we don't really have any other choice but to decompose down to a scale that is comprehensible to our limited faculties. Yes, the rhetorical and procedural holes in extrapolating local comprehensibility onto a map of the total structure may be exposed by later, more sophisticated, systems of analysis, as when Robert Adams can discover pre-

---

33. The mechanisms are, according to Casti: "logical tangles" (producing the "surprise effect" of "paradoxical conclusions"), "catastrophes" (producing "discontinuity from smoothness"), "chaos" (producing "deterministic randomness"), "uncomputability" (producing an "output [that] transcends rules"), "irreducibility" (producing "behavior [that] cannot be decomposed into parts"), and "emergence" (producing "self-organized patterns"). Textual study tends to reverse the causality, with a phenomenological observation of, say, "discontinuity from smoothness" leading us to postulate "catastrophe" in the transmission of the text, but Casti's main point— that it is the interposition of the observer between these two classes of epistemic phyla that produces the relationship—remains valid for any phenomenological and epistemological enterprise, including textual study.

computer logical inconsistencies in some of Kane-Donaldson's arguments for a
Piers poetic and for the specific exemplification of this poetic in individual lections.[34] But it is difficult to play the textual God or unmoved Prime Mover when
one can never get outside the tangle one is analyzing. Recognizing the value of
Poul Anderson's caveat on complexification in the eye of the beholder, I nonetheless retreat slightly from the godlike pretensions of my argument so far, and suggest some practical taxonomies for this critical moment in the epistemological
evolution of our discipline.

᪄   ᪄

All such attempts at a sort of anthropological "thick description"[35] of a cultural
moment partake of both the liabilities and the advantages of any local systemic
analysis.[36] The entropic condition toward which Lachmann's stemmatics
aspired[37] would indeed remain constant, if described in perfect and complete
detail. And it may be that during the period Donald H. Reiman has described as
the "brazen age" of textual editing,[38] the empirical positivism derived from an
association of textual study with science might have encouraged such entropic
pretensions of stability and stasis. Murray Gell-Mann has argued that, despite the
seductiveness of such mathematical entropics, "[i]n fact . . . a system of very many
parts is always described in terms of only some of its variables, and any order in
those comparatively few variables tends to get dispersed, as time goes on, into
other variables where it is no longer counted as order" (p. 226). To this extent,
Patterson is correct in suggesting that all editing is a form of circular reasoning
(variant-order-variant-order^n; see n. 27 above), and, as Gell-Mann would have it,

34. For example, Adams points out in "Editing *Piers Plowman B*" that the formula "me it + transitive verb"
(in the phrase "for kynde wit me it tau3te") is rejected as stylistically improper at B iii. 284 (just as Kane
had rejected the analogous phrase in A); but that at B xviii. 351 exactly the same phrase is allowed as authorial, as is the general formula at other places in B where an analogy from Kane's A "offers no reading and
thus no potential embarrassment" (p. 50).

35. For an account of the textual and editorial significance of the "local knowledge" derived from "thick
description," see the "Culture" chapter of Greetham, *Theories of the Text.*

36. As Murray Gell-Mann has noted, everything from "effective complexity" to the kind of "algorithmic
information content" we have already seen in the reduction of the 34,000,000 possibilities of the genealogical placement of the Germanic languages "depends on coarse graining—the level of detail at which the
system is being described"; see Murray Gell-Mann, *The Quark and the Jaguar: Adventures in the Simple
and the Complex* (New York, 1994), 226. Subsequent page references are given in the text.

37. With every page of the nonextant archetype of Lucretius being reconstitutable by a deft relation of the
formal system F successfully decoding the natural system N.

38. Donald H. Reiman, "The Four Ages of Editing and the English Romantics," *TEXT* 1 (1984): 231–55,
esp. 240–50.

a demonstration of the "real significance of the second law of thermodynamics."
But it is exactly this movement outward from the few variables to order and back
again that Kane-Donaldson employed in their adjudication of lections.[39] For this
present discussion of phyla, trees, rhizomes, and cross-fertilization, the apter figure for dispersal of (textual) authority is that suggested by Gell-Mann in terms of
the entropic relation between macrostates and microstates:

> A system that is initially described as being in one or a few macrostates
> will usually find itself later on in a mixture of many, as the macrostates
> will get mixed up with one another by the dynamical evolution of the sys-
> tem. Furthermore, those macrostates that consist of the largest number
> of microstates will tend to predominate in the mixtures. For both these
> reasons, the later value of entropy will tend to be greater than the initial
> value. (P. 226)[40]

Recognizing that my report from the frontline of textual taxonomy will therefore
be neither fully entropic (I do not aim to describe any system in its full detail)
nor even a complete macrostate, I can nonetheless hazard a few speculations on
the task confronting a (textual) discipline of classes.

As I perceive it, there are three basic challenges for biologists, historical linguists, and genealogical textuists: to differentiate among a) linear, parentally
derived features, b) the effects of immediate environment, and c) idiosyncratic
aberrations, what we may call (after Pliny) *ingeniosa natura,* or the monstrous.[41]

---

39. Kane-Donaldson's "scientific" method was to establish unambiguous moments of a transmissional "norm"
    in the evaluation of authorial versus scribal practice, and then to extrapolate a poetics from this norm in
    order to formulate rules of order. I think it is important to note that Kane-Donaldson attempted to
    "neutralize" the qualities of the putative norms they discovered by shedding any immediate influence of envi-
    ronment and descent—perhaps an inevitable strategy, designed to reduce the evidence of cultural and biblio-
    graphical "noise" in order to observe the entropic features more clearly.

40. While I accept the usefulness of this formulation for the dispersed bibliographical macrostates of many
    medieval texts (especially anthology manuscripts, *florilegia, compendia,* and the like), I recognize that the
    entropic value given to the cumulative power of microstates in Gell-Mann's hypothesis is countermanded by
    the stemmatic dictum that witnesses must be weighed, not counted (see p. 102 above). On the level of social-
    ized (i.e., evolutive) entropy and stasis, Gell-Mann's thesis works perfectly well, for the more microstate
    copies of a macrostate exemplar that are in circulation, the greater the value of the later textual states. But in
    systems emphasizing Big Bang or intentionalist entropics, the later value—even of microstates reproducing
    in multiple macrostates—will always be less than that of the initial state.

41. On *ingeniosa natura* and the monstrous, see D. C. Greetham, "The Concept of Nature in Bartholomaeus
    Anglicus," *Journal of the History of Ideas* 41 (1981): 663–77. On the transmissional ramifications of these
    arguments on the aberrant and the norm, see Greetham, "Models for the Textual Transmission of Translation:
    The Case of John Trevisa," *Studies in Bibliography* 37 (1984): 131–55.

Now let us turn to these three challenges and see how the phylum-tree-rhizome figure may illuminate the discussion.[42]

1. *Linearity.* Seeing the traits of the parent embodied in the child has been one of the main operative strategies for text-editing for several centuries. Thus, when Eugène Vinaver cites his "F" as evidence for resolving variance between "C" (the Caxton print) and "W" (the Winchester manuscript), he is presumably confident that genetics will establish a link between the textual DNA of a parent and that of its child. For the microstates of Vinaver's *Works of Sir Thomas Malory,* the problem was whether the two children maintained a consistent genetic relation with the parent or whether the relations might shift, from one macrostate to another or even within a macrostate. The ideal entropic stasis would have been one in which, as Gell-Mann suggests, every detail of the genetic system was mapped with mathematical security so that the system could not increase. Could Vinaver achieve this happy state? In the case of the *Morte Darthur v. The Works of Sir Thomas Malory,* the shape and teleology of the total system were, of course, further complexified by the transdiscursive interference of "translation" (whatever that meant, to Vinaver, to Malory, and to Caxton) from one language-system to another[43] and by the differing bibliographical formats (manuscript or printed book). But Vinaver's basic genealogical rationale of "kind" was essentially the same as that motivating *Altertumswissenschaft* (the reconstruction of the historical past through a positivist "science" of empirical observation) as a whole: that phenomenological features could be placed on a linear path from sameness to difference according to the principles of divergent variation. That is, phenomena become less "kind"—less singular, and more multiple, complex, and different as history progresses. According to Gell-Mann's map of complexification, such

---

42. The fraught and contentious history and taxonomy of the Germanic languages have already shown some of the ideological and cultural ramifications of these features (one need only imagine what the response to the "double bastardy" thesis for Germanic would have been under the Third Reich to see how cultural conditions may be less or more hospitable to certain textualized concepts). See especially the chapters on "History" and "Culture" in Greetham, *Theories of the Text,* for an examination of this "contingency" theory of textuality—even of textual contingency itself.

43. A complexification I have tried to formalize in my essay "Textual Transmission of Translation," using my work on Trevisa's translation of Bartholomaeus Anglicus' *De Proprietatibus Rerum* as a trove of examples from which to generate ideal stemmatic models. See the critique of this attempt in Mary Hamel's essay "Sources" in Douglas Moffat and Vincent McCarren, eds., *A Guide to Editing Middle English* (University of Michigan Press, forthcoming). My subsequent demurrals against my own practice appear in the "Interweave" to the reprint of the Trevisa essay in *Textual Transgressions.* For Vinaver's theory and practice, see the textual introduction to his *Works of Sir Thomas Malory,* 2d ed. (Oxford, 1967), esp. c–cviii.

"frozen accidents" as a fossil or a coin of Henry VIII (or a medieval manuscript reading) can be interpreted under not only the second law of thermodynamics but also "the initial condition of the universe." He maintains that "we can then utilize the tree of branching histories and argue, starting from the initial condition and the resulting causality, that the existence of the found coin or fossil means that a set of events occurred in the past that produced it, and those events are likely to have produced other such coins or fossils" (p. 228).

The problem (or one of the problems) of this model is that it assumes a relation of causality behind the dynamics, whereas (as we have already seen) convergent variation can produce the effects of causal relations without the substance (those winged bats and birds and insects). While the research of Valla into forgeries might successfully expose the bibliographical inauthenticity of the Donation of Constantine, and while the work of Mabillon and the Maurists might equally successfully place specific scripts on a map of orthographic development according to the dictates of evolutive development, this pre-Foucauldian concept of "archaeology" is always layered. It involves further digging further *back*, and it assumes causative and gradually evolutive parental relations, without epistemic disjuncts and without convergent variation. Contamination can no more be represented in Valla's distinction between the forgery and the original than in Maas's stemmatic model for textual transmission.[44] I suggest not that Valla's early formulation of a linear *Altertumswissenschaft* is improper or inaccurate, but that it is a conceptual and methodological mistake to regard it as the only transmissional game in town.[45]

Recension (especially as it is regarded as conceptually and methodologically distinct from *emendatio* and *divinatio*—with the attendant problems of circular reasoning already touched on) is therefore based in a post-edenic biology: it assumes an ideal state of deathless, invariant, nonproductive textual *quidditas* from which the bibliographical expulsion into the corrupt world of transmission

---

44. For an account of Foucauldian archaeology and its implications for textual study, see the "History" chapter of Greetham, *Theories of the Text*.

45. Causality was so regarded in my neophyte work on the (translated) text of Trevisa's *De Proprietatibus*. The editors were instructed that they should always attempt to find a paleographic explanation for why an original (correct) lection *x* in the Latin might have produced the deformed and corrupt translating text's *y*, using the evidence of causal paleography. A. E. Housman, of course, was notoriously impatient with such conservative historicity: "The practice is, if you have persuaded yourself that a text is corrupt, to alter a letter or two and see what happens. If what happens is anything which the warmest good-will can mistake for sense and grammar, you call it an emendation; and you call this silly game the palaeographical method" ("The Application of Thought to Textual Criticism," *Collected Prose,* ed. John Carter [Cambridge, 1961]: 142).

is a falling off, and by no means a *felix culpa*.[46] In my own work, such a predilection in favor of the uncirculated and unworldly was seen in our editorial disdain for ms C (Cambridge University Library, MS. Ii.v.41) in the transmission of the text of Trevisa's late-fourteenth-century translation of Bartholomaeus Anglicus' thirteenth-century *De Proprietatibus Rerum*.[47] This paper manuscript showed all-too-many signs of socialization and worldly accommodation: it was clearly not a memorial presentation copy; it was undecorated, sloppily written, full of erasures and interlineations and changes of mind. And, most pertinently for our editorial philosophy, it was less "kind" than the other manuscripts, for its variants contained many more *hapax legomena* than any other witness, more divergencies from the common stock as its text was adapted to a new social environment. These days, I might look at such a manuscript as the most interesting of witnesses, for it shows a scribe actively participating in the construction of a text. In those days (the early 1970s), such scribal meddling was an inevitable reduction in the authority of the witness, for it placed the document either further down the genealogy than a more "faithful" witness or off in a Neanderthal-like collateral and unproductive branch.[48]

I doubt that even the peculiarities of C would have led us to declare it a new and aberrant textual phylum (that is, too unlike any other witnesses to be mappable at the same level of classification). The *Cycliophoras* of this world, the new

---

46. It is with this edenic, "Romantic" view of composition and transmission that the so-called social textual critics (and specifically Jerome McGann in *A Critique of Modern Textual Criticism* [Chicago, 1983; reprint Charlottesville, Va., 1992]) take issue.

47. My editorial/textual narrative has traversed the critical and methodological topography of our cultural moment, beginning with a recensional editing of Trevisa's encyclopaedia *De Proprietatibus Rerum (On the Properties of Things)* in the late 1960s to early 1970s, moving to a still-linear ethic but often rhizome-like method in setting up the editing protocols for the normalization of Hoccleve's *De Regimine Principum (The Regement of Princes)* in the late 1970s to early 1980s; from there to a concern with the "network" of citation that is so endemic to medieval texts, and then to a full espousal of a postmodernist hypertextual and hypermedia environment of constantly shifting links in my current work on the *Hypermedia Archive of Citation*.

48. This narrative is illustrated and analyzed in *Textual Transgressions*. As I remark in "Reading *Piers,*" there are traces of traditional-print genealogical approaches even in the initial methodology and aims of the electronic *Piers* archive, for the eight manuscripts originally selected for digitization were those "necessary to establish the B archetype" (Hoyt N. Duggan, "The Electronic *Piers Plowman* B: A New Diplomatic-Critical Edition," *Æstel* 1 [1993]: n. 15); and it was only at a later stage of the project that full transcriptions of all witnesses were to be included, extending to the two "spurious" and "unauthoritative" manuscripts (Huntington Library, MS. HM 114, and Tokyo, Toshiyuki Takamiya, MS. 23) that had previously been rejected by Kane-Donaldson (more or less on the same grounds that we Trevisa editors regarded the evidence of "C" as untrustworthy). Fidelity in the *Piers* archive was thus partly inherited from print culture, until it was recognized that even the less than "faithful" witnesses might "represent two kinds of reader response to the poem" (Duggan, "The Electronic *Piers Plowman,*" n. 10).

phyla, are potential embarrassments to classificatory system itself, which loses its claims to entropy every time an unrecorded phylum has to be plotted on its axes. That is, a perfect Linnaean system of ecological niches should be able to account for, even predict, the proper biological disposition of any witness, documentary or inferred.[49] Indeed, the historical linguistics that was one of the most productive results of the linearity of *Altertumswissenschaft* placed a predictive premium on the construction of forms that happened to have no exemplars in extant documents. Just as according to Grimm's or Verner's "laws" one could predict the phonological mutations from a parent language to its descendants and collateral branches, so a textual scholar could [re]construct the grammatical form that ought to be found in a specific linguistic ecological niche even though there was no such form empirically available either in the document being edited or in any other witness to the text (or language). The innocuous-looking [*] that conventionally marks such reconstructions is testimony to the residual force of the historical linearity of philology, a linearity that can therefore look both backward and forward on the putative line of development. Varro did no less in filling in the blanks in Latin documentary testimony for the complete (that is, entropic) mapping of his *De lingua latina*[50]; and the analogists of Alexandria used the same systemics in both the construction of the perfect Homeric line and the rejection of "spurious" lections by a code of marginal sigla.

So a transmissional version of Wordsworth's apothegm that "the child is father of the man" has motivated much of the history of Western editing, from the third century B.C. to the positivist and idealist editions of nineteenth- and twentieth-century fiction produced under the auspices of the MLA's Center for Editions of American Authors and its successor, the Center/Committee on Scholarly Editions. The basic challenge is one of perspective: find out where one

49. An ideal entropic system should thus account not only for the *extant* niches—those biological and bibliographical phenomena that happen to have survived, as living, usable entities or as fragmentary or fossilized *remaniements*—but also for every intermediate *nonextant* stage in the evolutive history. That is, by convention the stemma should include both the Latin sigla for actual documents (ABCD and so on) and the Greek sigla for inferred witnesses (αβχδ, etc.). It is when the system has failed to account for these "missing links," or, worse yet, has not even allowed for their existence, that the level of embarrassment rises when the new phylum is discovered. An inferred hyparchetype is therefore just as systemically necessary to a stemma as is an archetype, and bibliographically the existence of the Winchester manuscript was just as necessary to complexifying the meaning and status of the text as was the Caxton print, or as necessary as any other putative copy-text or collateral manuscript of a printed book.

50. See Elaine Fantham, "The Growth of Literature and Criticism at Rome," in *The Cambridge History of Literary Criticism: Classical Criticism* (Cambridge, 1989), esp. 241–243, for an account of Varro's methods of analogical grammatical/textual formation.

is standing in the developmental phylogeny of the text; look both backward and forward along the branches and trunk of the stemmatic tree; fill in the blanks caused by scribal incompetence or the effects of time; discover which way is up (in the upside down tree) or down (in the archaeology of the transmission); and resuscitate either a lost physical archetype (as per Lachmann's Lucretius) or a "text that never was" (as per Greg-Bowers platonism).[51] Throughout this perspective analysis the textuist will be charged with separating the legitimate from the bastardized, the patrilinear descent from the collateral, in a biological typology that is Darwinian, evolutive, and both originary and teleological. So much for lines.

2. *Environment*. If the philology and predictiveness of *Altertumswissenschaft* is truly Darwinian, then it must also recognize the impact of environment on the survival and mutation of species. The Lamarckian biological heresy is heretical only because it conflates the two processes of genetics and environment (giraffes get long necks, which are then passed on to their offspring, as a *result* of straining upward to reach for the leaves at the tops of trees) not because of its invocation of environmental stress. Such stress is what informs the twin disciplines of textual bibliography and codicology.[52] The bibliographer and codicologist look for signs of environmental pressure not only at the level of the macrostate (in affecting the likelihood of production or obliteration of texts) but also at the level of the microstate (the dubious lection or print variant that can be more plausibly produced in one bibliographical environment than another). The first level can obviously have enormous ramifications for the construction of trees, and every major technical shift in production (from oral to written media, from roll to codex, from script to print, and now from print to electronic storage) has its casualty list of those species that did not adapt and therefore did not survive into the next age of transmission. The existence of palimpsests, the discovery of putative scroll exemplars for codices, the corrected proof or marked-up manuscript fair copy for the printer: all of these intermediate stages (especially in their comparative rarity) are testimony to the devastating effects of the shifts in production environment and the effects on linear transmission. The second level is such a staple of textual editing that we have perhaps taken its cognitive and epistemological principles for granted. For while some systems of linear analysis

---

51. See the "Ontology" and "Formalism" chapters of Greetham, *Theories of the Text,* for an account of the platonism of Greg-Bowers editorial theory.
52. Philip Gaskell, in *A New Introduction to Bibliography* (Oxford, 1972), defines textual bibliography as "*Textual Criticism* adapted to the . . . problems of editing printed texts" (p. 337). In the "Textual

(Greg's algebraic calculus, Dearing's rings, Quentin's collational tables) have attempted to separate the lexical from the physical transmission, the effect of environment on the production of specific textual variants is usually an unconsidered or unarticulated *modus operandi* for textual scholars of both manuscript and print. But while we may know that, say, a *c* and *t* are more likely to be confused in a textura script than a humanist, and that problems in casting off copy in folios in sixes may cause verse to become prose and vice versa, it is still rare for students of such transmissional aberrations to try to map out the procedures and results of textual slippage within a specific environment. Vinaver's attempt to construct an entropic template for all transmissional errors between exemplar and scribal copy[53] is, to my knowledge, still the only systemic model for the most fundamental unit in textual reproduction in a manuscript environment. I have elsewhere remarked on the absence of similar studies of, say, QWERTY-board errors.[54] Moreover, a systemics of electronic transmissional variance is still at a very clumsy and disorganized stage. While I have tentatively suggested some models for variance that could occur only within electronic environments,[55] other scholars, notably Tanselle, have emphasized the cognitive and procedural continuities in the production of error from one medium to another, claiming that electronic text-production merely exacerbates or modifies the transmissional and presentational functions of text.[56]

A major question still to be fully addressed is thus whether the move from the *Stammbaum* of fixed print stemmatics to the rhizome of structural tags and hypertextual links changes not just the technical medium of recovery but also the very epistemology of text. While we may recognize that some of the earlier environmental shifts acted as cognitive as well as material filters,[57] responses to hyper-

Bibliography" chapter of *Textual Scholarship*, I extend this definition to cover manuscript study, particularly with regard to the environmental "stress" that Gaskell records for the transmission of texts.

53. Eugène Vinaver, "Principles of Textual Emendation," in *Studies in French Language and Medieval Literature Presented to Professor M. K. Pope* (Manchester, 1930). See the analysis of Vinaver's methodological template as an important aspect of textual bibliography in Greetham, *Textual Scholarship*, 279–80.

54. See the "Psychoanalysis" chapter of Greetham, *Theories of the Text;* and see also Jonathan Goldberg, *Writing Matter: From the Hands of the Renaissance* (Stanford, Calif., 1990), esp. 281–91, for an analysis of Barthes's position on typewriter keyboarding errors.

55. See Greetham, *Textual Scholarship*, esp. 289–91.

56. This argument—that there are fundamental principles that remain constant throughout shifts in medium and genre—is one of the basic themes (with some carefully calibrated distinctions) of Tanselle's *Rationale of Textual Criticism.*

57. For example, patristic discourse was dependent on a citational complex of authority very difficult to accomplish in the roll format as opposed to codex; the interreferentiality of the codex therefore encouraged or perhaps even created the dialectic, the *sic et non,* and Scholasticism.

text as a transmissional environment range from Tanselle's insistence on continuity to McGann's messianic enthusiasm,[58] to Duggan's similarly optimistic claims for the *Piers Plowman Archive* and Peter Robinson's for the *Canterbury Tales Project*,[59] with Arnold Sanders occupying a middle ground in an attempt to link the manipulation of electronic text to cognitive and even mechanical paradigms drawn from manuscript culture.[60] David Kolb has argued that some of the most basic of our cognitive processes (as, for example, the tripartite and sequential structure of the syllogism) cannot operate in an electronic medium of headless, rhizome structures.[61] While it is clearly too early to predict how this cognitive battle will play out, I think we can already recognize that in an electronic environment it is difficult to see how the secure parental genetic features necessary to the project of recension could not become irrecoverably blurred and, yes, "contaminated" in the shifting multilevel and idiosyncratic traversal of a hypertextual coding of relationships. All parent-child affiliations would become contingent and temporary, the product of an individual and nonreplicable linearity that would be no more than the onscreen "history" of a series of "visits" to certain "sites." So while it is true that computer analysis can be parsimonious and reductionist—using algorithms to render the infinite visible and comprehensible—so too can hypertext exponentially explode the number of models available, with every visitor to the archive/museum of interwoven texts constructing a nonce taxonomy peculiar to themselves.[62]

By the standards of phylogenic biology, historical linguistics, and recensionist editing, such conditions will produce an existential anxiety. Will it be differ-

58. See, for example, McGann's "The Complete Writings and Pictures of Dante Gabriel Rossetti: A Hypermedia Research Archive," *TEXT* 7 (1994): 95–106 (a descriptive analysis of the cognitive and structural shifts involved in constructing and navigating his archive of Rossetti); and his "Rationale of Hypertext," in Marilyn Deegan and Kathryn Sutherland, eds., *The Electronic Text: Investigations in the Method and Theory of Computerized Textuality* (Oxford, forthcoming).

59. See Duggan "Electronic *Piers Plowman B*," and "Creating an Electronic Archive of *Piers Plowman*," at http://jefferson.village.virginia.edu/piers/report94.htm. See, too, Peter M. W. Robinson, "Collation, Textual Criticism, Publication, and the Computer," *TEXT* 7 (1994): 77–94; Murray McGillivray, "Towards a Post-Critical Edition: Theory, Hypertext, and the Presentation of Middle English Works," *TEXT* 7 (1994): 175–200; and Daniel W. Mosser, "Reading and Editing *The Canterbury Tales*: Past, Present, and Future (?)," *TEXT* 7 (1994): 201–32.

60. Arnold Sanders, "Hypertext, Learning, and Memory: Some Implications from Manuscript Tradition," *TEXT* 8 (1996).

61. David Kolb, "Socrates in the Labyrinth," in George P. Landow, ed., *Hyper/Text/Theory* (Baltimore, 1994).

62. See D. C. Greetham, "Morphin,'" in Deegan and Sutherland, *The Electronic Text*, for an examination of the cognitive effects of multiple, even infinite, states of intertextuality.

ent in kind from the sort of anxiety D. F. McKenzie has inferred from the production shifts during the seventeenth century from speech to script to print?[63]
Will our children find the click of a mouse such a "natural" way of entering, traversing, decoding, and encoding a text that the very idea of the secure fixity of
the codex will be as foreign to them as the bibliographical impenetrability of the
roll or the unreliable authority of oral transmission is to us?[64]

3. *Idiosyncrasy.* However our descendants construct and react to text and its transmission, their negotiations with textuality will be the result of an interplay
between cultural determinacy and personal production, in biological terms the
reconciliation of environment and genetic makeup. Medievalists have often
found the character analysis (even psychoanalysis) of textual transmitters a puzzle
and a challenge, just as textuists in later periods have done studies of the personal idiosyncrasies of compositors.[65] In fact, even the most technically severe attributes of analytical bibliography as a component of history of technology (cyclotron
analysis, collation formulae) are usually in the service of some level of intentionality—authorial, compositorial—and are therefore aimed at some sort of recon-
stitution of the personal, even the idiosyncratic. There has been a wide spectrum
of critical responses to such characterological studies, from James Willis's dismis-
sive diatribes against scribal follies[66] to Derek Pearsall's acknowledgment of
scribes as the first authoritative editors of Chaucer, with a creative engagement in

63. D. F. McKenzie, "Speech-Manuscript-Print," in Oliphant and Bradford, *New Directions.* But see the examples
    of a similar cultural anxiety in earlier (i.e., medieval and Renaissance) text-production in my critique
    of McKenzie in "Enlarging the Text," esp. 16–18.
64. I have only anecdotal evidence as yet, but it is telling. As I was writing this passage I received a phone call
    from one of my graduate students complaining that his high hopes for intertextual manipulation had not
    been met by any of the Institute for Advanced Technology in the Humanities projects at the University of
    Virginia (and specifically the Duggan *Piers Archive*) or at such other medieval sites as Georgetown's
    "Labyrinth." In his language, they were "just printed books in an electronic form. There was nothing new to
    do with them." In other words, they were not hypertextual enough for this young textuist. And again, while
    writing this note, I have had my four-year-old son on my lap insisting that it is time for Daddy to give up
    boring old text-entry and let him get into his digital "paintbox" to construct purple pterodactyls, green rab-
    bits, and other phenomena "unimagined yet in prose or rime," and all with a wrist action that I can only
    envy. My young graduate student may have underestimated the hypertextual involutions of *Piers* and my son
    is still an avid consumer of codices; but both their dissatisfaction and their facility with an electronic medium
    are salutary warnings of things to come.
65. On editors see E. Talbot Donaldson, "The Psychology of Editors of Middle English," in *Speaking of Chaucer*
    (New York, 1970); and on producers and transmitters of text see the "Psychoanalysis of the Text" chapter of
    Greetham, *Theories of the Text.*
66. Willis is particularly hard on their "pernicious desire to do good" (*Latin Textual Criticism,* 3).

the construction of the text.[67] In general, originalists and idealists will regard any scribal interposition as inherently corrupt (things can only get worse in this worst of all possible worlds), and social textual critics will see the continued involvement of scribes as testimony to the living organism of the work.[68] For the idealist, the more species that diverge from genera, genera from families, families from classes, and classes from phyla, the less edenic the textual situation becomes. It is therefore the task of the idealist to use the interactions among environment, transmission, and (putative) originary intention in order to reconstruct a psychoanalytic case-profile of the author. For the social-ist, the more species and the more cross-species fertilization, the more resilient the organism will become to changing environments, as a mark of its distance from the biological Big Bang. The psyche of the author is thus only one among many possible psychical profiles that can inform our continued rehabilitation of the work.[69]

Just as recent feminist critics have recalled us to a personalist criticism that celebrates rather than hides the narrative of the storyteller;[70] just as folkloristic and anthropological studies have placed the participant/observer back into the critical matrix from which textual meaning is generated;[71] just as the New Historicist analysis of Renaissance texts has emphasized the history of the anecdote as the fictional medium for the telling of history;[72] so recent bibliographical

67. See his arguments in "Editing Medieval Texts" for the "activity of intelligence" (p. 95) and "wealth of insight" (p. 103) to be found in the fifteenth-century "editors" (i.e., scribes) of Chaucer.
68. One caveat here. By involvement I do not necessarily mean the mere replication of text, a sort of unthinking cloning of an organism, but rather the critical intervention that we see in the transmission of such texts as *Piers*. In the terms of Barthes's distinction, the *Piers* scribes were confronting a *scriptible* or "writerly" text, one that invited construction and misconstruction, whereas virtually the same *number* of scribes who participated in the transmission of Hoccleve's *De Regimine Principum* obviously regarded that text as *lisible*, or "closed," and rarely offered the sort of speculative or interrogative coauthorship that *Piers* seems to have encouraged. Again, it is a matter of witnesses being weighed not counted, and it is not simply the raw number of descendants that a parent witness may have but the degree of evolutive distance from that parent and adaptation to changing bibliographical, cultural, and ideological circumstances that is the real challenge to the textual biologist and geneticist. I confess that there were times during the dreary collation of the forty-odd manuscripts of the Hoccleve when I fondly wished for a scribe with a bit of the *Piers* spirit.
69. See, for example, Jerome McGann, *Critique of Modern Textual Criticism,* passim; "In each case, so-called author's intentions is one of the factors to be weighed and studied" (pp. 114–15).
70. See, for example, Nancy K. Miller, *Getting Personal* (New York, 1991). I coopt Miller's "personalist" method in the autobiographical "Interweaves" of my *Textual Transgressions.*
71. See the account in John Miles Foley, "Folk Literature" (Greetham, *Scholarly Editing*), esp. "The Performance Approach" 611–14; and see Clifford Geertz, *The Interpretation of Cultures* (New York, 1973), and *Local Knowledge: Further Essays in Interpretive Anthropology* (New York, 1983). I demonstrate the textual significance of these maneuvers in the "Culture" chapter of *Theories of the Text.*
72. See, for example, Joel Fineman, "The History of the Anecdote: Fiction and Fiction," in H. Aram Veeser, ed., *The New Historicism* (New York, 1989).

work has begun to recognize the function of the idiosyncratic in the formation of a textual narrative and a textual discipline.[73] When Seth Lerer offers a critique of Malcolm Godden's "Wordsworthian" account of William Langland's rewritings of *Piers Plowman,* he challenges not only the applicability of the Romantic model of the life work to medieval texts but the authority of literary documents in our constructions of authorial biography.[74]

Such personalist intervention can therefore have enormous ramifications in the adjudication of textual authority,[75] especially when the personal is reinforced by the apparent neutrality of history or nationhood. I have dealt elsewhere with the textual symptoms of this sort of prejudicial reading of evidence: Lachmann's use of the term *itali* as synonymous with a Mediterranean (that is, humanist) disrespect for the lineage of medieval manuscripts, or Alberto Blecua's disdain for the failures of "Anglo-Saxon" textual critics to recognize the virtues of genealogical analysis of medieval Spanish texts.[76] A. E. Housman's English-commonsensical disdain for the benighted German stemmaticists having mistaken textual criticism for mathematics,[77] and Bédier's famous repudiation of Germanic genealogy in favor of French best-text theory[78] are just further symptoms of the setting of a personal perspective within a national prejudice that has come down to us in the culture wars of Anglo-American analytical bibliography and French *bibliologie*

73. See Donald H. Reiman's call for a "personalist bibliography" in *The Study of Modern Manuscripts: Public, Confidential, and Private* (Baltimore, 1993), esp. xii; and see my writing of Reiman's method into the recent history of textual scholarship in "Getting Personal/Going Public," *Review* 17 (1995): 225–52.

74. Seth Lerer, "Medievalist Mayhem," *TLS* 4 January 1991, 17, reviewing Malcolm Godden, *The Making of Piers Plowman* (Harlow, England, 1990).

75. See, for example, James L. W. West III's argument that editing is essentially a form of biography in "The Scholarly Editor as Biographer," *Studies in the Novel* 27 (1995), special issue on *Editing Novels and Novelists, Now,* ed. Alexander Pettit, 295–303. West claims that, working from exactly the same documentary evidence, an editor may construct two totally divergent biographical explanations for the evidence (he cites the "censorship" of William Styron's first novel, *Lie Down in Darkness,* as his primary exhibit). He concludes that editors will "sometimes find themselves working in reverse order—deciding first what texts they want to bring to life and then creating authors who will approve of what they wish to do" (p. 302). See my analysis of West's argument in "If That Was Then, Is This Now?" in the same issue of *Studies in the Novel* (pp. 427–50, esp. 436–37).

76. On Lachmann, see Tarrant, "Classical Latin Literature," esp. 110; on Blecua versus the Anglo-Saxons, see "Medieval Castilian Texts and Their Editions," in Greetham, *Scholarly Editing,* esp. 468. On nationalist prejudices in textual editing, see "Textual Imperialism and Post-Colonial Bibliography," in Greetham, *Textual Transgressions.*

77. Housman, "Application of Thought to Textual Criticism," 132.

78. Joseph Bédier, "La tradition manuscrite du *Lai de l'ombre:* Réflections sur l'art d'éditer les anciens textes," *Romania* 54 (1928): 161–96; 321–56. Reprinted as a pamphlet (Paris, 1929).

and *l'histoire du livre*. For our purposes, the best exemplum might again be George Kane, but this time the Anglo-Americanist (modernist, intentionalist, originalist[79]) sets himself against the Gallic structuralist, for whom the post-authorial complexes of textuality are not an embarrassment but a source of pride. Thus Kane, having already committed apostasy against the stemmatics of Knott-Fowler and having constructed a hermetically sealed A-text obeying a specific theory of transmissional corruption, then remakes the B-text in the light of his previously constructed A, as he must do if his earlier editorial credentials are not to be vitiated. It can be no other way, unless, like McGann, in the case of his evolving attitude to his Byron edition, an editor foreswears his misspent textual youth and declares that, if he had it to do over again, it would be very different.[80]

And so it is time for me to do the same thing. In brief: as an older man surveying earlier and current involvements in textual production (especially as they exemplify the basic phylum-tree-rhizome figure of this essay), what do I understand myself to have done in the matter of textual transmission, and how might it have been different? The story is all too easily told: brought up in a patriarchal culture, I did not question the linear assumptions about transmission made during the editing of Trevisa in the '60s and '70s. Our aim was obviously to cut through that scribal kudzu, work our way back up the tree and, via such other linear postulates as palaeographic error from exemplar to copy, reconstruct an authorial voice

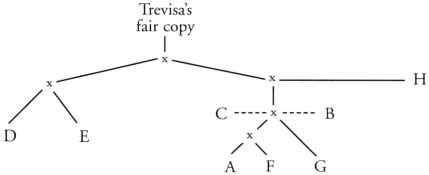

Fig. 2
Stemma for Trevisa's *De Proprietatibus Rerum*

79. See Patterson, "The Logic of Textual Criticism," where he describes the Kane-Donaldson *Piers* as a New-Critical "modernist" text, esp. 80–89.
80. See Jerome J. McGann, "Theory, Literary Pragmatics, and the Editorial Horizon," in *The Textual Condition* (Princeton, N.J., 1991).

in its edenic, uncorrupted space (fig. 2). And all of this was so, even though the external "correctives" applied to the linear descent of the Middle English text (reference to Latin texts of Bartholomaeus, one a print later than Trevisa's own translation) disturbed the logic of this linearity. I have since recanted, or at least re-rationalized the affair. My work on Hoccleve initially inherited a stemmatic, patriarchal system but had to account for contamination. Therefore, while a fairly conventional stemmatic model of transmission (fig. 3) was constructed by Marcia Smith Marzec (complete with the displaced and thus unmappable manuscripts that showed evidence of contamination and bastardy), we also relied in the actual normalization of text on an editorial flowchart that was part linear, part cyclical (fig. 4). This flowchart thus modified the tree-model of strict recension, but could still be read as a reinforcement of Marzec's *Stammbaum*. My current work on a hypermedia archive of citation presupposes some degree of linearity (cited and citing texts must ideally be differentiated as belonging to different phyla, and an individual user's following the path of citation, while nonteleological, is still a system of links); but a model of embedding rather than descent forbids any resolution of citationality. Each traversal of the hypermedia archive is by definition idiosyncratic, even when replicable by accident or by following the "history" of visits: such a "history" of sites visited is not history in the *Altertumswissenschaft* sense of linear evolution but a Foucauldian archaeology of *couches* or epistemic disjuncts.[81] I like to think that there is an intellectual as well as a procedural development in this series of models: one supersedes another because it better describes the documentary circumstances. But I retain enough cultural modesty to recognize that changing intellectual environments have made each model more or less plausible, and that I am by no means the sole, idiosyncratic constructor of these entropic representations of data. I also like to think that the hypertextual model of free-floating links is a better simulacrum of medieval textuality than the fixed critical text of the codex ever was; or at least of some types of medieval textuality, the *scriptible* rather than the *lisible*. If Bernard Cerquiglini is correct that *mouvance* is

81. See Michel Foucault, *The Archeology of Knowledge and the Discourse on Language,* trans. A. Sheridan Smith (New York, 1972): "History has long since abandoned its attempts to understand events in terms of cause and effect in the formless unity of some great evolutionary process, whether vaguely homogeneous or rigidly hierarchized. It did not do this in order to seek out structures anterior to, alien or hostile to the event. It was rather in order to establish those diverse converging, and sometimes divergent, but never autonomous series that enable us to circumscribe the 'locus' of an event, the limits to its fluidity and the conditions of its emergence" (p. 230). For an analysis of the textual and bibliographical significance of Foucault's noncausal theory of history, particularly as it illuminates theories of transmission, see the "History" chapter of Greetham, *Theories of the Text.*

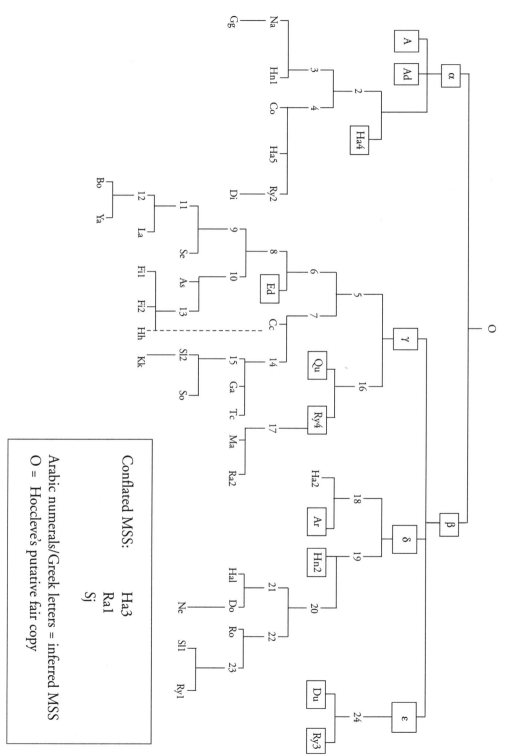

Fig. 3
The genealogy of *Regement of Princes* manuscripts

Conflated MSS: Ha3
                  Ra1
                  Sj

Arabic numerals/Greek letters = inferred MSS
O = Hoccleve's putative fair copy

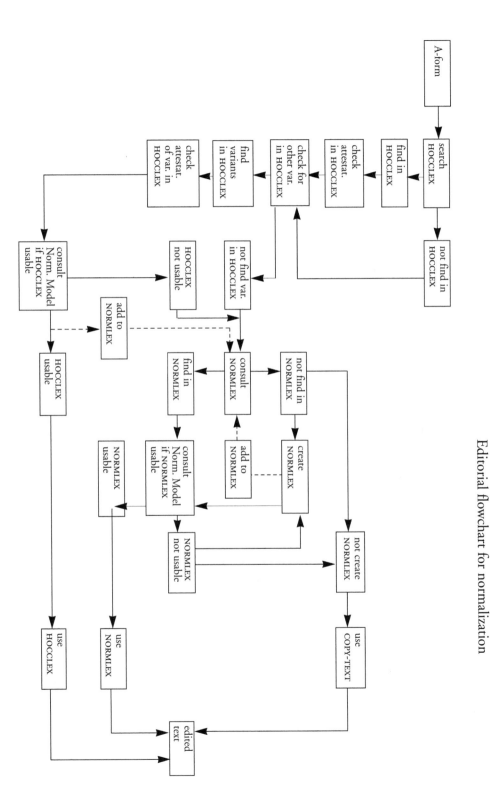

Fig. 4
Editorial flowchart for normalization

not merely a form of medieval textuality but that very textuality itself,[82] then a hypertext (and ideally a hypermedia) representation of textual relations is surely a more accurate and more honest reflection of these conditions. And yet I still keep thinking of those new editors and new projects: what is the first thing they address themselves to? Is it the construction of the rhizomes of hypertext? Probably not. My guess is that it's the possibility of finding the right tree on which to hang their witnesses. Phylum-tree-rhizome . . . tree.

City University of New York

---

82. Bernard Cerquiglini, *Éloge de la variante: Histoire critique de la philologie* (Paris, 1989): "Medieval writing does not produce variants, it is variance. . . . Variance is its foremost characteristic: fluidity of discourse in its concrete alterity, the figure of a premodern writing, to which editing should give primary recognition" (pp. 111–12), cited in translation by Suzanne Fleischman, "Philology, Linguistics, and the Discourse of the Medieval Text," *Speculum* 65 (1990): 27—re-cited by Stephen Nichols, "Introduction: Philology in a Manuscript Culture," ibid., 1; re-cited by Pearsall, "Theory and Practice," 124, n. 41.

Notes and Documents

The Bindings of the Ellesmere Chaucer

ANTHONY G. CAINS

DISBINDING AND CONSERVATION

The process of disbinding any elaborately decorated parchment manu-script that is in a modern trade binding is a parlous task. The first step is to study the text and its binding closely in order to overcome one's apprehension and to formulate a plan of action. Together with my colleague Maria Fredericks, conservator of rare books at the Huntington Library, and observers, I made a leaf-by-leaf assessment of the parchment and the pigment of the Ellesmere manuscript, MS. EL26C9, and studied the structure of the bind-ing, made by Rivière and Sons (ca. 1911).[1] This showed us that the general condition of the calfskin parchment was excellent and that, although there were areas of earlier loss, the pigment was generally well adhered to its surface, with-out evidence of recent flaking. The twenty-three pilgrim figures, along with some representative areas of the decoration, were examined under a binocular micro-scope. We determined that the pigments could withstand the stress from the disbinding and from the reprographic processes for the facsimile.[2] I judged the condition of the manuscript to be strong enough and flexible enough to with-stand the manipulation necessary to separate the gatherings from the animal glue and the thread binding them.

I am grateful to Nicholas Hadgraft of Corpus Christi College, Cambridge, for sharing his knowledge of fifteenth-century English bookbinding; to Maria Fredericks and Robert Schlosser of the Huntington Library for their careful recording of evidence; and to my colleague John Gillis for his help in preparing the figures. A summary of this report was published in Martin Stevens and Daniel Woodward, eds., *The Ellesmere Chaucer: Essays in Interpretation* (San Marino, Calif., 1995).

1.   The Rivière and Son repair and rebinding were apparently undertaken in conjunction with the facsimile published by the University of Manchester in 1911, printed by W. Griggs and Sons; the cover of this edition, however, is stamped "1910." There are no records extant of the Rivière and Son binding.
2.   The photography was undertaken for a facsimile of the manuscript, a copublication of Yushodo Co., Ltd., and the Huntington Library. The color facsimile appeared in 1995, and a monochromatic version follows in early 1997.

~ 127

We began on 4 April 1994, and the time available to us for the disbinding and treatment was two weeks. After the photography was complete, the repair and rebinding would take place in two additional phases scheduled for the following year. A crucial aspect of our work was to observe and record any evidence of the earlier bindings of the manuscript and earlier treatment and trimming of the leaves. All aspects of our work were also recorded photographically by Robert Schlosser, principal photographer at the Huntington Library, and by myself and Fredericks.

❧ Pigments

Using a binocular microscope connected to a video monitor, we examined the pigments and inks, chiefly to determine their ability to withstand disbinding and photography and to identify areas requiring treatment.[3] We also found evidence of the sequence of application, observed some characteristics of the pigments, and tentatively identified some of them.[4]

The text ink is an amorphous transparent organic brown in a clear medium, with no crystalline or particulate matter present. The ruling is a transparent medium stained pink by an organic (crimson) red; fine amorphous clumps of the red pigment are irregularly dispersed in the medium.

The blue color in the decoration is ultramarine (lapis lazuli)—either as a pure pigment or mixed with an inert white to give a lighter shade. It is also occasionally overpainted with an inert white (or painted over inert white). The orange-red pigment is almost certainly red lead. It has darkened when overpainted onto the ultramarine and oxidized in some areas to a brown color—a typical characteristic of the aging of lead-containing pigments. The transparent nature and the stability of the white suggests that it is chalk rather than lead white. There is certainly carbon black and possibly brown-black asphaltum, and a transparent amorphous green—transparent green particles, resinate or verdigris, suspended in a matrix of a transparent medium, perhaps copper. There is a rich, transparent crimson red, an organic color that was typically produced from such materials as madder, kermes, or orchil. This is used as a glaze over red lead and ultramarine and mixed with the inert white to give an opaque pink. (This rich crimon may be the same organic red as the one used in the ruling ink.) There is a transparent amorphous purple red in a clear medium that is generally referred to as folium or turnsole;

3.   A complete report of treatment is on file in the Conservation Laboratory of the Huntington Library.
4.   Scientific analysis was not undertaken because of the tight schedule, but the new binding, because it allows full opening of the manuscript, will allow safer access for such work in the future (see fig. 11).

this was also sold to limners in the form of dye-stained rags. Various complex mixtures of pigments were noted in the pilgrim portraits; for example, a transparent amorphous red, with a bitumous black and a transparent red-brown. The transparent red-brown had a resinous, shellac-like appearance. An opaque yellow pigment was noted on folio 138^r (Pardoner); the degraded condition of the binding medium suggested that it was orpiment. (Appendix A contains Fredericks's summary of the treatment of pigments and gesso.)

The gilding in the decorated areas has a very polished, "professional" quality to it. It is always on a white gesso base and burnished. Some of the figures have points of gold leaf applied directly to the parchment or pigment base and are not on gesso, and probably not burnished. These could also be gold leaf flakes in a medium such as albumen (glair) or vegetable gum and applied with a brush (also known as shell gold). Comparing the pigments suggested different techniques and perhaps different levels of skill among those who decorated, illustrated, and gilded the manuscript. The work of the illustrators appears technically less accomplished than that of the decorator and gilder. We noted that the ultramarine used by the limner is of a dark, rich hue; it has a coarser aggregate than the pigment prepared by the decorator.

In the course of an examination of the pigments with M. B. Parkes, I was able to demonstrate that the text was written before the decoration was applied. It had been thought previously that the decoration had been erased to allow space for text, but it was now clear that pigment had been applied over the text ink and that particles had simply detached due to poor surface bonding and consequent separation of the layers.

One of the most important aspects of the production of the manuscript that Parkes and I discussed was the famous crease that runs through the entire manuscript. I suggested that a likely explanation was that the skins had been folded by the parchmenter into either bifolia or quaterniones—and then simply refolded to produce a longer, intermediate format; the offcut would have been usable for a smaller-format book.

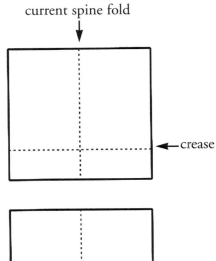

current spine fold

crease

Fig. 1
The position of the crease visible throughout the manuscript suggests an original fold by the parchmenter (into halves or quarters), and a possible offcut (shown below).

❧ The 1911 Binding and Sewing: General Description

The cover of the manuscript, in the Rivière binding, was full, heavily grained, green goatskin (of the type known as Cape Levant), highly polished. There were six large raised bands on the spine, each about 9 mm wide, with the following spacing:

head	1	2	3	4	5	6	tail
0	58–66	114–23	172–81	229–38	283–92	339–48	410 mm

It could be seen that the lacing-on of the book boards coincided with the bands, and this immediately suggested some form of flexible sewing. That the cover was adhered directly to the spine confirmed that view.[5]

The Rivière endleaves, made from heavy calfskin parchment, consisted of two flyleaves and a pastedown. Examination of the inside joints showed a gusset and indicated that the endleaves had been oversewn onto the text block after the text block had been sewn (fig. 2). Easing and lifting the gusset revealed the web of fine

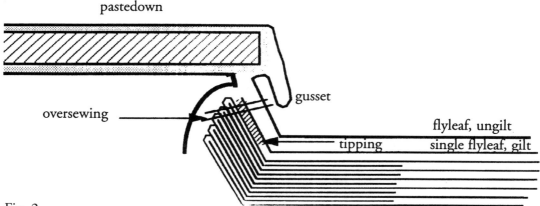

Fig. 2
The construction, attachment, and gilding of the modern parchment endleaves in the Rivière binding. The considerable backing crease is also evident in the diagram.

5. "Flexible sewing" refers to a comparatively strong structure in which each folded book section, or quire, is sewn around single- or double-cord supports that rest on the spine. The ends of these supports lace the book boards onto the text block. When covered, the supports appear on the spine as raised bands. As early as the seventeenth century and frequently in the nineteenth, cheaper bindings often employed a sewing structure using supports that were recessed into sawcuts made across the spine. To simulate the look of flexible sewing, "false bands" of cord, leather, or cardboard—which did not necessarily correspond either in number or location to the recessed supports—could be stuck onto the spine of the book prior to covering.

threads of the oversewing. The remaining two modern single-sheet, calf parch-ment flyleaves were left attached at this point, held by the original tipping of animal glue applied by Rivière. The threads of the oversewing were then cut one by one with a scalpel, and the first flyleaf was then pulled clear from the joint to reveal the ends of the sewing supports, or "slips," traversing the gap between text block and cover.

These intact slips were severed at each sewing station. A thin bone folder was inserted between the thick, claret-colored leather spine linings and the spine folds. These separated readily, leaving a fine deposit of leather fiber still adhered. By this means the cover was removed intact from the text block. It could be seen at this point that thick leather strips, or "dummy bands," had been adhered to the top of the sewing supports. It appeared that these had been added to bulk up the profile of the cords, which had been significantly reduced by Rivière's incorpora-tion of thick spine linings. The double, three-color silk head- and tailbands were removed and retained, along with the sewing cords and threads. At this point too the regular nature and reassuringly good condition of the spine folds became evi-dent, along with the perforations of an earlier sewing.

The Rivière parchment pastedowns and conjoint flyleaves are ungilt; they therefore must have been attached to the text block after gilding; however, the fly-leaves tipped by Rivière to the text block—that is, to the original pastedowns —are gilded. These flyleaves also reflect the narrow sawcut that Rivière made at the head and tail of the text.

The method of sewing used by Rivière was a surprise. Each station showed sewing through three holes (sometimes more) instead of the more usual one (or two) holes (fig. 3). The text had been sewn by Rivière on six thin double cords. These were in turn sewn through three (or four) nee-dle perforations at each station with a thick seaming twine. This method produced a very heavy spine swelling and a backing form with a shoulder actually deeper

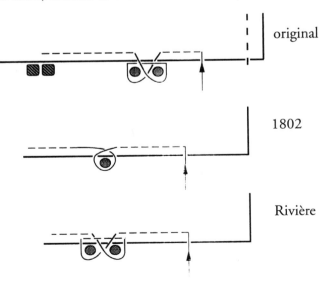

Fig. 3
The Rivière sewing employed three to four perforations and a cross-over thread.

Fig. 4
The gatherings of the manuscript after disbinding.

than the thickness of the boards (by about 8 to 10 mm).[6] The spine margin, especially of the outer gatherings, was characterized by a considerable backing crease. At the subsequent flattening stage, in preparation for photography, this was in fact the only significant distortion to be dealt with. Some decoration was within the area of the backing crease and being damaged by it; disbinding the manuscript was the only way that this could be discovered and treated (fig. 4).

✆ Separating the Gatherings

The animal glue and leather fiber was first removed from the exposed spine folds with a poultice of viscous methyl cellulose and scraped with a bone folder. The deep penetrations of animal glue between the gatherings (and to some extent into the earlier sewing perforations) made the process of separation a potentially dangerous one. Each gathering was opened to the center fold and the severed threads removed. Normally one would remove the entire gathering intact—the whole unit being stronger than its parts and better able to resist the stress of manipulation—but because of the excessive penetration of glue this was not possible. The three interior bifolia were removed one at a time without any difficulty, but this left the outer bifolium still adhered to the adjacent quire. Simply hydrating the glue to a point that it became soft would have meant overwetting and disfiguring the parchment. A compromise had to be found. A controlled amount of moisture was introduced by swabbing the spine fold with damp cotton wool and applying water in ethanol on the inside of the fold following the width of the glue line. The ethanol was allowed to evaporate. This gave the parchment a certain elasticity and also softened the animal glue. Where the penetration of the

---

6. This would have been recognized at the time as a major imperfection in the binding. Below I suggest the problems that the sewing may have been designed to solve.

glue was to a depth of only 2 or 3 mm, the parchment could be peeled away from the glue layer without undue shear stress. A thin bone folder was inserted between the folds and used as a lever to help with the separation. Some parchment fiber remained on the glue layer still adhering to the next gathering.

All gatherings were separated without new tears or losses. Before the removal of the glue from the folds and before the flattening of the spine margin commenced in earnest, a map was made to analyze perforations, sawcuts, and thread marks evident on each gathering. This indicated that the manuscript had been sewn twice or, more probably, thrice. As we have seen, the Rivière sewing was accomplished on six double cords through three needle perforations (which is in my opinion over a previous sewing, ca. 1802) at each station; the original sewing, however, had been accomplished on seven double supports (probably of tawed leather) through a single needle perforation (fig. 5).

The lumpy fillet of animal glue still adhering to the folds was removed by first paring, chipping, or scraping the glue layer to a regular film thickness of a few microns. To this film a poultice of viscous methyl cellulose was applied and covered with a moisture barrier. As soon as the glue had softened it was scraped away with a bone spatula, along with the methyl cellulose. This was repeated until the surface of the parchment was reached. If the parchment showed signs of going translucent from excess moisture the process was stopped and the fold allowed to dry under blotting paper and weights. The glue was then scraped again if necessary to remove the final traces. The glue layer had to be removed completely, both because it encroached on the decoration in many places and because it inhibited the flexibility of the spine fold. The residual moisture from this process had an additional benefit: we were able to reduce the backing crease by placing the dampened fold between blotting paper and glass weights.

The inner three bifolia of each gathering were treated in a different way. The spine folds were hydrated with damp blotting paper through a layer of Gore-tex and then placed between blotting paper and glass plate weights. Fredericks had prepared a set of padded clips and pins in readiness for a full flattening process, in which each bifolium was humidified to relax the creases and distortion over its entire area.[7]

7.   See Anthony G. Cains, "Repair Treatments for Vellum Manuscripts," Paper Conservator 7 (1982–83): 15–23.

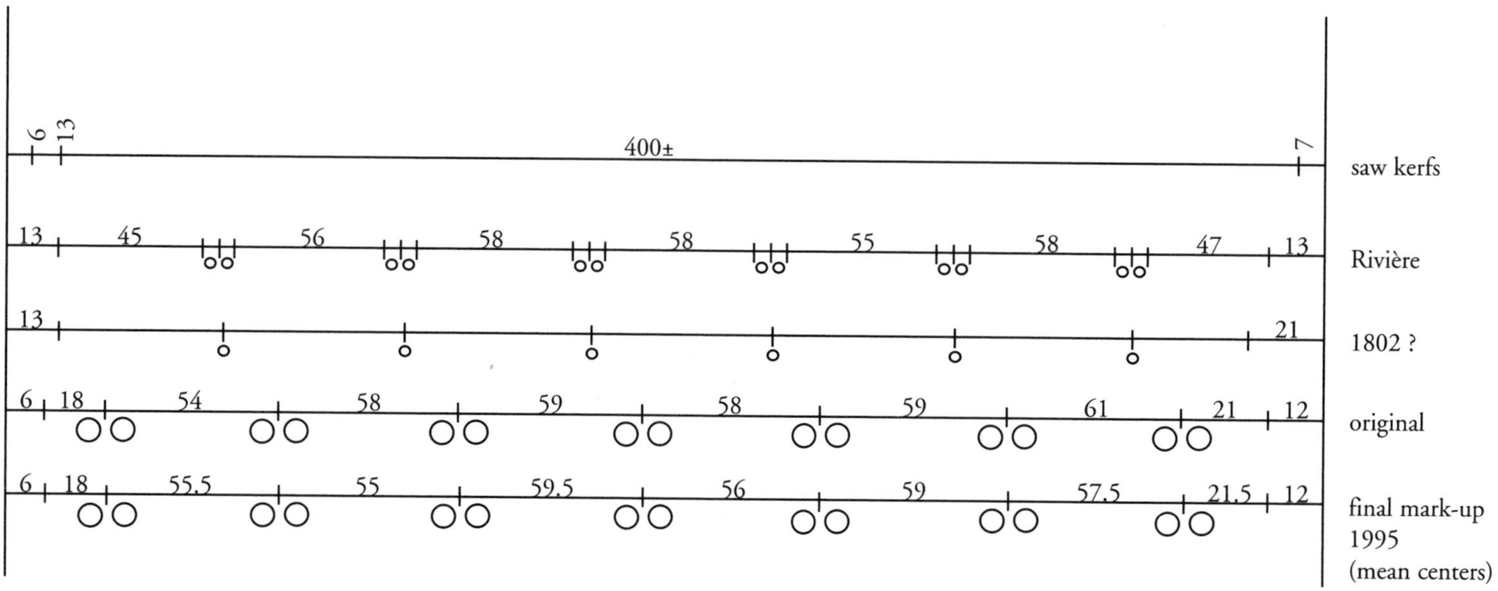

Fig. 5
The perforations and sewing stations of the various bindings.

✌ The Rivière Repair and Rebinding

The color and appearance of the parchment suggested processes it must have undergone at the time of the 1910/11 rebinding (there is no record extant of this treatment). I suspect that the warm color of the parchment and its translucent quality is the result of a flattening process that the binder performed for the printer. Another clue is the texture, feel, and handle of the parchment: the flesh side still retains a smooth feel but the more heavily scraped and "pounced" hair side[8] has a relatively abrasive tactile quality compared to contemporary material in original condition.

The flattening process would have entailed hydration and light pressing between absorbent blotting paper, and indeed we discovered paper fiber embedded in or attached to some areas of pigment (fol. 206, red lead, Parson; and fol. 169[r], Monk; also fols. 203[r], 223[r]; there were particularly large deposits in the black pigment in the border of fol. 231[r]). The hydration would have activated the adhesive quality of the binding medium (that is, gum arabic, albumen) and caused the loose fiber of the unsized blotting paper to adhere to the pigment. Pigment could also be lost during this process if the pigment bond to the parchment was weak.[9]

The flattening process likely resembled that still used in the 1960s at the British Museum, which drew on the tradition of London's West End binderies of which Rivière was very much a part.[10] The size water (dilute warm gelatine solution) was sprayed onto both surfaces of the bifolium. This hydrated and softened the parchment but did not make it thoroughly wet. The softened and pliable leaf was then placed between sheets of blotting paper on a pressing board and light flat weights were slid from the center fold out until the entire area was covered with weights. After a short period to set, the weights were removed and replaced with another pressing board and the process repeated. There was occasionally some offset evident on the blotting paper, but the remaining text and pigment were well secured to the now more translucent parchment substrate.[11]

---

8. In this process, the hard, slick surface of the hair side was rubbed with pumice to produce a velvety napped surface ready for writing or painting.

9. It has been observed by several leading manuscript conservators, in particular the late Judy Segal of the Bodleian Library, that heavily pounced parchment of this period is very vulnerable to moisture, leading to changes in texture, appearance, and refractive index—the way light is reflected. The pounced surface fibers of the parchment partially gelatinize in the presence of free water and become translucent.

10. I worked at the HMSO British Museum Bindery during the 1960s. It may be useful to describe the flattening process, which probably varied little, in some detail.

11. Fredericks has observed that areas of gilt gesso have a rather crushed appearance, which would follow from such a process (see appendix A).

Some evidence of previous binding was inevitably removed by Rivière's work. The pasted surfaces of the original endleaves had been cleared thoroughly of most of the adhesive deposit, leaving a small residue in places but no remnants of wood or leather fiber that I could discover. Fortunately a discernible impression, or differential staining, remains on the endleaves, indicating the channel and peg locations of the original board attachment system, two distinct sets of leather turn-in stains, and marks from brass clasp-plate nails. Other important evidence of the original binding was found on the reverse side of each of these two surfaces. This evidence will be analyzed below (see figs. 7 and 8).

It was apparent that the spine folds had been repaired by Rivière with paper patches and that the text and endleaf gatherings were often crudely infilled with various parchment types (some of these patches may be earlier; for example, on folio 218^r is a fine vellum-maker's repair). In addition to the general fixing there appears to be evidence of local fixing of the gesso gilding and pigment system.[12]

On completion of the flattening and repair work, Rivière tipped with animal glue a single leaf of new, thick, covering-weight calfskin parchment to the first and last leaves, gatherings A and B. The text block would then have been placed between boards and "knocked-up"; that is, gatherings were aligned at the head and spine folds so that the natural irregularity in format would be evident at the tail- and fore-edge (each skin would have different dimensions because of both natural aging and previous restoration). This variation, now no longer evident, would have been considerable—on the order of several millimeters.

At this point three narrow kerfed sawcuts were made into the spine, two at the head and one at the tail (now located 6 mm and 13 mm from the head and 7.5 mm from tail, each to a depth of between 2 and 4 mm).[13] The purpose was, I believe, to bind the text block temporarily for the purpose of trimming and gilding the three edges. Glue was applied to the sawcuts and its penetration caused the bifolia of each gathering to adhere to each other securely. Thread may have been inserted into the cuts to strengthen this bond and lock the entire book block together for the subsequent processes.

Edges can be gilt without excessive loss simply by knocking-up, each edge in turn to be scraped smooth, with a loss of only one-half millimeter or less, leaving the odd short leaf ungilt (as can be seen on fol. 193 at head-edge and fol. 201 at fore-edge; these short leaves indicate that the manuscript had not

---

12. Evidence of previous repairs requires further investigation.
13. This sawcut slot is visible in the endleaf gathering B section of the 1911 facsimile and less clearly, perhaps, in the reproduction of gathering A.

been gilt previously). The present text block is not exactly square but has been cut with a fair degree of accuracy: the head and tail dimension hardly vary through the entire manuscript, at 399.5–401 mm and the fore-edge spine dimension similarly constant at 285–286 and 286–288.5 mm (at 50 percent RH, 21 degrees centigrade). To achieve this accuracy and solidity of edge for gilding, all irregularities must have been removed. In the context of trimming, ancient edge damage and other wear and tear must also be considered. Furthermore, in the fifteenth-century binding there would have been a shallow back corner at the head and tail of the spine, where the single primary core of the original endband was seated; but this feature, along with the catchwords, was evidently lost in trimming before the 1910/11 binding.

A nineteenth-century facsimile of the Ellesmere manuscript provides some clues about the trimming.[14] The facsimile reproduced just a short length of the contemporary edge at the spine margin at the head. It showed only the curve of the leaf into the spine fold of the bound text; the rest is masked. This reveals nonetheless that the major cropping had occurred before the Rivière rebinding of 1910/11. In the preface to the facsimile of 1911, Alix Egerton refers to a previous rebinding of about 1802. We must therefore conclude that the cropping and the loss of the original binding were the product of this event. Thus far I am certain that the edges were cropped excessively by the 1802 binder and to a minor degree by Rivière but can only guess the exact amount. The evidence we have studied is the surviving catchword fragment, noted by Parkes in folio 184[v]; and the present relationship of the kettle stitch positions to their respective edges (fig. 6). We have also noted the profile of turn-in stains on the pastedown (of which more below); the secondary stains are probably from a board-edge repair rather than from the leather used in the 1802 rebinding.[15]

Evidence of the original sewing suggests the dimensions of the cropping. The seven-support station mark-up is not exactly symmetrical in the extant manuscript—that is, the bands are set roughly equidistant from one another, but they are all together about one-half inch closer to the head. This suggests that slightly more was lost at the head than at the tail. An estimation of the total loss can

14. Parkes first called to my attention to a reprint of folio 53[v] of this facsimile. The complete facsimile was edited by F. J. Furnivall and published by the Chaucer Society in 1885 (ser. 1, no. 74), *Autotype Specimens of the Chief Chaucer Manuscripts,* pt. 4.
15. The board-edge repair was probably necessitated by decay and worm infestation (about which more below). This work would have required the binder to lift the pastedown along its margins to a depth that would allow him to insert a narrow strip of leather to wrap the damaged board edges. It is not possible that the edges of the text block had been trimmed at this point.

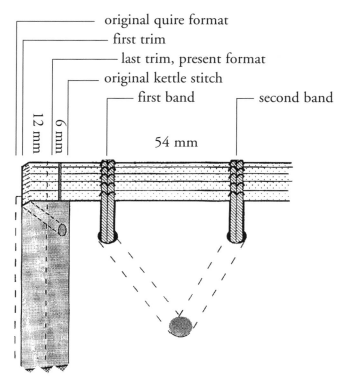

original quire format

first trim

last trim, present format

original kettle stitch

first band

second band

12 mm

6 mm

54 mm

Fig. 6
The trimmings of the manuscript.

be made by assuming that the kettle stitch was set half way between the first band station and the untrimmed head-edge of the text and again between the seventh band station and the untrimmed tail-edge. The first band is between 23 and 28 mm from the present head, and the kettle between 6 and 8 mm from it; the average distance between the kettle and the top band is 18 mm. This suggests a loss of 13 mm at the head. The distance between the seventh station and the tail kettle stitch is about 22 mm, suggesting a loss of about 10 mm—thus a total loss of 23 mm or 7/8", giving an original untrimmed height of 423 mm (16 5/8"). There are other clues evident on the pastedown (to be discussed in full below): the present geometry of the original turn-in corner; and the absence of any nail marks for the clasp plates at the fore-edge (see fig. 7). Other oxidation stains, and their relative alignment in endleaf gathering B, provide evidence of a loss of about 5 mm at the fore-edge, following the discarding of the original boards.

At this point, after gilding, the manuscript was likely sent by Rivière to the printer of the facsimile, Griggs. We note that he does not reproduce the old paste-down surfaces. I believe that the single parchment flyleaf tipped to each endleaf did not hinge back readily for photography. He does reproduce the deep sawcut made by Rivière, evident on several of the endleaf openings reproduced. One is able to discern the board channel system on the verso of the first leaf. The saw-cuts and the glue would have allowed Griggs to separate the gatherings one at a time from the text block while maintaining the register of each bifolium within the gathering; they would open like a tacketed pamphlet.

On its return to Rivière, the manuscript would have been sewn and the spine glued (with hot, fluid animal glue, as was the standard procedure at the time) and then rounded and backed. The endleaf bifolia (with their ungilt edges) were then oversewn onto the first and last gatherings A and B, the threads of which embraced the single flyleaves previously tipped on. The work was then completed by the standard forwarding and covering procedure of the time.[16]

The unusual character of the Rivière method of sewing cannot be overemphasized (see fig. 3).[17] Finding it was most unexpected; the method is not discussed or illustrated in any contemporary manual.[18] Furthermore, the Rivière firm could have made their work much easier by adopting a recessed cord sewing, as frequently employed by the West End trade at that time. In adopting a flexible sewing system (see n. 5, above) they were certainly reflecting the influence of T. J. Cobden-Sanderson and Douglas Cockerell; but I am convinced that the method was adopted in an intelligent response to a technical problem unique to the task.

It is clear from the 1885 Chaucer Society facsimile that the nineteenth-century binding opened reasonably well; on folio 53^v, for example, one can see this from the curve of the head-edge spine margins. (The only tangible evidence of the 1802 binding phase is a double-thread tie-down of brown silk in the fold of fols. 58^v/63^r, exiting 21 mm from the tail.) Early nineteenth-century practice would suggest that the sewing was light-weight, either on single cords or double cords sewn single-flexible, with a carelessly placed and erratic kettle stitch. At each cord station the result would be a needle-perforation pattern of one or two holes. However, we observed that the present three- or four-hole stations are damaged: the bridges between the perforations are torn in some quires, suggesting that they have been under shear stress in use. Now it is clear that this stress cannot have been the product of Rivière's sewing because the system could not be stressed. It was locked solid by the glued leather and paper linings and the enormous dummy bands glued to the cords. I suggest that the problem of resewing through a weakness in the folds at each station was specifically countered by the Rivière sewer, who made two extra perforations through undamaged material, thus ensuring a

16. See Bernard C. Middleton, *A History of English Craft Bookbinding Techniques* (London, 1963).
17. The pattern of perforation it produced may be seen in medieval texts but the sewing method would be entirely different, and this has only been recently understood. See Christopher Clarkson, "English Monastic Bookbindings in the Twelfth Century," in M. Maniaci and P. F. Munafò eds., *Ancient and Medieval Book Materials and Techniques*, Studi e Testi, 357-58, 2 vols. (Vatican City, 1993), 2:81.
18. See Douglas Cockerell, *Bookbinding and the Care of Books*, 5th ed. (London, 1954), originally published about 1900; and J. W. Zaehnsdorf, *The Art of Bookbinding*, 6th ed. (London, 1903). Although I have considered the method Rivière used as a theoretical possibility, I cannot recall that I have ever seen it.

solid sewing structure. The disadvantage of the method, as mentioned before, was the excessive swelling created by the crossover thread, so that the joint would have protruded above the level of the boards.[19]

The Original Binding

❧ Sewing and Endbands

The very clear impression made by the sewing thread—clearly of a robust gauge—and the needle perforations show us that the text was originally sewn on seven supports. The sewing perforations are pricked, or pierced, rather than slit.[20] The supports would almost certainly have been of a white tawed leather, rolled thongs or straps. In this technique, the supports were sewn through one hole at each station, and there were two kettle-stitch positions, one at the head and one at the tail, from whence the sewing thread moved from one gathering to the next after a kettle stitch was made. As we have seen, the present position of these kettle-stitch perforations in relation to their respective edges gives us an important clue to the amount of cropping the text block has suffered in the two rebinding phases.

The impressions left by the endband tie-down threads are, on the other hand, rather faint—unlike the clear thread impressions to be seen on rebound Romanesque texts (such as the Winchcombe Psalter, Trinity College Dublin, MS. 53)—and not evident in every gathering. Nicholas Hadgraft suggested that the material used for the sewing of the primary endband was apparently lighter in color and softer than that used for the primary sewing of the text block; furthermore, it was apparently the practice not to tie down through every gathering. For a manuscript of thirty gatherings, perhaps seventeen to twenty-three would be tied down to the kettle stitch.[21] Hadgraft further suggested that this thread was two-cord flax with an easy twist. This form would provide a flat profile over the single white tawed leather endband core—therefore a smooth surface on which a secondary decorative sewing could be formed.[22] The cover's turn-ins at

---

19. Apart from this imperfection, the forwarding, headbanding, covering, and finishing of the Rivière binding are first-class extra quality of the period.

20. There are iron oxide stains in the parchment that have the profile of a needle in the joint margin of folio 65[v].

21. This evidence was reviewed by Christopher Clarkson, who then referred me to our mutual friend Nicholas Hadgraft of Corpus Christi College, Cambridge, currently studying English bindings of the fifteenth century.

22. The simple covered endband of the period, illustrated by Middleton in *English Craft Bookbinding*, is more usually to be found on bindings that were not intended to be double covered. As will be seen below, the fifteenth-century binding of the Ellesmere Chaucer did have an overcover.

the head and tail of the spine were probably cut off level with the laced-in primary endband, and a decorative secondary sewing of silk or linen made over the endbands and through the spine cover. An exposed silk endband—that is, one sewn through the cover and not protected by a "cap" (a later development)—would have been more vulnerable to abrasion damage than either the simple covered type or a triple-crowning core endband composed of tough linen thread.[23]

⟿ Pastedowns

In most manuscript collections, there are examples of rebound parchment texts bearing clear evidence of the original binding on the pastedown surface of the parchment endleaves. The surfaces frequently retain, in the layer of residual adhesive, fragments of the original covering material and wood cell fragments or splinters, spine lining fragments, or offset text from such linings. The adhesive layer also records very clearly the turn-in profile and the channel and peg locations of the board attachment system. In the case of the Ellesmere manuscript, although the pasted surfaces have been thoroughly cleaned by a previous binder, a great deal of evidence has survived.

⟿ Board Attachment System

At our request, Schlosser produced two sets of raking-light photographs of the surface of the two pastedowns and four eight-by-ten color transparencies of the verso and recto of the same leaves. These were enlarged to actual size. From the original endleaves Fredericks prepared two tracings giving the outline of the channel and peg locations. The tracings and photographs also recorded the two sets of cover turn-in marks, the verdigris points indicating the clasp positions, the profile of the envelope pocket of an overcover, and a tawed leather fragment adhering to the residual paste (of which more below). The photographs also recorded the network of surface channels and perforations created by wood-boring insects (figs. 7 and 8).

The "gothic" lacing schemes illustrated by Michael Gullick suggest two common forms: the parallel form, where each thong enters the board and exits through a single hole or slot from a channel parallel to the head; and the "vee,"

---

23. I noticed one of the latter type in the collection of Corpus Christi College, Cambridge (Archives XVII-4, East Field Teiners).

or chevron, form, in which the thongs enter through single holes and exit in pairs. In Gullick's example, six thongs exit through three pegged holes.[24]

Our subject, however, has seven thongs exiting through four "stepped" and pegged holes,[25] and it therefore combines both "gothic" forms. The boards have been channeled in an identical manner; thus, the front and back boards both show the pattern "VIVV" (fig. 9); and the stepped locations of the pegs, furthermore, are not dissimilar. The diameter of the pegs would have been about one-half inch. All the thongs appear to have entered the board through holes drilled about one inch from the spine edge (not staggered, as in Gullick's example). Reading from the head, thong stations one and two exit together on both boards from a vee channel as do stations six and seven. Station three on the front board has a single exit from a parallel channel, and on the back board it is combined with station four and exits from a vee channel. Stations four and five exit together on the front board and station five has a single exit on the back board.

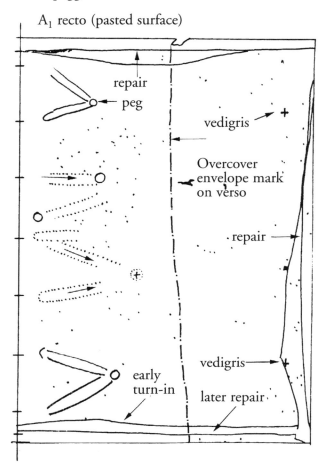

A₁ recto (pasted surface)

repair
peg
vedigris
Overcover
envelope mark
on verso
repair
vedigris
early
turn-in
later repair

Figs. 7 & 8
Evidence of previous bindings and repairs has survived cropping and overcleaning. The scattered dots represent perforations made by insects.

24. See Michael Gullick's contribution on the bindings in R. A. B. Mynors and R. M. Thomson, eds., *Catalogue of the Manuscripts of Hereford Cathedral Library* (Cambridge, 1993). See also *The Canterbury Tales . . . : A Facsimile and Transcription* (Norman, Okla., 1979), xi and xii, on the board attachment system of the Hengwrt manuscript.

25. To protect the integrity of the boards, the holes were staggered in relation to the vertical grain axis.

There is no evidence of an endband lacing system. This lack of evidence may be owing to the fact that the primary cover turn-ins overlaid the channel and peg positions so that they did not mark the pastedown. Another consideration is that the heavy cropping may have removed some evidence of endband lacing and of the back-corner form, just as it has impinged on the corner turn-in profile. Despite the lack of hard evidence, contemporary practice suggests that the single-cored endbands must have been laced in. There may have been a channel ending with a peg,[26] as in the case of HM 35300, a manuscript of Bede's *Historia Ecclesiastica* in the Huntington's own collection.

As we weighed the clues provided by our scrutiny of the pastedowns, we were fortunate to discover that this manuscript had a binding similar to the one that Ellesmere must have had (for a full description of HM 35300, see appendix B). One of the most interesting features of this manuscript is that it retains several fragments of its original overcover. The condition of the primary cover of tawed sheepskin is so good, in fact, that one can conclude that the overcover was hacked away in modern times. Although restored, the binding retains a large intact portion of triple-crowning core endband in indigo and white linen thread. In the case of the Red Book of Ossary, a late-fourteenth-century Anglo-Irish binding originally covered in a red surface-stained tawed leather, the only surviving fragment is the mechanically

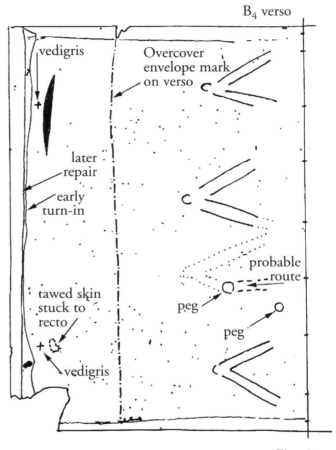

Fig. 8

26. See Dag-Ernst Petersen, *Mittelalterliche Bucheinbande der Herzog August Bibliothek* (Wolfenbüttel, Germany, 1975), plates 3 and 4.

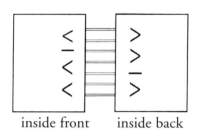

inside front   inside back

Fig. 9
The "vee" and chevron forms.

tough covered endband, of the type mentioned above.[27] I first thought this an appropriate model for the new binding but following discussion with Mary Robertson, curator of manuscripts at the Huntington, we decided to adopt a number of features suggested by HM 35300 (see fig. 13).

Gullick also illustrates a typical section of a "gothic" board.[28] This cushion-beveled form gives a relatively light weight without undue loss of strength and preserves the rigidity of the panel.[29] Middleton notes that the boards would not have projected much beyond the text block; that is, they did not have the "squares" introduced later in the century (and still, of course, part of modern practice). The pastedown therefore could have provided an almost perfect "negative" of the original boards—except that the information has been degraded by cropping and overcleaning.

✐ Primary Cover and Overcover

We do not know for certain the species of wood used for the boards or the material used for the primary covering. However, the profile of the original turn-in is evident on the pastedown, along with a much darker and parallel brown stain. I first suggested that the turn-in profile might be from a vegetable-tanned leather cover, although it could also be derived from a reaction between the dye and a flour paste adhesive or between the adhesive and tawed leather (containing oxidized animal fat and potash alum and salt). On the other hand, I feel that the much darker and roughly parallel turn-in marks must be the product of a vegetable (oak) tanned leather; the neatness of the line suggests a board-edge repair of the eighteenth or early nineteenth century rather than a complete recovering of the old boards.

27. The Red Book of Ossary is a fourteenth-century manuscript in the collection of St. Canice's Cathedral Library, Kilkenny.
28. This form is also exemplified by the binding (Corpus Christi College, Cambridge, Archives XVII-4, East Field Teiners) I referred to in reference to endbanding; like HM 35300, it displays the chevron channel form and is covered in white alum-tawed sheep- or goatskin.
29. This is the form generally preferred by modern English and American binders influenced by the Arts and Crafts/Cockerell School of bookbinding, in particular by the late Roger Powell in his work for Trinity College Dublin and the Royal Irish Academy.

On the front pastedown the turn-in marks are evident on all three edges but on the back pastedown only at the fore-edge. The turn-in impressions indicate a mitered or slightly overlapping form. It must be appreciated that both sets of turn-in profiles are now reduced in width by the binder's cropping; the front fore-edge turn-in profile is completely lost at the top corner. Nonetheless, the geometry of the impression of the two surviving cover miters—at the front tail corner and the back head corner—supports the evidence of the degree of cropping provided by the present kettle stitch-to-edge relationship. The lack of any nail marks near the fore-edge for retaining the clasp plates suggests that this evidence has also been trimmed away.

I have observed that the overcover of a typical English Romanesque binding is in fact made of a heavier substance than the primary cover it protects or, rather, complements; and it has been suggested that this is also true of English bindings of the early fifteenth century.[30] Hadgraft indicates that the overcover of this period is of heavy, reversed, white alum-tawed leather, and that it would have extended beyond the edges of the boards to form a protective skirt for the edges of the text block. The skirt edges may have been edged with a narrow border of vegetable tanned leather (sewn on) or left as a raw-cut edge.[31]

On the reverse surfaces of the pastedowns of the Ellesmere manuscript, we have a clear profile of the envelope pockets that secured the overcover to the boards and a residue of the paste adhesive that fixed them to the pastedowns. Whether this fixing was accomplished in the early fifteenth century or not is difficult to say, but what the adhesive has done is to retain a precious fragment of the overcover's material—a pink-stained piece of leather. This was discovered by Fredericks within the pocket area of the lower board and it has been left in situ. It tells us that the overcover was a white tawed leather, we think sheepskin, with its grain surface stained with an organic red dye; and as this grain side was facing the pastedown, the white flesh side would be to view. It is therefore not unlikely that the primary cover was the same type of leather, but with the grain side outermost.

30. For example, a late twelfth-century Fountains Abbey manuscript in Clongowes Wood College near Dublin (one of the few of this period I have access to in Ireland) is complete with its original overcover. See Graham Pollard, "The Construction of English Twelfth-Century Bindings, *The Library,* 5th ser., 17 (1962): 7; Gullick, in *Manuscripts of Hereford Cathedral Library;* and Clarkson, *English Monastic Bookbindings.*

31. The proportions of the skirt differ from the Romanesque form in that each has more or less equal margin width sufficient to meet and cover the edges. It is not uncommon to find that these skirts have been trimmed to allow storage on modern vertical shelving.

❧ Worm Holes

The overall wood-worm infestation of the original boards is recorded as the pattern of exit holes and ramification of tunnels etched into the parchment's pasted surface. This initially suggested to me that the original material was beechwood, because in my experience this wood is readily attacked by the common furniture beetle (Anobium punctatum). Oak is less frequently infested, and to a lesser degree than our subject.[32] Hadgraft has suggested, however, that beechwood is not a likely candidate for the period and area of production and that quarter-cut oak was the commonly used material. The practice of the time was to place the softer sapwood toward the spine for ease of working—boring the holes and carving the channels—and Hadgraft has frequently found this area to be worm damaged.[33]

❧ Clasps

Not unexpectedly for a manuscript of this period, there is evidence of two fore-edge clasps. On each pastedown there are two verdigris copper alloy–stained points about 25 to 30 mm in from the present fore-edge and in alignment with the second and sixth sewing stations. These indicate the locations of clasp or strap plate and catch-plate nails. A single nail that far in could never have worked alone, of course, and there must have been at least one other nail near to the fore-edge to retain each plate securely. The straps would be set into stopped rebates cut into the fore-edge of one of the wooden boards (probably the front) and secured, after covering with a plate of brass. The symmetry of the nail marks suggests that clasp or strap plate and catch plate had similar form and dimension. This symmetry suggests an all-metal clasp. The clasp and catch would have passed through slots cut into the board envelopes of the overcover but not through the skirt of the overcover to the exterior (see fig. 7). In HM 35300, a small bit of the chemise remains under the catch plates, so it is clear that the clasps were mounted over the chemise (see fig. 12).

---

32. My experience of ancient structural oak in the London area (St. Albans) is that the sapwood of oak, but not the heartwood, is often infested, but by a much larger animal, the death-watch beetle (Xestobium). Harold Plenderleith has noted that wood-boring insects may be identified either by the size of the holes they leave on emerging to lay eggs or by the material attacked. See Norman Hickin, *Bookworms: The Insect Pest of Books* (London, 1985); and Plenderlieth, *The Conservation of Antiquities and Works of Art* (London, 1956).

33. A German binding in the collection of Trinity College (MS. 10811) from the same period as the Ellesmere has beechwood boards infested in a similar way. In my view the question of the board material remains unresolved. HM 35300 shows minor infestation but we have not identified the type of wood used.

REPAIR AND REBINDING OF THE ELLESMERE CHAUCER

Following the completion of the photography and color correction for the fac-simile, the manuscript was preconditioned at a high relative humidity to render the parchment pliant and flexible. The bifolia were then folded, gathered into quires, and interleaved with thin paper tissue; the quires were stacked in order, and the text block placed under moderate weight. The manuscript was then placed in storage at the normal ambient RH of the Huntington Library and allowed to come into equilibrium.

The text block had taken on a very satisfactory solidity as a result of the pre-conditioning process. The spine folds were again examined and remaining significant traces of animal glue removed by scraping and swabbing with damp cotton buds. Some ingrained heavy soiling along the spine folds that had been fixed by the Rivière hydration process was reduced but not removed by pouncing with pumice powder.

Each bifolium was examined for damage to the parchment and a tracing made of all lacunae, cuts, and tears to be treated. Around each of these tracings a profile of the patch form was made allowing a flange beyond the lacuna of between 3 and 5 mm. This series of tracings records all repair zones for patching with either calfskin parchment or transparent gold-beater skin.[34]

From the tracings, the profiles of about 140 separate patches were transferred onto the repair parchment using a hard pencil; the profile of the lacunae onto the hair side and the flange profile onto the flesh side. The repair parchment was selected on the basis of a clear overall follicle pattern, indicating that a good, sub-stantial portion of this tough grain layer had survived the parchmenter's knife work. This selected parchment was then reduced by scraping the flesh side until it was thin and pliant. The patches were then all cut out and mounted on cards with the sequence head to tail kept in order. They were then reduced even further along the flange and made as thin as feasible. This was achieved by grinding the flange area with an abrasive ruby tool bit held in a flexible shaft-driven drill. In some cases the flange was given a further dressing using sanding sticks, but gen-erally the machining was found sufficiently precise. This work was done over a light box on a surface of thick tracing paper.[35]

---

34. Some transparent membrane repair patches were not traced, such as those on folios 105 and 106, but are noted in the record on file in the Conservation Laboratory of the Huntington Library.

35. An important advantage of the tracing procedure, of course, is that the handling of the manuscript is kept to the minimum.

During the first phase of repair, a number of crude and disfiguring parchment repair patches were removed from endleaf gatherings A and B. Some inappropriate repair patches in the text were also removed subsequently with the agreement with Robertson, mainly on technical grounds. For example, on folio 85 a crack and crease in the fore-edge margins had been patched with thick inflexible parchment on a thin and fragile area. This was replaced with transparent membrane. Another example is the lower corner patch on folio 105; this was again inflexible and its color too light in tone, and it was replaced on aesthetic grounds. The majority of the Rivière repairs, however, were left untouched, except to reattach them with gelatine. Some Rivière patches over ancient lacunae did obscure evidence, and these were also removed. For example, a patch on the lower corner of B4 aligned with an oxidation stain on B2, which then revealed the extent of loss from cropping at the fore-edge.

The new spine patches were attached with a solution of edible gelatine and dried under padded weights. The opening of each fold was checked and the flanges of each patch scraped with a sharp knife until the right degree of flexibility was obtained. Repairs to the text area were then applied with the same solution. Membrane rather than parchment was used to repair knife cuts and lacunae that needed to be reinforced or bridged but remain transparent (as, for example, B4). Creases that had been slit by Rivière (for example, on folio 100^r)or sometime before were also reinforced with membrane, usually on both sides of the damage.[36]

On completion of the repair work a number of spine folds needed to be hydrated and flattened to correct the slight contraction of the longer repair patches. None of the folds was repaired with a single strip along its entire length. The contraction of the spine was on the order of less than 1 mm and easily corrected.

❧ Sewing

As we have seen, the relationship of the edges of the text block to the original sewing perforations has been altered by cropping in two ways. The kettle stitches are closer to the head and tail than they should be—5 mm and about 12 mm, respectively, and are not parallel. Thus the perforations, if followed exactly, would tilt the angle of the bands by several degrees. It was decided that the best course of action was to keep the bands as square and parallel as possible by finding the

---

36. It was noted that the original parchment in the areas we repaired with membrane showed very little sign of translucency from penetration of the gelatine adhesive. This reinforced my belief that Rivière had sized the parchment.

mean of all the perforations at every station. After some experiment a mark-up pattern was produced that embraced the vast majority of the original perforations (see fig. 5). In practice it was found that because of the enlarged size and oval shape of the original perforation zones, our sewing registered very well while maintaining the squareness of the new bands.

The gauge of the double cords we used was determined by the evidence presented by the original pastedowns, that is, according to the width of the lacing channel. The gauge of the sewing twine was based on the impression of the original thread, to be seen in most of the center folds, but in any event as thick as we could possibly use. We chose a 7 cord, which has a diameter of 1 mm. From this thread we cabled the seven double-cord lengths required following the method described by Robert Espinosa.[37]

A standard sewing frame was set up with a packing of hardwood and a base board shaped along the edge abutting the cords to accommodate the anticipated swelling from the sewing thread. The frame maintains the symmetry and tension of the cords. The packing block was inserted to elevate the text block during sewing, and thus to preserve a suitable length of undistorted cord. A line of thread was tied across the frame where the gatherings could be clipped during the sewing process. A copy of the mark-up sheet functioned both as a guide for the sewing and as a protection sheet for the surface of the center-fold margin and text.

The work was divided thus: Each gathering was checked for the alignment to the edge and adjustments were made. The gathering was then prepierced to the mark-up pattern through the new repair patches. The collation was checked at every stage. As this work progressed the text was being sewn. Each length of thread was waxed with beeswax and flattened with a bone folder. This loosened the cabling of the thread and gave it an oval shape, to bed well down into the folds and thus to reduce the swelling of the spine. The sewing was link-stitched at every station to the previous gathering, forming a herringbone pattern of threads at each double cord, and the lengths of thread were joined at the kettle-stitch position with the standard weaver's knot. On completion of the sewing the kettle stitch was pack-sewn to wrap the thread ends. The hard, compact nature of our cabled cords meant that despite the herringbone link stitching and tight sewing tension, the spine remained square when the tension of the cords was released. The ends of the slips were frayed, glued, and twisted to a point, to aid in the lacing-on of the boards.

---

37. See Robert Espinosa, "Specification for a Hard-Board Laced-in Conservation Binding," *Book and Paper Group Annual* 2 (1983): 25-49.

~ Boards

From my small stock of quarter-sawn oak I was able to find a board of sufficient width and thickness for the manuscript. The model for the general shape of the board was HM 35300. The boards were cut to the same height as the Rivière binding, at 410 mm giving a projection of about 5 mm on each edge. The inside spine edges were cushioned to accommodate the spine swelling, and the outer edges shaped in a similar manner (fig. 10). The boards seated well and in parallel to each other. From the mark-up pattern the entry holes were drilled and taper-reamed to produce a tight interference fit for the double cord. Entry centers were approximately $5/8$" from the spine edge of the board on the outside and angled to exit at about 1" centers. The four peg locations were found, centered, drilled, and reamed, and the channels gouged out following the evidence of the original paste-downs. The boards were temporarily laced on and the text block wrapped in a bandage to keep it under pressure in storage. We thus reached the conclusion of the second phase of our work, on 16 March 1995.

~ Cover

As we have seen, the specifications of the binding evolved during the course of our work, informed by both the conservation needs of the text and the discovery of historical evidence. At an early stage it was decided that no new parchment fly-leaves would be added and that the inside board surface would remain exposed, so that the new sewing supports and channel and peg system would be to view—where they could be seen to reflect the marks on the original pastedown. The

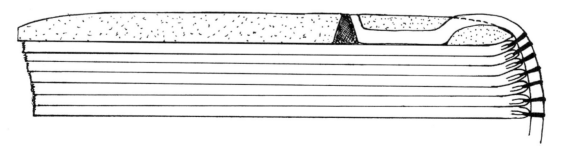

Fig. 10
The board was chamfered to accommodate the slight spine swelling.

choice of the new covering material, a white tawed calf, was made before we tentatively identified the pink-stained leather fragment on the recto of B4 as sheepskin. Although a goatskin leather with a grain similar to sheepskin is available, it lacks the quality of calfskin for our purposes. The thread we used is probably more tightly cabled than the original thread, and it is somewhat thicker as well. The turn-ins of the new cover will be recessed along their edges so that they do not mark the surface of the original pastedown leaves.

Goatskin parchment was used to line the spine, partly for aesthetic reasons; its tone and texture blend with the color of the oak boards where they meet at the hinge. The lining was slotted to fit over the bands without adhesive, and it extends beyond the hinge to form an inside joint. Once this slotted lining was attached, the boards were finally laced on and pegged.[38] The primary core of the endbands was sewn through the lining and the sewing slips were laced in and pegged.

The cover was adhered with cooked wheat-flour paste to the boards and the slotted spine lining. This system ensures that the text will open well and in a controlled way but without any paste adhesive touching the text's spine folds. The secondary decorative endband is in fact not only decorative; it allowed us through a choice of core materials to fine-tune the opening of the book (fig. 11). The endband was the subject of extensive discussion; my initial plan had been to use a simple covered endband but following an examination of HM 35300 (see appendix B) it was decided that a triple-crowning-core secondary endband would be a much more interesting solution. I rejected the use of modern silk on conservation grounds. The endbands in the Corpus Christi College and Huntington bindings, with their two-color linen thread, were thought the most appropriate model.[39]

✑ Boxing

On preservation grounds we urged that the manuscript, traditionally on display, should be closed whenever the opportunity presented itself. It was then agreed that a carrying and storage case should be made for safety and ease of transport.

---

38. See Nicholas Hadgraft and Katherine Swift, eds., *Conservation and Preservation in Small Libraries* 12 (1994), especially the essays by A. Cains, "Roger Powell and His Early Irish Manuscripts in Dublin"; N. Pickwood, "The Conservation of Corpus Christi College, Cambrdge, MS. 197B"; and M. Jefferson, "The Rebinding of Corpus Christi College, Cambridge, MS. 280.

39. Robertson proposed that the Corpus Christi example might reflect East Anglian practice, but HM 35300 seemed to suggest that the endbands were consistent with London practice, where the Ellesmere would have been bound.

I built a padded pressure-box from aged mahogany, based on the model of the box designed by the late Edward Barnsley for the late Roger Powell's binding of the Book of Kells. The lid of the box is fitted with a phenolic resin spring that, when locked into place, applies firm and uniform pressure on the book, simulating the action of fore-edge clasps. Our work was completed in October of 1995.

Trinity College, Dublin

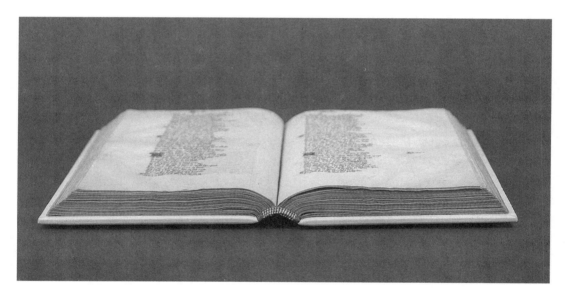

Fig. 11
The Ellesmere manuscript in the 1995 binding.

Appendix A

❧ *Summary of Pigment and Gesso Consolidation*

The stability of the accessible areas of pigment and gesso was determined by eye and under a binocular microscope prior to the disbinding of the manuscript. Although numerous areas of cracked pigment and/or lost gesso were noted, all of the pigment and gesso accessible for examination was found to be well adhered to the support. After the bifolia were separated, unfolded, and relaxed for photography, a detailed reexamination of all the gilt and pigmented areas on every page was carried out, again under the binocular microscope. Additional areas areas of cracked, loose gesso and pigment were discovered, particularly where the parchment had been required to "flex" when pages were turned within the tight Rivière binding—that is, at the vertical axis along the gutter, especially at the front and back of the book.

Unstable areas were consolidated using the following techniques: Working under the binocular microscope, reagent alcohol was fed under the loose particle of gesso or pigment using a 00 sable brush; this was followed immediately by an application of 3 percent (3 grams per 100 ml) edible gelatin in filtered water, kept in a liquid state on a hotplate. The initial application of alcohol helped to draw the gelatin solution to the underside of the loose or detached media, rather than having it settle on top of or between damaged areas, where it would not have the desired effect of reattaching the media to the support. The alcohol flowed into the desired areas easily due to its relatively low surface tension and created a capillary action that helped to draw the consolidant into place after it. In gessoed areas, very light pressure (a fingertip through silicone release paper) was applied until the gelatine had cooled enough to set. In areas of pigment alone, the consolidant generally softened the pigment slightly and drew it back into contact with the support as the gelatine cooled and dried. In these areas pressure was applied. This phase of treatment was carried out before photography for the facsimile, so that particles of media would not be lost during handling.

The consolidation was done by Susan Rogers, conservator of manuscripts and photographs, and Maria Fredericks, conservator of rare books, following general guidelines given by Anthony Cains. The choice of gelatin rather than an acrylic resin (such as Paraloid B-72) as the consolidant was based on both its compatibility with the materials in the original artifact and the conservators' greater familiarity and experience with it. The gelatin was effective in readhering loose particles to the support and did not create an undesirable synthetic gloss or shine.

Following is a list of areas consolidated with 3 percent gelatin as described above. Areas of gesso described as "loose" were generally cracked into "tiles" of gesso or pigment that were still attached to the support on the bottom but showed potential for becoming detached from the support; "flaking" is used where particles of media and/or gesso had already been lost and/or were almost entirely detached from the support.

1R	Loose pieces of gesso in *demivinet* near bottom edge and at foot of initial A
1V	Flaking blue and white pigments around initial W
2R	Gesso, initial T
2V	Loose gesso, initial A; gold paraph near fore-edge
3V	Cracked gesso, 2 initial A's, gold paraph
4V	Loose gesso, gold paraph
5R	Gesso, left foot of initial A; cracked gesso in initial W
6V	Gesso, gold paraph
7R	Gesso, initial T, initial A
9R	Gesso, gold paraph
136V	Flaking gesso, *demivinet*
151R	Flaking gesso, *demivinet*
187R	Loose gesso and pigment, *demivinet*
194R	Loose gesso, bottom left corner *demivinet*
196V	Flaking gesso, *demivinet*
217R	Loose gesso, gold paraph
217V	Gesso, upper corner *demivinet*
218V	Gesso, gold paraph

Prepared by Maria Fredericks

APPENDIX B

❧ *Description of the Binding of Huntington Library, MS. HM 35300.*
BEDE, HISTORIA ECCLESIASTICA
Oxford or London Binding (?)

Cover: White alum-tawed sheepskin with tongued corner miters. Head corners repaired but tails in original condition. Modern infilling of worm holes now discolored.

Chemise: (fragment) Similar to material of primary cover. Envelope pocket survives under back-board pastedown. Stitching perforations evident at the head; other edges cut. Adhesive residue in the area of the pocket on front-board pastedown. Modern paper lining under front pastedown. Back pastedown largely undisturbed. Chemise material also survives under clasps and label on the back board.

Clasps, back board: The two catch plates are attached, each by two brass rivets passing through back-board cover, envelope pocket, and pastedown. Two modern brass pins have been added to each plate but do not pass through the board.

Front board: Modern metal work and straps secured by the same type of brass pins. The original plates and straps were secured with two iron nails each station. Iron nail perforations at the tail strap rebate have been infilled.

Boards: Wood (probably quarter-cut oak not to view), cushion-chamfered on all edges, giving continuous semi-elliptic curve to board surfaces.

Lacing pattern: VIV (see *Sewing*) Boards project very little at the tail; 2 or 3 mm at the head; fore-edges 4 mm on the front and 1–3 mm at the back. Thickness estimated at 12–13 mm with 5 mm edge flats.

Fig. 12
The back of HM 35300. Traces of the overcover can be seen under the label.

Sewing: Five rolled double-tawed thongs sewn herringbone link stitch. Lumps at kettle stitch position suggest threads joined at this point (centers not examined).

Mark-up: The gatherings are possibly back-cornered slightly but certainly compressed by the endband tie-downs. Would appear to have been tied down every gathering. Measuring from the head:

(0-5)	14	41	84	130	177	219	249	(258–62)
(Compress)	K	1	2	3	4	5	K	(Compress)

Endbands: Primary endband of rolled tawed skin, each slip attached by single channel and peg. *Decorative:* Triple crowning cores of skin material (?) secured to the primary by four double wrapping turns of indigo linen thread with one crossover and then worked with alternating doubles of white and indigo, ending with four doubles of indigo wrapping the cores. Crossovers under lower spine crowning core. For the purpose of making a model I suggest that the method of construction was roughly as follows (facing the primary from the fore-edge): thread needle with a double length of indigo thread and knot ends together. Enter needle about 4 mm from the right and bury knot under primary core, reenter perforation and form loop; position the three crowing cores in the loop, tighten and continue to wrap cores with four double threads of indigo. Having exited near the board to the right return the double thread to the first loop position and pass the needle under the spine crowning core and primary core exiting toward the fore-edge. Place the double thread between the primary and book-edge core. Insert a double thread of white and bury the knot under the primary and exit under the spine core. Figure-of-eight the double indigo over the three crowning cores to the spine; cross over and figure-of-eight the double white back to the book-edge core and return to the spine under the primary. Cross over and repeat, ending with the four double core wrapping turns of indigo.

Fig. 13
Headband of HM 35300.

Headband: Only the back board side of about two-thirds the total width appears to be in original condition, the remaining third a good reworking in similar threads starting at a break in the core (?).

Tailband: Modern replica in silk (?), and incorrect in that the threads have been worked singly over the cores.

Pastedowns/endleaves: Sheepskin parchment of coarse quality, quaterniones. *Front:* The first is a pastedown stub about 25 mm wide; the second is the pastedown conjoint to the third leaf, a narrow stub and the fourth a leaf conjoint to the first stub. *Back:* First a stub conjoint to the fourth leaf, the pastedown. Conjoint leaves two and three are narrow stubs.

Label on back board: MS Parchment turned over transparent horn or membrane and secured through both covers with various forms of copper-alloy nails, twelve in number. Turn-over lost at sides and lower edge. Overcover cut away along profile of label.

Text: Sheepskin parchment.

Dimensions:

Height of board at spine:	265 mm
Height of board at fore-edge	268 mm
Width of board at head	192 mm
Width of board at tail	195 mm
Thickness: Text block	about 30 mm
Book block	about 55 mm

Huntington Library Press of San Marino, California
and Yushodo Co., Ltd., of Japan
are pleased to announce the publication of

THE ELLESMERE CHAUCER:
A New Monochromatic Facsimile

∼❧∼

The Canterbury Tales
Huntington Library, MS. EL 26 C 9

edited by
Daniel Woodward and Martin Stevens

available November 1996
from Huntington Library Press

Contributors

Seth Lerer is a professor of English and Comparative Literature at Stanford University. His books include *Chaucer and His Readers: Imagining the Author in Late-Medieval England* (1993), recently awarded the Beatrice White Prize of the English Association of Great Britain. He is the editor of *Literary History and the Challenge of Philology: The Legacy of Erich Auerbach* (1996), and his book on early Tudor literature will be published by Cambridge University Press in 1997.

❧ ☙

Julia Boffey teaches in the School of English and Drama, Queen Mary and Westfield College, University of London. She currently holds a British Academy Research Readership in support of her work on the collaborative revision of *The Index of Middle English Verse*.

David Lorenzo Boyd teaches English at the University of Pennsylvania. He is the author of articles on Chaucer, medieval English literature, and medieval manuscripts that have appeared in *South Atlantic Quarterly*, *Fifteenth-Century Studies*, and *Essays in Medieval Studies*.

Ardis Butterfield is a lecturer in English at University College London. She has published widely on Chaucer and medieval French poetry and music, and she is currently completing a book on Chaucer and thirteenth- and fourteenth-century French culture.

Anthony G. Cains is director of the Conservation Laboratory at Trinity College, Dublin.

Joseph A. Dane is a professor of English and comparative literature at the University of Southern California. His most recent book is *The Critical Mythology of Irony* (1991), and he is the author of articles on Chaucer and medieval studies in recent and forthcoming issues of *Publications of the Bibliographical Society of America*, *The Library*, *Scriptorium*, and *Analytical and Enumerative Bibliography*.

A. S. G. Edwards, a professor of English at the University of Victoria, is a Guggenheim Fellow and a Fellow of the Society of Antiquaries. He has recently coedited volume 1 of the Yale edition of the works of St. Thomas More, and he is currently engaged in the collaborative revision of *The Index of Middle English Verse.*

David Greetham is Distinguished Professor of English and Medieval Studies at the Graduate School of the City University of New York. He is the author of *Textual Scholarship: An Introduction* (1992), and his *Theories of the Text* and *Textual Transgressions* were published this year. He is founder and executive director of the Society for Textual Scholarship and coeditor of its journal, *TEXT.*

Ralph Hanna III is a professor of English at the University of California, Riverside. He has written widely on manuscript transmission and its cultural implications, and his most recent book is *Pursuing History: Middle English Manuscripts and Their Texts* (1996).